Praise for F̶a̶r̶r̶a̶h̶ ̶G̶r̶a̶y̶

"I congratulate you on learning [...] entrepreneurship and the free ente[...] you are making it happen."

Stedman Graham

"Farrah Gray is among those [African Americans] with out-standing accomplishments. He has founded and fosters companies as diverse as food manufacturing and venture capital. He donates regularly to after-school and summer literacy and mentoring programs."

Sacramento Bee

"Farrah is an example of what is achievable. . . . His financial drive at such a young age makes him an invaluable role model."

Aubrey Stone
executive director, California Black Chamber of Commerce

"A savvy entrepreneur, Gray is CEO and founder of NE^{2}W, his flagship organization, with five other operations going at the same time. His mission is to educate youth about the career opportunities in business and, at the same time, lead by example in the area of social responsibility. He wants to make the world a better place . . . Farrah Gray—ordinary teenager with extraordinary success."

MBE (Minority Business Entrepreneur) **magazine**

"Farrah is refreshing and inspiring."

Suzanne L. Casupang
executive director, YMCA of Southern Nevada

"This Teen Tycoon is making his mark."

CBS News

"[Farrah Gray is] a very handsome, well-groomed and polished black teenager. As the saying goes, 'You can pick them out of a crowd.' It's as though success carries an energy of its own. You can see it, you can feel it—Farrah has it all. . . . Farrah Gray is a role model for both youths and adults."

***Las Vegas Image* magazine**

"Farrah displays great poise and has learned to successfully divide himself between his entrepreneurial pursuits and his education."

Carlton Jenkins
partner, Yucaipa Corporate Initiatives Fund

"You are on a very focused path and succeeding in your quest to bring entrepreneurship to young people. For this I congratulate you and say, 'Keep up the good work.'"

Shahara Ahmad-Llewellyn
vice chair, America's Promise

"Most kids his age are like, 'Let's go to the mall.' Farrah's like, 'Let's build a mall.'"

Wendy Day
cofounder of The Rap Coalition

"Farrah can teach me anytime about business; I will teach him the violin."

Olga Breeskin
international recording artist

"Farrah Gray makes me proud."

The Honorable Percy Sutton
chairman emeritus, Inner City Broadcasting Corporation

Reallionaire

Nine Steps to Becoming
Rich from the Inside Out

Farrah Gray
with Fran Harris

Health Communications, Inc.
Deerfield Beach, Florida

www.hcibooks.com

Library of Congress Cataloging-in-Publication Data

Gray, Farrah, 1984–
 Reallionaire : nine steps to becoming rich from the inside out / Farrah Gray, with
 Fran Harris.
  p. cm.
 ISBN 0-7573-0224-6
 1. Finance, Personal.   2. Financial security.   I. Harris, Fran, 1965–
 II. Title.

 HG179.G7218 2005
 332.024'01—dc22

                                                                    2004062555

HCI, its Logos and Marks are trademarks of Health Communications, Inc.

Publisher: Health Communications, Inc.
        3201 S.W. 15th Street
        Deerfield Beach, FL 33442–8190

R-06-05

Cover design by Larissa Hise Henoch
Inside book design by Lawna Patterson Oldfield
Inside book formatting by Dawn Von Strolley Grove

Reallionaire:

Someone who has discovered that there is more to money than having money. A person who understands that success is not just about being rich in your pocket; you have to be rich on the inside, too.

Dedicated to

the five generations of the past and present . . .

Great Great Grandma Birdie
Great Grandma Dalia
Grandma Audrey
Mother Paula
Sister Kiki

The residual of your collective 317 years of wisdom, humanitarian spirit and unwavering compassion is the foundation upon which I stand.

CONTENTS

ACKNOWLEDGMENTS

First I want to thank God and his cocreators of me, Mom and Dad.

To Greek "Kiki" Gray, my beautiful one-and-only picture perfect sister, for the profound impact you have had on my life. Prayers are answered, for your battle with cancer had me visiting God quite often, asking him to pull you through. As a family, we won the battle and the war. You are a Sistah Soldier, Woman Warrior, Female Fighter. I love you, Big Sis. You keep on being a no-limit soldier!

To my brothers Andre, Jonathan and Alex, thank you for your love and respect.

Danielle Jean Jacques, my spiritual aunt, you truly have an angelic nature. You opened up your heart and home to me to experience the richness of an extended family. You urged me to weigh in at 100 percent to write the book I had in me.

My spiritual Grandma Rosette, thank you for being so loving and always serving the right amount of Haitian soup for the soul.

Jahdi, Malaikah, Tariq, Cheyenne, Trinity, Madison, Micaya, Grace and Isaiah, you kids never cease to amaze; you inspire me to want to be like you when I grow up!

Yaa-Asantewa Nzingha, there would be a void in my life of learning if I was not blessed to draw from your well of wisdom.

The invaluable motivator behind the motivator, Alicia S. Thibou. Thank you for being you.

Thanks for the work, backing and faith of a handful of good people who believed in me and who used their "pulling and drawing power" or the investment of time to assist or make introductions on my behalf: Barbara Belle Newman, Nan and Grace, Kimberly Bailey-Tureaud, Axal Admas, Erykah Badu, Deborah Campbell, Yvonne Atkinson Gates, Isabella Laforet, Minyon Moore, Roi Tauer, Tim Ralph, Dr. Glen Yago, Kwame Brown, Pierre Sutton, Percy Sutton, Karen Malone, Alice Huffman, Carlton Jenkins, Beverly Swanagan, Stedman Graham, George Ginder, Ertharin Cousin Moore, Gary Campbell, J. Michael Rush, Mary Beth, Bret Witter, Fran Harris, Kim Weiss, Randee Feldman and the whole HCI family. Your faith and direct and indirect support have been far-reaching.

Last and least, thanks to those who made promises they never intended to keep. You helped me learn that my word is my bond; it represents the content of my character.

INTRODUCTION: Know Yourself

I'm a nineteen-year-old African American male who grew up in a single-parent household. And if you believe in statistics, I'm supposed to be either in jail or dead. Instead, from the jump, I was a kid who was all about possibilities. I'd sit by the window in our tiny apartment, dreaming of the day when I'd look out of my office onto the manic streets of Manhattan. I dreamed of igniting audiences of thousands, even millions of people, with speeches that rivaled Dr. Martin Luther King Jr.'s. I dreamed of making enough money so that my mother could stop working her two, sometimes three, jobs to take care of us. I knew that no matter what my current circumstances, it was possible for me to dream outside of what anyone I knew personally had ever achieved.

You see, the Chicago neighborhood I grew up in didn't appear to be brimming with potential for success, but to my surprise, it was full of possibilities. Thankfully, things are not always as they seem. The block where I lived was always lined with empty beer bottles, old cars and street peddlers. The broken-down apartment we lived in frequently had no running water. The toilet was constantly jammed, and roaches seemed to have signed a long-term lease in our place.

But that wasn't all there was to my community. In the shadow of the most notorious housing projects were all the makings of Ivy League students, biochemists, corporate executives, lawyers, educators, engineers, media moguls and entertainers. What was missing in most cases wasn't a shortage of brainpower but rather a shortage of hope. Hope that things would one day be better. Hope that one day kids wouldn't have to walk past a crack house to get to school. Hope that parents would be able to establish business enterprises and acquire funding to see those ventures grow and sustain themselves until they could be passed on to their children.

Hope. I didn't live in a neighborhood full of that. But I did live in a household where ideas and inspiration were abundant and, more important, where excellence was expected. My mother planted a tiny yet powerful seed in me before I was born: *that I could become and do anything I set my heart and mind to.* Thank God I believed her.

My journey to this point has been mostly about the inner strength, faith, focus and drive it takes to make it out of a difficult situation and see myself on the other side of that mountain. The old folks used to call this "a way outta no way" attitude. And make no mistake, we all possess the ability to reach the top of our own unique Mt. Everest. I've learned that true success isn't so much about being talented as it is about what you do with that talent. Real success isn't about a bulging bank account, a second home or a customized jet. It's not about the size of the house or the make of the car. It's about how we recognize and actualize our unique gifts. That's what will take us to that next level of achievement and abundance. For me, that's when you become a "reallionaire"—someone who pursues his or her passion with authenticy, sincerity and honesty.

The process of writing this book has given me the chance to revisit my journey in a way that actually makes me appreciate it much more. Some people say of their past that they look back on it "and laugh." Not me. I look back on the starting blocks of my life, and I nervously change the subject. There's nothing funny about being poor, trust me. But I would not change one thing about my life. Not one thing. I've been blessed, and had I not been dealt this hand, I wouldn't have had the amazing life I've had. And I'm just getting started!

My business success has given me the opportunity to touch lives that I would have never touched, to see places I may have never seen except in my dreams. The tenets that were instilled in me by my mother and grandmother led to my achievements as a businessman and philanthropist and eventually put me at the table with influential leaders who are changing the world one day at a time. My story has thrust me into a speaking career that's taken me to neighborhoods, schools and communities that are starving for inspiration, and for that, I'm eternally grateful.

Now, I didn't become a millionaire by age fifteen so I could keep all of my secrets to myself. That's never been the plan. Over the next few hundred pages, I'll share my personal method of turning lemons into lemonade (including my tips on how to market, package and sell it!). You'll find not only my story, but my Real Points—important concepts and reminders that will help you both in business and in life. I know you're going to experience your share of ups and downs, and I know you're going to have moments of doubt and self-evaluation. These Real Points are milestones you can use to make sure you are still on the right road. My Reallionaire Exercises aren't mileposts; they are wheels I hope will speed you on your reallionaire journey.

My story, though unique, is not unlike others who began with nothing more than a dream fueled by sheer determination. Even if you've never walked the streets of a housing project or seen food stamps up close, I believe my story will remind you of the kid in all of us who knows no limits and believes anything—and every-thing—is possible. This is my story, but in a way, it's your story too.

Understand the Power of a Name

how the love and support of family and community helped put a young African American with big dreams on the path to success

By the time I made my entrance into the world on September 9, 1984, my mother, Paula, had left my father and was well on her way to caring for five children on her own. I grew up near the South Chicago housing projects, where drug deals gone bad and people being shot to death were commonplace. It was a good month if nobody you knew got killed. Those months were few and far between. You see, the inner city wasn't a place for the weak or weary. Thank goodness Mom was a warrior.

My mother was thirty-six years old when she gave birth to me. At five feet, seven inches tall and a petite 125 pounds, she looked like Grammy Award–winning singer Erykah Badu. The oldest of four siblings and descended from three generations of hardworking women, Mom was a product of "old school" rearing and sensibilities. She grew up during a time when children were to be seen and not heard. You worked hard and valued education.

I was the baby of the family, curious, outgoing and precocious. In other words, I got on everybody's last nerve. My brother Andre was seventeen years old when I came home and invaded the household. He was already the anointed surrogate father in our home. Then there was my brother Jonathan, who was six; Alex was five; and the queen of the royal palace, my sister Kiki, was fourteen years old. She was the quiet and unassuming swan that all of my friends swore they'd marry one day. Living in Phoenix, in the backdrop but hardly in the background, was Grandma, the strong, silent matriarch who later blessed me with very valuable business know-how and wisdom that ultimately led to my first million-dollar deal.

Mom had grown up during the '60s, a time when black folks were extremely socially conscious and heavily engaged in a high-octane struggle for human and civil rights. She and my father had been activists who marched in the streets and participated in sit-ins on a regular basis. Our house was often the setting for meetings and marches. It was a place where people could voice their opinions and organize to bring about social change. Mom and Dad have never been labeled wallflowers, and they were officers in the great fight for equality. Some might have called them agitators. We called them our heroes.

Mom hadn't come from a wealthy family. Her upbringing was similar to mine. She grew up in a home where there was a lot of love, discipline and spirituality but not a lot of material wealth. Still, she always believed that it was better to be respected than rich, and she raised us with the same sensibility. Little did she know that I was striving to be both—rich and respected. My name in Arabic means "burden bearer," the one who leads and shoulders great responsibility. Maybe that's why I came into the world raising Cain, asking questions and challenging the status quo. So be careful what you name your children!

Even in the projects, birthdays were special occasions. You could always tell when it was someone's birthday in the 'hood because the barbecue grill would be fired up, and there would be lots of laughter and soul music piping from one of the apartments. My sixth birthday was no different than any other in the neighborhood, except for one unusual and prophetic gift. Four different family members presented me with a copy of a videotape of the 1986 movie *The Golden Child*, starring Eddie Murphy. What a strange gift for someone my age. I didn't get it. Did they think I was interested in becoming the next Siskel or Ebert? What ever happened to cars and footballs? What about good old-fashioned cash? In my book, those were respectable gifts for a six-year-old.

Mom had raised us to respect grown folks so I didn't dare say what I was thinking, which was, *Why in the world would seemingly intelligent folks buy me videos, of all things? A gift I hadn't even asked for?* It seemed odd. Okay, let me be real, it seemed crazy. And as much as I tried to pretend to be happy, I wasn't feeling those gifts. But I did what I'd been taught to do: I smiled and said, "Thank you." Mom didn't tolerate a lack of gratitude. If you were unappreciative, Mom "gave you something to be unappreciative about," which was usually a tap on the rear end. She didn't believe in sparing the rod. And since I valued my life, I flashed my pearly whites and said, "Thank you."

For those of you who don't own the Eddie Murphy Filmography Collection (he should have stopped at *Beverly Hills Cops 2*, by the way) or who weren't fortunate enough to get one, let alone four copies of the *Golden Child* video for your sixth birthday, let me tell you what the movie's about. Eddie Murphy plays a detective who specializes in finding lost children. He is told he is the Chosen One who will find and protect the Lost One, also known as the Golden

Child, a Buddhist mystic who was kidnapped by an evil sorcerer.

There's the old Chinese saying: "When the pupil is ready, the teacher will appear." Looking back, I can see that my loved ones were giving me the highest compliment by giving me those videos. What I then perceived as a less-than-thoughtful gesture on their parts was really a promise of what lay ahead for me. They were calling me the Golden Child. What an incredible metaphor. It took me years to absorb the subtle power in those gifts, but ultimately, I got it.

When the pupil is ready, the teacher will appear.
—Chinese saying

And when I got it, I realized the tremendous power parents and guardians have over their children's legacies simply by the words they choose to speak. Had my family showered me with negative and unaffirming sentiments, my life would be drastically different today. I know that for a fact. I've seen it too many times. I saw it in my neighborhood, and yes, I experienced it in my extended family. Surprised? Don't be. My rock is my immediate family, and they have been supportive from day one, but nobody's inner circle is perfect. You can't grow without some strife. So never believe the hype.

There were people who, I'm sure, thought that I'd grow up in prison simply because of where I lived. Children of single-parent households come to accept the world's perception of their supposed plight. There are certain stereotypes you have to combat from the day you come out of your mother's womb. That's a given.

Some kids in my 'hood came to believe that no matter how hard their parents worked, they'd never be more than half a paycheck ahead, if that. The unspoken code in the inner city teaches you one thing: a nine-to-five is a way of life. Get used to it. If you make it to adulthood, you'll always be working a J-O-B, which means you'll always be Just Over Broke! In our case, it became one paycheck away from being evicted. Maybe that's why my mother worked so darn hard. Actually, I know that's why she worked so darn hard. That's probably why I work so darn hard.

You see, although I lived in a single-parent household, the bonds within my family were like steel. And there was plenty of "can do" conversation in my house. People tend to think that single-parent homes, especially minority homes, somehow lack love, respect, discipline or vision. That's not always the case. There were tons of single mothers and fathers raising their children in the projects. And the bonds in our community were actually quite alive and vibrant. Still, there was an enormous sense of overwhelming hopelessness that engulfed the children in my neighborhood. There was so much despair that they were turning guns on each other and themselves. It was a challenging time to be growing up black and male. No doubt about that. But the old folks used to say the main reason black people didn't commit suicide was because you couldn't jump out of the basement window. I understood this saying quite well because everywhere I turned I saw my friends succumbing to the streets. Selling drugs, joining gangs and dropping out of school. Mom was witnessing the same thing. That's why she reminded me every day that I was destined to become her golden child.

After the birthday bash, the golden child moniker followed me wherever I went. But that was just one of the names I was called. Black folks are notorious for creating nicknames for their family members. I was "little fella," "little big man" and "old soul." I didn't know what any of these names meant so I asked lots of questions. So many questions, in fact, that people would beg me (sometimes pay me) to stop. In what I'm sure was partly a strategy to get me to take a break, one grown-up answered in response to my "What's a golden child?" question by saying, "You are destined for greatness, young man."

"I am?" I answered.

"Yes, sir," he said beaming. Even with my missing front tooth, he believed this of me—and he made me believe it, too.

Hard Work and Hard Love

For years, I never saw my mother sleep. I'm not lying. When I would go to bed at night, she would kiss me and leave for work. While I was getting dressed for school the next day, she would return home from one job and begin to get dressed for another. Always working. In fact, I saw much more of my mother's back than any six-year-old should see. As I reflect on those days, I can see that her dedication and commitment to caring for our family was her driving force, but back then I hated that she worked so much. I wanted my mom home with me. I cherished those days when I got to snag a few moments with her, reading, laughing, just being a kid.

My siblings and I called Mom many names: Superwoman, Wonder Woman, Wondermom. She was all that and a side order of potato salad. Oh, we knew she couldn't leap tall buildings in a single bound. Because if she could, she was the kind of mom who would have told us about it. Her work ethic left an imprint on us all. And for at least twenty-three days out of the month, she was pure, tender loving care. We learned to stay out of her way on those other six or seven days of the month!

Whenever she was home I usurped every bit of time I could squeeze in with Mom. If she was cooking, I'd be right beside her, talking her ears off and watching her culinary genius. In fact, I got my first taste of being a chef from Mom, who was not only a great cook but also a magician when it came to providing food for our family. She could make a bag of potatoes, a can of beans, a package of ground beef and a loaf of bread go a long way. Most people would look at those four items and see only one meal but Mom turned them into a week's worth for us. Day one might be mashed potatoes and ground beef. Day two might be hamburgers with a side of beans. Day three might be leftover hamburgers with French fries. You're starting to get the gist, aren't you? Mom was working it!

And she had an amazing way with words. When we'd thank her for turning our morsels into meals she'd say something like, "A rich woman with a full pantry and refrigerator can't beat my cooking because she takes for granted that the meal will come out just right. Me? I gotta get it right the first time. Plus, I've added the main ingredient—a little TLC—because my cupboards only have just enough to feed my family." That's how Mom made miracles.

Of course, there were certain times during every month when we'd have a serious shortage of food. In other words, no food. That's no exaggeration. People think that poor people embellish the degree of their lack, but there were days that our cupboards were completely bare. There were days on end when the only thing in our refrigerator was the light that came on when you opened the door. That's how desperate things got sometimes.

> *A rich woman with a full pantry and refrigerator can't beat my cooking because she takes for granted the meal will come out just right. Me? I gotta get it right the first time.*
>
> —Mom

When food was scarce, we had to be creative. We were always lacking one staple item or another. If we had bread, we had no

butter. If we had cereal, there was no milk. If there was peanut butter, you guessed it, no jelly. That's probably where I honed my
cooking skills. We were poor so there were no cookbooks in our
house. In fact, when it came to cooking, experience was the best
teacher. Thankfully, I wasn't the kid who sat at the table waiting for
Mom to bring the food over. I was the kid who pulled up a chair
and watched every single move she made as she prepared meals.

And when the hunger pains hit, man did they hit! It was during
those times that I wanted most to be rich. *Rich people always had
food*, I thought. *Rich people didn't have to go to bed hungry.* There
were many nights that it was much easier to go to sleep rather than
feel the pain of hunger. For once I wanted us to be able to go to the
grocery store and shop without looking at the price tags. I dreamed
about that day.

While Mom was busy making miracles, the rest of us did our
part. Everybody in the family was expected to contribute to the
household, something that I think is missing in many homes today.
Kids laugh at doing chores. Everyone's so busy that they don't take
time to have dinner with the family. I think our humble beginnings
actually forged a closer bond within my family. We all learned to
cook, clean and do laundry. Some of us were better at some tasks
than others. I had a natural affinity for cooking, but the others took
turns burning something every now and then. There were no such
things as "gender-appropriate" roles in our house. If it needed to be
done, you did it. Kiki took out the trash. Andre did the laundry.
Jonathan and Alex mopped and cleaned the bathroom. As the
youngest, I couldn't really do much more than help wash the dishes.
But I observed carefully, and when it was finally my turn to assume
certain responsibilities, I gave it the army "spit and shine."

The fact that my mom was the main role model in my life was

more a matter of circumstance than of choice. Like most of my friends and acquaintances in the neighborhood, I grew up in a single-parent household. We never talked about why or how our families had gotten that way, either inside or outside the house. A silent code seemed to dictate that we never discussed our father-lessness. In fact, I don't think I had a conversation with my friends about my father until I was in puberty. In my 'hood, boys learned to play the role. No emotions outside the home. We might cry in the privacy of our rooms, but we never cried outside those doors.

In that respect, I was one of the lucky ones. I had a somewhat close relationship with my father, although I never lived under the same roof with him. We spoke by phone, and on occasion I'd see him at family gatherings. He was a kind, thoughtful man who believed in hard work. He ate and slept activism, so I did not see much of him. I appreciate the fact that although my father didn't have a consistent physical presence in my life, he and Mom main-tained a civil, courteous relationship. There wasn't much baby mama drama in my house, and I'm grateful for that. I loved my father, and I know that he loved me.

I had two solid role models with Mom and Dad, but I especially welcomed the chance to sit at the feet of my mom's mom, Grandma, whenever I could get her to slow down for a moment. She was definitely my mother's mother, proud and smart, and like most independent black women, she worked a lot and complained little. I remember hearing Mom on the phone with one of her girl-friends saying, "Nothing's going to change unless I change it, so what's the point of complaining?" I wrote that one down: that atti-tude was my family's legacy to me.

A Taste of the Good Life

One day, after school, I heard Mom talking to Andre about having a little extra money. I dashed from around the door with a big grin on my face. "Can we go to the Chinese all-you-can-eat place?"

"How long have you been standing there?" Andre asked.

"Long enough. Can we, Mama?"

Mom agreed that it was time to give our stove the night off. So we went to a Chinese restaurant that was known for its great selection. I'd secretly put a Tupperware container under my jacket because I knew I'd want a doggie bag. My own doggie bag. Those Styrofoam containers most restaurants used weren't enough for my ample appetite, so I came prepared—a lesson Mom had taught me early in life. "You always wanna have a plan B, Farrah," she'd say. I'd nod yes even though I had no idea what that meant.

At the restaurant I ate until my stomach almost popped. I looked like a little chocolate Buddha with an Afro. I told Mom that I had a surprise gift for her.

"What's pink with black writing on it, Mama?" I asked. She'd once told me that "big money" people always asked this question of the new kids on the block in the financial world.

"What is pink with black writing?" she repeated. It was a joke that Mom knew well. The smile on her face disappeared when I pulled out a newspaper.

"How did you . . . ?" she said, looking around at Andre, Kiki, Jonathan and Alex, then back at me.

I pushed the pink *Financial Times* newspaper toward her. "Where did you get this?" she asked. My brothers had hopped on the train downtown to the financial district newsstand to pick up a copy. "Only big-money people read that paper, Mama," I said as I walked over and planted a kiss on her cheek.

"That's right, baby," she said, hugging me.

"And one day, we're gonna be big-money people, ain't that right?" I said.

Mom's chest swelled with pride, and the smile on her face was as wide as the one worn by a kid in a candy store. On that night, I vowed that one day I would be able to put that same smile on her face again. One day I'd be able to take her to eat wherever she wanted, no matter how expensive the restaurant.

That night, as I had on many occasions, I lay in my bed staring at the ceiling. Only this time I wasn't counting the cracks. Suddenly the ceiling became the surface for me to visualize what I desired for my family and how I would get us there. It was the canvas, and I was da Vinci. I was only six years old, but I was already becoming the Energizer Bunny. My mind was racing with possibilities and dreams. I didn't allow any thoughts of lack and negativity to enter my brain.

Watching my mother toil away at job after job made my thirst for success insatiable. Yes, insatiable. At age six, my deepest desire may have been to treat Mom to dinner at a Chinese restaurant, where for about five bucks you could eat well and drink a lot of green tea, but it's not the size of the dream that counts. My

> *You go on or die.*
> —Harriiet Tubman, "conductor" of the Underground Railroad

dream ate me up and filled me with hope because I really and truly wanted to give my mother a treat. She was always taking care of us. For once I wanted to take care of her.

The Sweet Smell of Success

I didn't *talk* a lot about being rich, but I sure *thought* about it a lot. That's what poverty will do for you. While some of our neighbors were taking their hard-earned money and throwing it at the lottery, my mother taught us to move beyond the lottery mentality. She showed us how to save for a rainy day—and we had plenty of those. In fact, we had so many rainy days we started walking around the house with umbrellas.

We could always tell when the floods were on the horizon. Mom was always honest about our situation. She didn't believe in pretending that things were better than they were. If the lights were about to be disconnected because we couldn't pay the bill, she'd say, "Let's whip out the candles." For the next few days we'd simply cherish the daylight and prepare to bump into each other when night fell.

I've never been poor, only broke. Being poor is a frame of mind. Being broke is temporary.
—Mike Todd

On one of those dark nights I remember Kiki listening to a small, battery-operated radio in her room. One of the songs from Janet Jackson's first hit album was playing. The track was titled, "Control." The song talked about how she wanted to move out of the shadows of her family and be the captain of her own ship. Like Janet, I wanted to call my own shots. I was an ordinary kid planning on accomplishing some very extraordinary things. I was feeling my Cheerios, as we used to say. Pretty soon, I began to let the whole world know that "little man" had big dreams.

One day while Andre was cleaning his side of the room, he ran across an interesting discovery: an envelope of old Polaroid pictures. He immediately started laughing. I walked over to see what was so funny. He showed me the picture. It was a snapshot of me when I was four years old. I was sporting my Sunday-go-to-meeting outfit. I had a tie draped around my neck. In my right hand were cutout cardboard business cards. In my left hand, I held an oversized crayon box that I believe I was using as a briefcase.

I remember staring at that picture for the longest time. It was clear that I was not planning on being a completely normal kid. Already I'd become aware of what poverty felt like. And suddenly I had two personas. The kid who loved candy and cartoons. And the kid who wanted desperately to know how the world worked so he could figure out a way to make enough money to support his family.

As fate would have it, my first successful business enterprise put enough money in my pocket to treat my mother to that dinner— almost. It was also a total fluke, which I've since learned is the way great things often come together. One night after bathing, I searched for a container of body lotion. What I found was bottle after bottle of near-empty containers. Frustrated with having to run around the entire apartment to find lotion, I brought all of the bottles into the bathroom and turned them all on their heads. All I wanted was enough to pour over my little bird body.

As I sat there waiting for the lotions to drain, it hit me. I could mix and sell lotions. After all, everybody likes to feel smooth and soft, right? So for the next few hours I squeezed every drop of lotion into its own glass bowl. Then I washed out all of the original lotion bottles and got them ready for resale. I went to the kitchen and pulled out a few more bowls. I would need to see which lotions mixed the best.

Andre stumbled into my laboratory and frowned. "Boy, what are you doing?"

"I'm gonna sell these lotions," I said.

Andre shook his head. "Nobody's gonna buy *old* lotion from you, Farrah."

"Yes, they are," I said. "And it's not old because nobody's used it yet. I'm going to start selling them tomorrow."

I didn't care what Andre thought, I was going to sell that lotion! I was so excited I could hardly sleep that night. The next day, while I worked feverishly to get the original labels peeled off of their bottles, I asked Kiki if she would help me with my own labels. "What's the name of your product?" she asked.

I hadn't thought about that. But I did notice all of the other labels. Vaseline Intensive Care. Jergens. Avon. A store-label brand.

"What about Farrah's lotions?" I asked.

She frowned and shook her head no.

I remembered that I'd once seen a billboard that read Taylor Enterprises.

"Kiki, what's an enterprises?"

She laughed a little. "You mean enterprise? It's a business."

"What about Farrah Gray Enterprises?" I asked eagerly. "Or FG Enterprises?"

"That sounds good." Kiki started to write my business name directly on the label. "Have you thought about how much you're gonna charge?"

"What about $5?" I said optimistically.

"I don't think so," she replied.

"Why not?"

"Because this bottle right here," she said, holding up a sixteen-ounce, empty lotion bottle, "cost less than $5, Farrah. You can't sell a teeny-weeny bottle like this for more than a big one."

"Oh," I said. "Well, what about $1.50?"

"That's more like it," she answered.

The next day was my first business day. With help from my sister and brothers, I came up with the name First Impression. My inventory consisted of three bottles of scented lotions. I had a name. A product line. And enough energy to light the entire block!

Next, I would have to find the perfect outfit. After all, part of selling a product is selling yourself. I was asking $1.50 per bottle. My sales pitch was simple. "Hi, my name is Farrah Gray. Would you like to buy a bottle of my lotion? It's called First Impression." I can remember the looks on my neighbors' faces. It was a mixture of shock and delight. I'm sure my family thought I'd lost my mind.

But forty-five minutes and three buyers later I returned home with my first paycheck. I'd made my first step toward my first million dollars. I didn't own a wallet, but I was sure it was time for one. I'd made $9, and the whole world was about to know about it. I must have danced around the neighborhood for at least an hour. I couldn't remember being that happy. The thrill of creating something all on my own and then selling it? I was hooked. Entrepreneurship wasn't going to be a one-time thing for me. I was in love with that feeling.

Now, you're probably thinking I'm a poor mathematician because three bottles at $1.50 has never totaled $9, right? Well, you're right. Two customers paid me $2 each because they didn't have the correct change. Of course, neither did I. The third and last customer paid with a $5 bill. "I don't have the right change, ma'am," I said.

"I don't want the right change," she said.

"You don't?" I responded quickly.

"Nope. I just invested in your future."

"Thank you," I said, then I jetted back to the apartment. As soon as my sister opened the door, I zoomed past her for her dictionary. "How did it go?"

When I returned to the living room, Kiki stared at me. "What are you looking for?"

I kept turning the pages. "In-vest. In-vest . . ."

"Farrah, what are you talking about?"

"My last customer said, 'I invested in your future.' What's 'invested' mean?"

"It means she believes in you," she said.

I beamed. I still wasn't 100 percent sure what "invested" meant, but it sure sounded good. And besides, I was nine dollars richer. Only 999,991 dollars away from my first million.

REAL POINTS: Before You Begin

Nothing happens without effort. You have to lay the foundation for success, even before you begin to plot your future.

1. **Watch those around you and learn from them.** If people are working hard but not getting ahead, don't dismiss them as role models. They have a lot to teach you, both about the realities of life and the values that can lead to a better life. If you can't find a role model in your family, find one in your community. They are there if you look.

2. **Accept your parents for what they are.** I was fortunate to have a wonderful mother to lead me by example, but you may not. Nonetheless, you need to make peace with your family. They can teach you—and unfortunately, sometimes that lesson is what *not* to do.

3. **A name provides insights into the future path.** Understand the meaning of your given name, listen to the names other people call you, then choose the name you want to be known by. When you choose a name, you are choosing your destiny. My mother chose Farrah; my family chose Golden Child; but as you'll see in the next chapter, I ultimately chose my own name, even if I only said it to myself: Twenty-First-Century CEO.

4. **Never underestimate the power of a name when setting up a company.** Cute phrases and puns will get you somewhere, but they won't get you everywhere. The end must be reflected in the beginning.

5. **Listen and accept positive reinforcement.** Don't listen to the negative. There are those who will say that you "can't." Ask them why not. You'll find that more often than not the reason is "because no one else has done it." That's not a dead end; that's a challenge. Don't let negative people drag you down.

6. **Great ventures start with small ideas.** Don't be afraid to experiment. Keep your eyes open, your mind working and your body ready for work. You don't have to hit a home run the first time, but you'll never hit a home run if you don't learn to swing. I only made nine dollars on my first "business," but it was probably the most important nine dollars I ever made.

7. **Invest in your future.** Don't make it just to spend it. You need to enjoy life, but you also need to think about your future.

8. **There are always people who will help you.** Just keep looking until you find them. Don't give up; keep asking for help. That's not begging, that's investing in your future. There are a lot of good people in the world. Don't ever let anyone tell you differently.

REALLIONAIRE AFFIRMATION

◆

I was put on Earth to fulfill a specific purpose.
I only have to name it to achieve it.

Reallionaire Exercise:
What's in a Name?

Names are powerful. Your name is something to help people distinguish you from the next person. I have a unique name. People typically have a hard time pronouncing it at first, but they never forget it. So let's explore your name and find the power that lies inside of you.

First, find out what your name means. Ask your parents why they named you your name. If they just "pulled it out of a hat," go to the Internet and do an extensive search. There are different meanings depending on the language you choose. My name in Arabic means "burden bearer." Imagine how affirmed I felt when I found this out. I'm put here to lead and inspire. That's not a burden in a negative sense; it's an honor.

Let's complete a quick exercise that will provide some insights about your specific purpose.

My given name is: _____

My parents named me this because: _____

_____

_____

My name means: _____

_____

_____

Sometimes people go by nicknames, but even nicknames carry meaning. Look inside yourself and find out if your name fits you. Why do you go by Bob instead of Robert? Do you really want to be called Missy, or would Michelle be your preference? Would you move through the world differently if you carried a name that was more aligned with your purpose? Think about it. The first step to becoming a reallionaire is to become real. That starts with your name.

Never Fear Rejection

how I became a real salesman by learning to see "no" as an opportunity, not a rejection

Muhammad Ali rubbed a lot of people the wrong way. He was outspoken, cocky and handsome. He was the proverbial thorn in white, middle-class America's side. And he knew it. Because he was also very intelligent. He read a lot. He studied great thinkers. He observed the world. He spoke out about the inequities in American society when that kind of behavior got you lynched. I admire people who aren't afraid to speak up in the face of hostility. Ali was unflappable, and I dig that.

Like Ali, it was time for me to start observing the world. After my first business venture, I stopped watching a lot of television. I was still a kid; don't get me wrong. I still loved cartoons and video games, but I also started to branch out by reading more books and watching the people around me. I was becoming more intrigued with the world. Like "the greatest boxer of all times," as Ali called himself, I questioned the way things had been set up in society.

Champions aren't made in gyms. Champions are made from something they have deep inside them—a desire, a dream, a vision. They have to have the skill, and the will. But the will must be stronger than the skill.

—Muhammad Ali

While flipping through the television channels I once heard a member of a black political party say "The rich get richer and the poor get prison." My brain did an about-face that day. Those words hit me like a ton of government cheese. It would be years before I was able to fully comprehend the severity of those words, but when I did, I began to rumble.

Right around the time I heard those "rich get richer" comments, I started to hang out with Mom a lot more. Mom was the oldest in her family and the first to start her own business. At age fifteen she started a full-service dry cleaners pick-up and delivery service in her neighborhood. By her twentieth birthday she'd opened a day-care center and even hired her former sixth-grade teacher to work with her. She ran this enterprise until she was twenty-five years old. Since then Mom has been a partner in many different businesses: insurance, executive search firms and an advertising agency, to name a few. Her tenacity is off the charts, but what I admire most about my mom is her hustle. Sean "P. Diddy" Combs says he's got the "right hustle," but Diddy's got nothing on Mom. I'm glad hustle is a part of our family's DNA. We do what we have to do to put food on the table because we know that nothing happens unless you get off your butt and get into action.

During the summer of 1991, just before I turned the big seven, Mom started to talk to me more about her business. As a freelance consultant, she helped entrepreneurs start their own enterprises and helped established businesses keep theirs running smoothly. "There are lots of things I can teach you about business," she said. "And there are lots of things you can teach me, too."

My eyes bucked out of my head. "I can?" Mom nodded yes. "Like what?" I asked.

"Like how kids think," she responded. "I'm very interested in what goes on in that little head of yours."

Word! Nobody had ever really asked me anything like that before. Mom turned back to her paperwork, and I turned back to my book. I could hear the television playing in the background, although I wasn't really paying much attention to the newscast. But then I heard something that made my antennae rise. The anchor said something about someone being a "twenty-first-century CEO." I turned to the television set to see a crowd of people erupting from their seats in applause. This "twenty-first-century CEO" walked proudly to the podium. I figured he must be somebody important because he was wearing a suit. And everybody in the 'hood knows that only preachers, pallbearers and important folks wear suits.

My eyes widened as the man in the expensive suit waved to the audience. What had he done to get to be on TV? Why were those people clapping for him? I wanted what that man had. *Maybe,* I thought, *I already had it.* As I sat gazing at the television, Mom walked over and turned it off. "Time for you to go to bed," she said, kissing me on the forehead. "I've gotta get ready for work."

Then she turned on her stereo and put in a cassette of one of her favorite songs, "Ain't No Stopping Us Now" by McFadden & Whitehead. Ironic, huh?

Things were looking up, I could tell. Mom's goal had been to show us by example what hard work could do, and she was delivering on every promise. She was going to be our Harriet Tubman, our Moses. She would lead her children out of poverty. And guess what?

Her golden child would be right beside her. Believe that.

Mom had told me the year before that when I was ready to learn more from her, she would teach me. So I decided to ask her to make good her promise of spending more time with me. I invited her to become my business associate. That's right, my business associate. Let the meetings, interactions and transactions begin. It was time for me to pull Mom to the side and try to wrap my arms around her occupation.

Things may come to those who wait, but only the things left by those who hustle.

—Abraham Lincoln

"Mama, what exactly does a consultant do?" I asked.

She placed her paperwork aside. "A consultant helps people. They look at a business to see what makes it work. If something is wrong with the company, they help that business figure out how to keep it running smoothly, so that it can make money and be profitable. Does that make sense?"

I nodded yes. "You're sorta like a doctor then, right? Doctors look at people and help them fix whatever's wrong with them," I said.

Mom smiled and shook her head yes. "You're something else. Yes, a consultant is a little like a doctor."

I understood. I finally understood what my mother did. She was a business doctor. My world made sense. I'd seen lots of folks who called themselves businessmen and women. And I'd watched enough television to know that in business there's one ironclad rule: it's all about the briefcase and the suit.

I learned early on that successful people had a certain look. They wore certain clothes. Walked a certain way. Carried themselves in a certain manner. And most importantly, possessed certain "toys."

One of the first things I noticed when I attended meetings with Mom was that, at the beginning or end of the meetings, the grown-ups always handed each other these small pieces of paper.

Clearly, I'd seen these slips of paper before because I had made one from cardboard when I was four years old. But I don't think I really understood what role they played in business. I was intrigued by these two-inch-by-three-and-a-half-inch slips of white, ivory or sometimes colored paper. I also noticed there was never a meeting where they weren't exchanged.

So, one night after we'd arrived home and I'd stayed up way past my bedtime, I walked into the kitchen where my mother was completing a presentation.

"What are you still doing up?" she asked, never looking up from her notepad.

"I wanna see those pieces of paper they gave you at the meeting."

"What paper?"

"Those card things," I responded.

My mother frowned. She had no idea what I was talking about. "Farrah, go to bed. I've gotta finish this presentation."

But I persisted. "Those cards, Mama. Those little pieces of paper that everybody traded." You see, to me, it looked like they'd swapped baseball cards, something I'd done with my friends. "They're like baseball cards," I said.

Finally my mother stopped writing. "Boy, what are you talking about?"

I walked over and grabbed her briefcase, which was almost as big as I was. "In here," I said, handing her the mahogany-colored contraption.

She opened it and moved some papers around as I looked over her shoulders. "Those," I said, pointing to a neat little stack of the cards she'd been given during the meeting that night.

"These?"

I nodded yes. "What are those?"

"They're business cards, Farrah. They tell everybody else who you are, what you do, what company you work for and stuff like that."

"Can I see them?"

She handed me a small stack. I began reading them one by one. I noticed that each one had certain words underneath the person's name. President . . . manager . . . vice president, and so on. Finally, I stumbled upon a card that caught my eye. A white one with the name "Bill Young" written in black letters. Bill Young, CEO.

"Mama, what's a CEO?"

"Chief executive officer. They run things," she said as she scribbled a few numbers on a legal-sized sheet of paper. "That's the person who usually makes the most important decisions in the company. I thought I told you to go to bed."

My eyes lit up. "Do they make a lot of money?"

She laughed. "Yeah, usually they make a lot of money. A whole lot."

I smiled and stared at the card. "Can I have one of your cards?"

"For what?"

"I wanna do something with it. Make something. Can I?"

"Just one," she said, never looking up again. "Now, don't let me tell you again to go to bed."

I knew when I'd gone past my limit with her, so I vanished into the hallway with my new possession. I headed to the bedroom and turned on the light. Andre screamed at me, "Boy, turn that light off!" So I headed for the bathroom. I was far enough away from Mama so she wouldn't know I was still awake, but close enough so I could hear her coming if I needed to bolt for the bedroom.

For the next few hours I scribbled away on sheets of notebook paper, designing my own business card. I tried a number of things.

"Farrah Gray, President." That was okay, but I thought people might get me confused with the president of the United States, and I didn't want that to happen. Besides, in my mind, that title was taken any-way. So I moved on.

One doesn't become great by claiming greatness.
—African proverb

"Vice President." Hmmm. Nope, all I could remember him doing was stand-ing in the shadow of the president. I wasn't interested in being the boy *behind* anybody, so vice president was out too.

"CEO. Chief Executive Officer." My mom said this was the man. The person who was the most powerful in the company. I liked the sound of that. Plus, I'd heard several people on television mention that we were approaching the twenty-first century. I knew that whatever I would do as a businessman, I'd do in the twenty-first century, whatever a century was. I took the black marker and traced my mother's business card about eight times, four in each column. And then I wrote the following:

Farrah Gray
21st Century CEO

Then I grabbed my round-tip scissors and cut it out. That was my first real business card.

The next day after I got home from school, I started washing dishes. My mother worked at least eighteen hours a day, so she insisted that we do our parts to keep the household running smoothly. A few days earlier I'd asked her if she would buy me a briefcase so I could be like the other businesspeople at our meetings. She laughed and told me she wasn't going to buy me a briefcase and that I needed to "be creative." So, that day as I rinsed the glasses and plates from breakfast that morning, I noticed my lunchbox sitting next to my books. That's when it hit me. I already had a briefcase.

I rushed over to the table, dripping water all over the floor, and I grabbed my hand-me-down Incredible Hulk lunchbox. After I washed it and polished it with a little Vaseline, it was ready for its debut as my briefcase. I practiced walking with it in my hand just like the businessmen and women did when they walked down the streets of Chicago. I was ready for my first business meeting. I had my business cards and my attaché; all I needed was a suit.

Look out, Armani!

One of the things I loved most about watching political debates or caucuses or even the ten o'clock news were the suits the men wore. I loved the ties, the cuff links, and the cool way the tailored jackets hung off of politicians, businessmen and anchormen. I'd sit for hours in front of the television admiring those suits. "One day," I told Andre, "that's gonna be me. I'm gonna make my suit look gooooood." I'd read somewhere that fortune does not change men but rather unmasks them.

That day had finally arrived. Now that I had the business card and briefcase, it was time to unveil the final piece of the business-boy ensemble. It was time for me to think about what I'd wear to my mother's next meeting. Most of the clothes in my closet fit into two categories: hand-me-downs or hand-me-downs. That was it.

There were years that I never got one new piece of clothing but instead got whatever my older relatives couldn't wear anymore.

But it was cool because in this particular moment, none of that mattered much. I was about to step out into the world of business, and I was going to be looking like a million bucks even if my total ensemble only cost around five dollars.

Now, at the time I didn't own a complete suit. I had what I now affectionately call "pieces of a suit." A pair of pants. A jacket two sizes too big. And a couple of cotton button-down shirts. None of which, by the way, were the same color. Most poor people possess one suit that they wear to funerals, weddings or graduation ceremonies. Not me. I had to connect the dots when it came time for dressing up. You just never knew what I was gonna come around the corner wearing.

Fortune does not change men; it unmasks them.

—Madame Necker

I put my lunchbox briefcase on the table and headed to my closet, where I stood in front of the near-empty space. Staring me in the face was an old pair of sneakers and a well-worn pair of brown "church" shoes. Church shoes are the shoes you only wear to events at church. On the rack were two shirts, one short-sleeve with blue stripes on it. The other one was white with long sleeves that had a space on the chest where a pocket used to be.

The pants category was even more dismal. Basically, I had four pairs of pants. One for each season, although I wore each of them year round. I knew I wasn't going to wear my jeans to the meeting. I'd never seen businessmen in jeans. I often wondered if they even owned a pair! I knew I wasn't going to wear the bone-colored corduroy pants my cousin had given me. They were so tight I could barely move without squeaking. So that left my navy pants or the black pants. It was a tough decision.

The navy pants had this huge hem in them. I wasn't that tall at the time, so Mom had to hem them so I wouldn't trip when I walked. The black pants were what kids in my neighborhood called "floods." Floods were pants that came above your ankle. Some people call them high-risers. They were called floods because the thinking was that if a flood ever came, you'd need to make sure your pants were pulled up high enough that they would not be damaged by the water. Wearing floods was always a cause for ridicule in the 'hood. So I wasn't sure I wanted to step out to the business meeting in a pair of floods. That meant I'd be wearing a pair of navy pants with the only suit coat in my closet. And it was brown.

Now, I wasn't the fashion Adonis I am today by any standard, but even at seven and a half years old I knew that wearing a brown jacket and a pair of navy slacks was not going to turn the fashion world on its head. But it was all I had, so I put them on with the long-sleeve white shirt.

There was still one missing link. A very important missing link. The tie. Had to have the tie. No business suit is ever complete without a fly tie. So it was off to Andre's closet. There I found the tie I wanted to wear. A black one with brown and ivory stripes. Perfect. I was almost ready but there was still one small thing: the tie wasn't a clip-on, and I didn't know the first thing about tying a tie.

That's when I remembered the immortal words of Mom: "Be creative." So I went into the bathroom, climbed on the back of the toilet onto the vanity, where I kneeled to work on my tie. For the next thirty minutes I fidgeted with the tie. Then I yelled for Kiki to come and assist me, but she wasn't much help. "I don't know how to tie a tie. I've never worn a tie," she said laughing. Finally, I got the tie around my shirt collar. And although it was cutting off my oxygen supply, at least it wasn't falling off. Business-boy was finally ready for the world.

Presentation, Presentation, Presentation

It was a breezy night in late October. I'd finished my homework and was waiting anxiously for my mother to come home so I could find out about her big presentation, which was taking place in a suburb of Chicago. I had placed a stack of my newly designed business cards next to my math book so I could look at them while I worked on my schoolwork. I also had organized my "briefcase" with cards, pencils and office supplies from my mother's stash, so I could look the part when I got to the meeting. I'd told all of my siblings and practically everyone at school that I was going to be unveiling the Farrah Gray, twenty-first-century CEO business card that night at "our" next business meeting. I could hardly concentrate on my lesson because I wanted so badly to get to that meeting to shove my business cards down people's throats.

A few minutes later, my mother walked through the door. I shot out of my seat like a cannonball. "Ready," I said. "My business cards are in here, in my briefcase." My mother glanced at the lunchbox and smiled. "Did you finish your homework?" she said laughing. I nodded yes. "Let's get going," she said.

Mom was a student of great thinkers. She was always reciting memorable quotes. One of her favorites was, "Don't be discouraged. It's often the last key in the bunch that opens the door." Before we entered the building that evening she quoted another of her favorite sayings, "Never let them see you sweat." Two minutes later, we entered a room full of people, most of them white. She introduced me either as her business associate or the CEO of FG Enterprises.

I said hello and took my seat. I knew to be well behaved. Never speak unless spoken to. But I checked out everybody, noticing their clothes, how they addressed each other, stuff like that.

At the opposite end of the table from Mom was a tall, thin man dressed in a black suit. His hair was pulled back into a graying ponytail. He was smiling as people entered the room, and everyone seemed to know who he was. I was curious. Who was this Sean Connery–looking dude who was getting so much attention? Most of the people around the table seemed to look down on Mom. But not the man with the gray ponytail. He had a different vibe and energy.

Meanwhile, Mom was in her "I'm about to present" mode. Very serious. She hadn't talked very much on the way over to the meeting, which meant she was preparing, and I shouldn't flood her with questions. She had managed to tell me that if the meeting went well, we would be able to move out of the projects and into a nice apartment downtown. I was praying the meeting went well.

> *Don't be discouraged. It's often the last key in the bunch that opens the lock.*
>
> —Anonymous

Even though I had said two prayers— one before and one during the meeting— I could tell people weren't responding to Mom's presentation. Some of them looked bored. Some looked at their watches. They had few questions and basically appeared to be uninterested in what she had to say. Mom closed the presentation, and almost instantly everyone was up and out of the door. They filed past Mom without so much as a boo, but they all went out of their way to say good-bye to the man with the gray ponytail.

Mom walked out into the hallway to talk to a few of the attendees. The mystery man watched Mom leave the room, then he walked over to me.

"Hi, I'm Roi Tauer."

"I'm Farrah Gray," I said, handing him my business card. He looked down at it.

"Twenty-first-century CEO, huh?" he asked as he handed his business card to me. I could read, but pronouncing his company's name was a stretch.

"That's Ideators," he said, laughing. "It's hard for some adults." The card said he was a twentieth-century CEO, founder of a think tank.

"What's a think tank?" I asked.

"A think tank is a group that meets to brainstorm and come up with strategies for a particular project or topic," he said. "Would you like to be in one of my think tanks?"

"Yeah, I mean, yes," I said. "But why would you ask me to be in your think tank?"

"First, you know to ask 'why.' Second, you're intuitive. Third, you're inquisitive. Fourth, you hear things on the ground. Fifth and sixth, you have no sense of limits, and you have a fix on the future," he said.

"Thank you," I said. How did he know all of that?

"Farrah, your mother's told me a lot about you. She said you have all the right intentions and motivation for wanting to become a successful businessman. Is that true? Do you want to be an entrepreneur?"

"Yes, I do," I said eagerly.

"Then it's your turn to blaze your own trail," he said.

Mom entered the room. She wore a pained facial expression, a look her children knew all too well. She had not gotten the outcome she wanted. Mr. Tauer walked over and patted her on the shoulder. "That was over in the first ten minutes. I was just telling your son that in business you have to . . ."

Mom just walked over to the table to pack her belongings. She high-fived me, which indicated that she'd been cast down but not destroyed. As Emily Dickinson once said, "A wounded deer leaps the highest." I knew Mom would bounce back.

"Farrah says he's an entrepreneur," Roi said.

"He tell you he made his first sale recently?"

"No," he said, turning toward me. "You're holding out on me?"

"I sold lotion. I made almost ten dollars too!"

"Good for you," he replied.

Mom motioned for me to get ready to leave. Roi walked toward the door with us. "Do you and your friends ever talk about what you want to be when you grow up, Farrah?"

I nodded yes. "What would you say if you and your friends came up with a business you could start together?"

"That would be fun," I said.

As we rode down on the elevator Roi asked, "What do you think about the name Unique for your business?"

"It's unique," I said, laughing.

"Run the name Urban Neighborhood Economic Enterprise Club past your friends."

"Urban what?"

"Urban Neighborhood Economic Enterprise Club. Ciao," he said as we exited.

"Chow," I said back. What the heck was Urban Neighborhood Economic Enterprise Club? And what did he mean by "chow"?

Unique UNEEC

A few days later I got to attend another meeting with Mom, and Roi was there also. I was glad to see him. I'd remembered everything he said at our initial meeting, although I hadn't had the chance to run the Urban Neighborhood Economic Enterprise Club or "unique" thing past my friends. At the end of the meeting we struck up another conversation.

"So, did you give any thought to our last talk?" Roi asked.

"Yes, sir, I did."

"And what did you think?"

"Well, I haven't talked to my friends yet, but I do want to start a business," I said.

"Good, good. Did you know that people will give you money to start your own business?"

My eyes got bigger than a stack of silver-dollar pancakes. "People will give us money to start our own businesses?"

Roi nodded yes.

"Do we have to give it back to them?" I asked.

Roi let out a hearty laugh. "No, Farrah, when you make money they make money. The people I'm talking about are called investors. Sometimes they're called angels."

"Cool," I said. "I have your card, can I call you? Will you help us?"

"Yes, I will. If you're serious about starting your own business, and you're willing to work hard, I'll be your mentor," he said. "You think you can get your friends together to discuss their business ideas?" I quickly nodded yes. If things went well, I thought, I would be able to help my mother with the bills around the house and maybe even buy a real suit.

Before Roi and I could talk any longer, my mother signaled for the meeting to start. Roi leaned over and whispered, "Call me."

"Really? I can call you?" I asked.

He shook my hand. "Farrah, we're gonna be business partners; of course you can call me."

My charge was to recruit other kids who had dreams of starting their own businesses. My years as a professional kid had taught me there are a few things that are guaranteed to get kids excited. One of those is free food. So, a few days after talking to Roi, I gathered about nine boys and girls to make the announcement. "I've got something that you're going to love," I said.

"What? What? Candy?" one boy asked.

"Video games?" another shouted.

"Better than candy," I said. "Better than video games."

Well, their eyes widened. What could be better than candy when you're eight years old? I knew I'd better get to the point before I lost my audience.

"Pizza. How would you like to have all the pizza and soda you want?"

They erupted with screams. "When do we get it? Where?" They had questions galore.

It was a chore to get them quiet again. "If we form a club and meet every Saturday, we can get all the pizza and sodas we want." They were in.

Later that evening, I phoned Roi. When he picked up the phone, I could feel the butterflies going crazy in my stomach. "Hi Roi, this is Farrah Gray. I just wanted to thank you."

"Thank me for what?" he asked.

"Are you really going to be my mentor?"

Roi answered quickly. "Farrah, I didn't have to offer to be your mentor. I'm serious about that, but be prepared to meet people that will smile in your face, shake your hand and make promises they don't intend to keep," he said. This sounded like very heavy advice for an eight-year-old, but I listened because I could tell he was quite serious. "Farrah, the benefit of having an experienced mentor is that

I've been there and done it. I've started lots of businesses."

Speaking of promises, I told Roi about the indirect promise I made to my friends to get them to start the club with me. "What did you tell them?" he asked.

I hesitated. Roi had told me to be direct and honest with my friends about why they would be meeting on Saturdays. I finally mustered up the courage to answer my new mentor. "Well, not what you told me to."

"Why not?"

"I don't know," I said quietly.

That didn't cut it with Roi. "I don't know" didn't appear to be one of his favorite phrases. "You have to give me a good answer, Farrah. An answer that will help me understand why your plan went in the opposite direction of what we discussed. Tell me why you didn't do what I suggested you do."

My mind went back to something my grandmother used to do. She would give us information and never bring it up again until she wanted to see if we remembered. She called it "putting your brain on display." This is exactly what Roi was doing. My first test, and I blew it! And he wasn't letting me off the hook very easily.

"Farrah, are you a leader or follower?" He didn't give me a chance to answer. "If you are a follower, you will travel the path of others." I didn't exactly know what he was talking about, but I knew better than to interrupt him. He continued. "Now, tell me what you told your friends again?"

I hated to repeat it. "I told them we could eat free pizza and drink lots of soda on Saturdays if they joined the club."

Roi's voice elevated. "The *club*? Did you mention that this was about starting their own businesses?"

"No."

"What is the name of the club supposed to be? Did you even give any thought to our meeting and talk the other night? Did you do anything we talked about?"

But before I could answer, Roi said, "Call me back when you have answers that I can relate to, young man—okay?"

Click. He hung up! I felt horrible. Not only had I disappointed my new mentor, but I'd also made a promise to my friends that I couldn't keep. No more than ten minutes later, I phoned Roi back asking if it was a good time to speak with him. He chuckled, "No. Take ten more minutes to think about it and then call me back."

_____

A wounded deer leaps the highest.

—Emily Dickinson

I sat near the phone thinking about everything that had just happened. I was ready to talk to Roi again. "Is this a good time?" I asked again.

"I don't know. Do you have better answers than you did earlier?" Roi asked.

"Yes, sir," I said.

"Okay, so let's start again. Why didn't you tell your friends that you were coming to them with an idea that involved business?"

I started to say "I don't know" but I caught myself. "I was afraid that they wouldn't do it," I said.

"Do you fear rejection, Farrah?" he asked.

"I don't have any fear, Roi!"

"You don't?"

"No, sir! Maybe I just didn't want them to say no."

"No to what? You never gave them a chance to say no, son," he said.

I'd never thought about that. He continued, "How do you know if they have dreams or not? They could have been just as excited about the club as they were about the free pizza, but you didn't give them a chance, did you?"

"No, sir."

"No, you didn't. Now, go back to your friends and let them see how excited you are about the business idea. They may become motivated to listen and ask questions. Let them know you are the cofounder with your mentor," he said. "Are you willing to do that?"

Roi rarely asked "can you do" anything. For him it was a matter of what someone was *willing* to do, not whether they had the ability to carry out a task. "Farrah, I'm very proud of you, and you should be proud of yourself. Go out there and prove to your friends that you believe in yourself and that you're willing to follow your dream. You just might infect them with your enthusiasm," he said.

"Yes, sir," I said.

"The next time we speak, I'll share some of my failures with you because they have been the key ingredients to my successes in life. Prepare yourself to fail; if you don't fail, you stop learning."

"You failed?" I asked, surprised.

"Of course, Farrah. You don't hit a home run every time you're at bat," he said, laughing. "Now, if you want to be taken seriously, go out there, get in the ring and get your nose bloody. Are you ready to have a bloody nose?" he said, still laughing. He always made me laugh.

"Yes, sir, I'm ready to get my nose bloody," I said, laughing as well.

"Good. Begin by calling restaurants out of the Yellow Pages. Ask to speak with the owner—not the managers, the owners. Let them know they've got a serious youngster on the other end of the phone."

The more Roi talked about my action plan, the more my nerves built. Why couldn't he call the owners for me?

And as if he could read my mind, he said, "And don't ask me to call for you. . . . It's your club members who you promised a free pizza and all they can drink."

"Okay," I said.

For the next fifteen minutes Roi gave me bullet points to discuss with the restaurant owners. The first thing I'd have to do was convince these adults that I wasn't just some kid playing jokes on the phone. I was a serious businessman.

"Do you like the name UNEEC?" he asked.

I frowned into the phone. "I sorta like it. What does it mean?"

Roi laughed. "It's an acronym. You know what an acronym is?"

"Is that when a word sounds like another word but it's really another word?"

"That's a homonym. An acronym is a set of letters that stand for something else. Write this down, U-N-E-E-C."

I grabbed my pencil and wrote the letters down. "UNEEC?" I repeated.

"Right," he said. "U-N-E-E-C stands for Urban Neighborhood Economic Enterprise Club," he said. You and your friends are entrepreneurs who are starting your businesses in your own neighborhoods. Are you ready for what's ahead?"

"Yes!"

Frank Leahy is credited with saying that when the going gets tough, the tough get going. The next morning I got up bright and early. I grabbed the Yellow Pages and took a deep breath. The first few people I called laughed. They thought it was a prank. *Click.* They'd slam down the phone. It was tough. Some of the folks hung up the phone in the middle of my pitch. But I kept calling. I left messages for more than ten owners, and finally, I received a phone call back from a restaurant owner who also owned a hotel franchise in the Chicago South Lake Shore Drive area.

"Is Farrah Gray in?" he asked.

I thought it was a joke. Instead, he introduced himself. "I have a message here that you're looking for meeting space, is that right, son?"

"Yes, sir, we have a business club called UNEEC, Urban Neighborhood Economic Enterprise Club."

"Well, I give entrepreneurs respect even if I can't figure out what they are doing or going to achieve. What are your ages?" he asked.

I told him I was seven years old going on eight, but the oldest member was going to be twelve years old. "When do you all plan to have your first meeting?" he asked.

"On a Saturday. As soon as we can get someone to say yes!" I replied.

"I see. Well, looks like I'm that someone. Call me back tomorrow at the hotel during business hours. You got a paper and pencil? Take down my direct line," he said. He gave me his phone number, and I wrote a big question mark on a piece of paper to remind myself to ask the gentlemen what was he expecting out of the deal. "Thank you, I'll call tomorrow, I promise." There I was, making promises again.

I couldn't sleep at all that night. I didn't want to tell anyone about the phone call until I knew for certain that I had a deal. The next day I called three times. I didn't want to leave a message because that would mean I'd go crazy waiting for him to call me back. On the fourth try, the hotel receptionist put me through.

"It's me, Farrah, the young man you spoke to yesterday," I said. "You said to call you today."

"Young man," he chuckled. "You did as I asked you to. I'm impressed! Now, I have arranged for you and your club to have meeting space every Saturday from 11 A.M. to 2 P.M. inside the main dining room."

I was momentarily speechless. Roi had told me that when you

cut a good business deal there has to be something in it for all parties. "Will that work for you, son?"

"Yes, sir. May I ask you a question? What do you want out of the deal?" I asked.

When the going gets tough, the tough get going.

—Frank Leahy

He seemed confused. "Didn't I get this right? You're looking for meeting space, free pizza and some sodas, right?"

"Yes, sir," I replied.

"Then what could be in it for me?"

He had me there. I didn't know what was in it for him. I was hoping he would tell me!

"Well, actually, there is something you can do for me," he said. I was relieved. "You can conduct a press interview to talk about your club once it is up and running. That'll give me some publicity for the hotel."

I didn't know what publicity was, but I agreed anyway. "Yes, sir, I can do that," I said.

"You ever talked to the newspapers or TV stations?"

"No, sir, but I can. I know I could do it," I said.

He chuckled a little. "I'm sure you can too."

One challenge down, another to go.

The Importance of a Good Ride

The next thing I'd have to do is take care of transportation from our housing project to the meeting, which was approximately two miles away. I made calls to cab companies, but this got me nowhere. Those calls went something like this:

"Yes, I'd like to get transportation for me and my business club. . . ."

"You live where?"

Click. I must have called ten or fifteen cab companies before the last taxicab dispatcher told me to try the airport shuttle vans. Not being an experienced traveler, I knew nothing about airport shuttles.

By the time I stumbled upon a company called Airport Transportation, I was already accustomed to the word "no" and being laughed at. Many of the airport shuttle companies were owned by small business owner–drivers. Some of them were family-owned businesses. Such was the case with this company. The man who answered the phone was the nephew of the owner. He referred me to the owner's son. The son then referred me to his older brother, and the older brother patched me into his father, who was driving a vehicle.

The owner listened very attentively and asked a few questions. He sounded like he was in his early fifties; I'd listened to enough "old schoolers" to recognize his age range. He grunted a few times after hearing my request and finally said, "Little fella, I'll see what I can do. Where do you live?"

I started to give him my address. "I want to meet you," he said. "Let me speak to a parent."

I told him my mother was at home, but I hadn't told her of my secret assignment. "It's not a real secret but I don't want to get her hopes up too high." Then I reminded him that we were going to a club of young people, not old people. He laughed loudly.

"Old people can teach you a thing or two. You know that, don't you?"

"Yes, sir, I do. I'm sorry if I offended you."

"No, son, you were just speaking your mind. Always speak your mind. You don't waste folks' time and they don't waste yours. Remember that!"

I called my mom to the phone. She had no idea what I was doing or who was on the other end, but she took the phone just the same. "Hello, may I help you?"

"Yes, ma'am, I want to stop by your place to meet your son with your permission."

Mom frowned. "Why?"

"I think I'm going to make an investment of my time and gas in this club venture of his. Time is money so I want to be sure that if I block my vehicle out of the service for nonpaying passengers that I feel good about it."

Mom turned to me with The Look. She nodded. "I see."

"Meeting that boy of yours will help me make up my mind. Would that be all right?"

Mom gave him the address, hung up the phone and looked at me. "Just so you know, you're on your own with this meeting. You can tell me about it when it's all over." Then she instructed me to put on my "meeting shirt."

Within an hour I'd bathed, brushed my teeth, used my brother's shoeshine rag and cleaned my fingernails. Then I went outside to wait for the airport shuttle to show up. People in my neighborhood rarely called airport shuttles. The only exception was when they were flying out for a family funeral. So I knew I would not have a hard time spotting my visitor.

Soon, a light yellow and brown ten-passenger bus pulled onto the street slowly, as if it were driving in a school zone. The van pulled to a stop in front of me and out stepped a tall black man built like a linebacker. His dark piercing eyes seemed to penetrate whatever he looked at. I extended my hand for a handshake. Then I handed him one of my homemade business cards. "Hello, I'm Farrah Gray."

He took the card with a smile. Then he shook my hand so hard that I thought my eyes would pop out of my head. "There are two types of firm handshakes, young fella," he said. "The white-collar handshake and a hard-working man's handshake. You are gonna have to use both to make it in this world with the competition that is out there now. None of the big boys are going to give you shelf space."

Instead of parking, we drove around the neighborhood. As he drove, he talked nonstop about his business. "I wish my boys had listened to me when they were younger. We could have a fleet of vans by now," he said a little sadly. "Where is your club going to meet?"

"The Ramada South Lakeshore."

"The Ramada? Boy, how did you pull that one off?"

"What do you mean, sir?"

"I service that hotel because black folks stay there. They can pay for three nights there for the price of one night at those big, pricey hotels."

I kept looking out of the window. I'd never been in an airport shuttle before. He looked in the rearview mirror at me. "Do you know the owner?" I asked.

"I've been doing business with them for years. Two shuttles running back and forth daily so I shouldn't lose any money on Saturdays while I'm helping you out."

Just as we were pulling back up to my apartment, his two-way radio went off. He opened the door and helped me out of the van. "I gotta go. Pick you here, right?"

I straightened my clothes a little. "Yes, sir, everyone will be standing right outside in the same place next week. Thank you."

"My pleasure. How many you think will be going?"

"I don't know yet. I haven't told them what I have planned."

"Can I join your club?" Before I could answer he chimed in, "I know, I know . . . no old folks!"

Mom and Kiki had been watching from the living room window, waiting for me to return. As soon as I walked through the door they bombarded me with questions. "What was that all about?" "Farrah, what are you up to now?" My mother smiled broadly.

I didn't stay long enough to chat. I had a job to do; I had to go back outside and round up my friends to invite them to our new club. I'd just made my second business deal in less than a week, and I was feeling pretty good about myself. It was time to add the final piece to the puzzle.

When I returned outside, all of the kids circled me much in the same way a football team gathers around its quarterback. When I had their attention I asked a simple question, "Who wants to get rich?" They all yelled, "Me! Meeeeee!"

I kept going, "Who wants to buy all of the candy they want, as much as they want, at any time?"

"Meeeeeeeeee!!!"

I had sufficiently warmed up my audience. Now all I had to do was convince them we could get rich together. I took my business cards from my pocket, ready to take a very big step for a young businessman: give my friends my card. I had accomplished three huge tasks. First, I'd secured meeting space. Second, I'd gotten us transportation. And finally, I'd had the confidence to stand before my friends and tell the truth about my dreams and what we could create together—this time without fear of rejection.

By dinnertime, when we all had to be in the house, club membership totaled four of my friends. The next day all four of us spoke to everyone else's parents about the club. I explained that the club was designed to help their kids become entrepreneurs, maybe even millionaires.

Within an hour of my arriving home from the visits in the neighborhood, our phone started to ring off the hook with calls from my friends' parents asking my mom, "What is your son feeding my child?" or "What big idea is he selling about starting their own businesses?" My mother let those parents know that I was very serious about my business endeavors. "My son will be retiring me before I'm fifty years old . . . will yours?" she asked. What could they say to that?

That night, my call to Roi was brief. "You did it," he said. "You infected them."

"Yes, I did."

"You should be very proud of yourself, Farrah," he said. "Call me tomorrow."

I was never in short supply of conversation, but that night my brothers let me share all of my plans with them. They showered me with encouragement: "Farrah, you can do it! You're the man! Pretty soon they'll be calling you Mr. Farrah Gray." Finally they said, "Go to sleep, little brother. Otherwise you will be talking to yourself."

But there was no chance of that, so I went to see if Mom was still awake. She liked to wind down by listening to music. I put my ear to her bedroom door. I could hear the soft music playing, and her light was still on.

"Mom?"

"They fell asleep on you, huh?" she said, laughing.

"Yeah. I'm still excited."

"You can come in for a few minutes, but I need to get some sleep before I have to get up to go to work," she said.

I remember my mother looking extremely tired. I didn't like

that. But that night when I hugged her good night I had a new sense of hope. I knew that what my friends and I were about to do would help me show my mother how much I loved and appreciated her. She wouldn't have to be tired for much longer. My new club was about to pop off, and more importantly, I was about to launch my empire and a relationship with a mentor who would change my life.

REAL POINTS: Getting Started

The first step is the hardest, because it's accompanied by fear, doubt and inexperience. But you've got to take it before you can take any more steps on the path to your dream.

1. **Opportunities are all around you.** Some people might think that being young and black was a disadvantage, and in some ways it was. But it was also an opportunity. You have to understand your inherent advantages and then sell them. Remember, people want to help. Give them a reason.

2. **Fear is False Expectations Appearing Real.** It is an illusion created entirely in our heads! You don't overcome fear, you embrace it and walk through your doubts, knowing you have the capacity to achieve your dreams *in spite* of your fears. Fear is the fuel of reallionaires. It's perfectly normal to be afraid—it's what you DO with that fear that defines you.

3. **Decide what you want to be—and aim high.** You'll never get further than you can dream, so dream big. Even if you just want to be a schoolteacher (a very noble dream!), then try to be the best schoolteacher in the world. What do you have to lose?

4. **Have the right look.** Your appearance is your first impression. Think about your style carefully, then take the time to do it right.

5. **Presentation is important.** Yes, your personal appearance is important, but all of your materials—from your posters to your handouts to the bag you carry them in—are just as important. It's got to be first class all the way.

6. **Watch everyone around you.** Some people obviously have more going for them than others. Get to know those people. They will lead you by example, and soon you will be one of them.

7. **Never be afraid of your idea.** I was so worried about what my

friends would think of UNEEC that I couldn't even mention it to them. That's a loser's mentality, which I quickly corrected. If you're ashamed of your dream or your idea, then it's not worth having. Talk about your ideas. Get feedback. Find supportive people. That doesn't mean you have to be a blabbermouth, but you have to be out there to get anywhere.

8. **Never say "I don't know."** Right or wrong, you always need a reason. If you didn't have one when the event or decision actually happened, then think about it afterward and determine exactly *why* you did what you did.

9. **Never take "no" for an answer.** Persistence isn't everything; it's the only thing. If you're going to be a success in life, you'll hear "no" thousands of times. Look at every "no" as an opportunity.

10. **Success creates confidence, which creates more success.** Remember that the first step is always the hardest. Once you've taken it, don't start walking—start running. Momentum is a valuable asset in life.

REALLIONAIRE AFFIRMATION

♦

Opportunities are everywhere. I can rise above any circumstance with hard work, integrity, faith and especially persistence.

Reallionaire Exercise:
What Can You Learn from Your Environment?

Where are you right now? Look at your current surroundings. What can you learn from your present situation or environment? There are lessons all around us if we just take the time to notice and appreciate them. I met my mentor Roi Tauer because I was in the right place at the right time. There are people like Roi in your life if you can just clear some of the clutter to see them. Here's a quick exercise.

There are six components to this exercise: clear the area, focus, be positive, visualize, celebrate and create. These six steps should be done over the next thirty days.

Step 1: Clear the Area

If your life feels like it's filled with too much stuff, get in touch with all the things you can clear out so you can better assess what you have to work with. Maybe you can't get anything done because your work-space is congested and messy. Take the time to organize yourself and get your lab in order; you'll find that your efficiency will improve significantly. Maybe your situation has to do with emotional clutter. Uh oh. Time for some relationship spring cleaning? If the people in your life aren't contributing in a positive way, there's a good chance they're bringing you down. Get rid of them! Emotional clutter is much heavier than mounds of paper on your desk. Negative people are like ticks. They drain the blood and leave you lifeless. Aren't your dreams worth more to you?

Step 2: Focus

Decide what it is you want and then focus like a laser beam. Keep your eye on the prize. Write down your desires and look at them every day over the next month until they are branded in your thoughts. Now that's focus!

Step 3: Be Positive

What you want may not come overnight, but it will come if you continue to be and act positively. In other words, it's not enough to just say "I want to be rich" or "I want to be healthy"; you must also do the things that will result in riches and health. Save or invest your money. Reevaluate your fitness plans.

Step 4: Visualize

When you believe it, you'll see it. Belief begins with a picture of what you want. Close your eyes and get an image of your goal or desire. If you want to be healthy, picture your perfect body. If you want to be famous, see millions of people applauding as you cross the stage at the Kodak Theater in Los Angeles. The more visualization you do, the closer you move toward actually having what you want.

Step 5: Celebrate Every Day

You are your biggest supporter. Don't look for someone else to tell you that you're doing a great job. Know that you are moving closer to your dreams. Tell yourself, *I'm doing good*, or *I'm proud of you*. It may sound crazy but it works. Pretty soon you'll find that these internal conversations are propelling you to greatness. Don't worry if people stare, just keep talking!

Step 6: Create Your "Grow My Success" File

Write down daily successes and review the list each morning before starting the day.

Build an All-Star Mentoring Team

how the experience and knowledge of others helped me craft a business club uniquely my own

Roi's enthusiasm for UNEEC had infected me. I was now having visions of moving out of the projects and taking Mom to a Chinese buffet every week. I wouldn't have to think of food stamps and welfare checks anymore. I could focus on my own business dreams. For a week, I worked on my speech for the meeting. I knew that since this was my idea, my friends would be counting on me to say something that made sense. I decided that the thrust of my presentation would be about making money. Poor kids can relate to making money. First we had to get psyched about the challenge at hand—our club. President Harry S. Truman said something that I've never forgotten. He said that he studied the lives of great men and famous women and found that those at the top were those who had done their jobs with everything they had in the way of energy, enthusiasm and hard work.

And I thought about the last few questions Roi had asked before we ended our most recent conversation: "What will you tell them UNEEC is? How will you explain the plan?"

"The what?"

"The plan. You need a plan. You think those kids could do those martial arts moves because they're lucky, Farrah?" Roi had invited me to a martial arts class a few weeks earlier. He wanted to make sure I understood that it was more than kids kicking each other, but a lesson in what hard work and focus could achieve.

"No," I said.

"They're learning from a master teacher. Where they are as students has nothing to do with luck. They work hard. Remember that. Good work, not good luck. Say it."

"Good work, not good luck," I said with Roi three times in a row.

"Now, before you can work on UNEEC you first have to answer these questions: Who's Farrah? What are his strengths and weaknesses? How strong are his mind, body and spirit? How well do you fight?"

"Fight? I don't fight my brothers or sister. My friends and I don't fight. I don't know how well I fight because I have never been in a fight," I told him.

Those at the top are those men and women who have done the jobs they had with everything they had of energy, enthusiasm and hard work.

—Harry S. Truman

"It's time for you to get ready to fight to win. I'm not talking about fighting someone with your fists but rather defeating whatever is inside of you that could stop you from achieving your dreams."

I was feeling the butterflies again in my stomach. I didn't fully understand all of Roi's metaphors, but he spoke in a way that awakened me. At seven and a half

I couldn't think about taking control of my life, but I could think about taking control of my mind because I was learning from the best. Roi had created a spark, a burning desire and a fire that wasn't going to be put out any time soon.

Up until then, I'd been surrounded by so much poverty and lack that the only thing my little brain could think about was money, money and money. But after that last conversation with Roi, I stopped thinking about having lots of money. Instead, I was beginning to understand what made a person rich. Money was only one piece of the puzzle. There was something else. I didn't have all the answers yet, but I knew it was something that happened on the inside. *Good work, not good luck*. Roi's words rang in my ears for the next few hours.

On the morning of our first club meeting, I was given the royal treatment. Mom prepared my favorite breakfast of eggs with cheese melted on top, turkey bacon and an English muffin. We were rubbing our pennies together so there was no jelly.

Andre pressed my clothes and shined my shoes. Kiki rewrote our meeting agenda. She created a few sample logo designs of UNEEC for us to choose from. She and Roi suggested that we get T-shirts produced. Not only could we sell them to make money, we could also promote our club by wearing them ourselves.

I was almost ready. The only thing I had to do was to call for transportation. I'd been so excited the day I secured the ride, I'd forgotten to get the owner's name or business card. When I called, the guy who answered the phone was in a mood. "May I speak to the owner, please?"

"You want my dad, kid?"

"Yes, sir!"

"Hold on," he said. I recognized the next voice on the line. "It's me, sir, it's Farrah. I left two messages that we were going to need to be picked up today for our first meeting." "Are you ready now?" he asked rather impatiently.

"No, because we're not supposed to be ready until ten."

"Young man, you and your friends should be waiting for me at ten, ya hear?"

It was a tone that carried special meaning. He didn't say it, but I'd heard that tone many times: don't be late.

"Yes, sir. And sir?"

"Ten o'clock," he said.

"I know, sir, I just wanted to know your name."

"Mr. Perry."

I hung up the phone and thought for a moment. Roi told me to call him "Roi," not Mr. Tauer. Why did I have to call him Mr. Perry? I didn't know this then, but as I look back now, that encounter makes me reflect on how black people sometimes look for ways to make sure people give them respect. They might say "Call me Mr.," or "I'm this or that," before they even state their names. At seven and a half, I was just as guilty. I was calling myself a "twenty-first-century CEO" before telling people my given name. It was a trait I now wanted to toss into the trash. I was still the twenty-first-century CEO, but I was going to be known by my name first. Farrah. I liked the sound of that.

I hadn't talked to my friends since Friday night. I was praying that when I walked out the door that I wouldn't be the only one out there. Thankfully, by ten o'clock there were fifteen kids ready to roll out of the projects to our new adventure. And an adventure it was. We were about to be exposed to a whole new world. A whole new set of people. Living in the ghetto makes you think that nothing exists outside of what you see on a daily basis.

This was, and still is, partially the fault of the media. There weren't that many positive depictions of black folks on television, even in the late '80s, and we all knew we weren't going to be Bill Cosby. Even though, as Baltasar Gracian said, "Nothing arouses ambition so much as the trumpet clang of another's fame," we still needed to see successful people who looked like us—otherwise what were we expected to be when we grew up? Where were we to look for role models? We'd heard about the Boy Scouts, the Girl Scouts and Junior Achievement. But those were organizations for them, not us. "Them" was anybody who didn't live in the ghetto.

UNEEC was not just a business club, it was also a place that we could call our own. Something created for us, by us. As we drove down the highway on that inaugural Saturday, you could just see the pride swelling out our chests. Here we were, fifteen little black children, stepping out on faith to

> *It takes time to succeed because success is merely the natural reward of taking time to do anything well.*
> —Joseph Ross

explore the unknown. I still get chills thinking about it.

Mr. Perry talked the entire drive from our neighborhood to the Ramada Inn. "We're here," he said. "Farrah, you're the ringleader. Let's move 'em out!" That was my cue to get up and lead us into the hotel lobby.

But first, I wanted to give Mr. Perry a handshake to thank him for his support. Mom raised us to say thank you, and Mr. Perry was about to get my sincerest gratitude. "Thank you, sir," I said. "We really appreciate it."

"You're welcome, little fella," he said, beaming. He stood in the background as we filed orderly into the hotel registration area. "May I see the owner, please?" I asked the registration attendant. The bifocaled desk clerk barely looked up from his paperwork.

"You want who, little boy?" he asked.

"The owner, sir," I repeated.

"What do you want? Are you selling candy for your church fundraiser?"

"No, sir, the owner is waiting for us," I insisted.

Mr. Perry knew something was up, so he walked up to the front desk as if he were the owner. "Hey fella, you must be new here? I haven't seen you before."

"I just started. I'm in training," the clerk replied.

"In training, you say? Well then, you shouldn't take liberties with your boss' guests."

"Guests? Who are these kids?"

"Kids? These are young businesspeople. Farrah, come up here and ask this desk-clerk-in-training his name so you'll be able to tell his boss how he treated you," Mr. Perry said.

The desk clerk looked down at his clipboard. "We're expecting a group of people for a special meeting but . . ."

Mr. Perry interrupted. "This is the group. Where's the room?"

Mr. Perry led us to our meeting space. He told me to ignore the desk clerk's treatment. "He doesn't think young kids are important enough to warrant his attention." I thought about what happened in my mom's last meeting. This is what she must have meant about having thick skin.

We arrived at our meeting room and were amazed by what we saw. A big room set up with plenty of soda, water, ice, paper cups, mint candy, paper and pencils. And it was all for us.

I was carrying a big envelope with paper and a bunch of BIC ink pens wrapped in a rubber band. Kids wrote with pencils, but businesspeople signed checks with pen. So it was important for us to conduct ourselves as businesspeople long before we launched our first enterprise. After we'd all taken our seats and gotten sodas (of course) we were ready to start the meeting. That's when it hit us. What could we talk about at the hotel that we couldn't talk about in the 'hood? And who was going to speak first?

I was so used to sharing and being polite at home that I didn't think to kick things off. That's when I remembered what Roi had told me. *You're a leader, Farrah. Leaders lead.* I went to the front of the room and stood. "Hello everybody. You all know who I am, and I know who you are. We are a bunch of poor kids who want to get rich . . . right? That's why we're here." It had become an inside joke that UNEEC was a group of "po" kids who were about to become rich kids. In the 'hood, "po" means that you can't even afford the extra "o" and "r."

UNEEC is a club to teach neighborhood children how to turn their ideas into business enterprises. UNEEC club members are big ideas in small packages.

I asked Twjuanna, a twelve-year-old, "Since you're the oldest, will you please read what's on the paper?" Twjuanna began to read:

"UNEEC is a club to teach neighborhood children how to turn their ideas into business enterprises. UNEEC club members are big ideas in small packages."

She took her seat. I stepped in. "First, raise your hand if you know what you want to be when you grow up."

A few people raised their hands and said things like "policeman," "football player," "engineer" and "teacher." I kept hearing Roi's words again: "Infect them." I looked down at the talking points list. "What kind of business do you want to start?" I asked. Nothing. Everyone just stared at me like I was E.T. or something. "Come on, haven't you ever thought about starting your own business?"

The waiter walked in, interrupting me, "Do you all want your pizza now?" The waiter took a seat as we told him what kinds of toppings we wanted on the pizza. When he left, I finished telling the group about the night I had made lotions and sold them. Some of them already knew about that story because some of their parents had been my customers. But most of them had not heard the story. They were impressed that I made almost ten dollars in less than forty-five minutes.

Twjuanna said, "You're the youngest, but I think you know what you're doing. What's going on with this club?" I was nervous. After all, most of them were older than I was. "We have to learn together," I said. "That's what my mentor says."

"What's a mentor?" someone asked.

As soon as that sentence flew out of his mouth, I realized that I'd forgotten one important ingredient: to invite a mentor to the meeting. We needed someone who could give us guidance, information and answer our questions. I'd blown it. I'd crossed all of my t's but I'd forgotten to dot that last i.

"A mentor is somebody who can teach us how to do what we're trying to do," I said. "They're like teachers or guardian angels. At our next meeting, I'll be sure someone is here."

They seemed fine with that, or maybe the aroma coming from the pizzas distracted them. It was hard to keep our minds on the meeting after the waiter came and asked us about food. Within the next thirty minutes we'd gone through our entire agenda. The pizza had arrived, and it was clear that we didn't have any more business to take care of. So, after we finished eating, I asked the group something Roi always asked me: "Are you proud of yourselves?"

"I know this is our first meeting but can we do something in here before Mr. Perry picks us up that we can tell our parents about? Something we can say we're proud of?"

Some of them wanted to wait until the next meeting, but I knew that I would have to give a report to Mom and Roi, so I wasn't leaving without accomplishing something. Someone blurted out, "We should be proud that we're here."

At first we all looked at him like he was crazy, but he was right. There were kids in our neighborhood who wouldn't have been caught dead in a Ramada Inn on a Saturday morning. We were a unique group of kids.

"That's it," I said. "Write down on your sheet of paper that we are proud because we are here." We talked about all of the negative things that were happening in our neighborhood, but we had still chosen to do something positive.

I immediately felt good about going home because I knew that as soon as I walked through the door, my mother was going to ask me what I learned, and I couldn't tell her that I learned how to eat pizza. She wouldn't go for that. If I came back with that answer, she'd make me go to the laundromat with her on Saturdays. And I couldn't have that! That was not going to happen. "Okay, we have about ten more minutes," I said. "We need to write down two more things: What kind of money do we want to make, and by when? And what kind of businesses do we want to start?"

Just as we were finishing this exercise, the waiter told us that Mr. Perry had to make a quick run, so he had ordered another pizza for us. While he was placing the soda and napkins on the back table, he asked, "What are you all trying to prove?" No one wanted to answer him, mainly because he didn't sound like he cared. He made us feel as if he didn't like or want us there. Like we had inconvenienced him. That made two people in the hotel who weren't taking us seriously. We didn't need to compare notes to know this.

Shortly after the waiter left, we heard Mr. Perry's voice as he burst through the door. He was a rather large man with a commanding but warm voice. "Kids, I've been working hard all my life, and I just like what I see in you all. Since I was your age I've been working. I've been my own boss since I moved away from home in Baltimore back in . . . well, a long time ago," he said, laughing. "For a while I lived like a hobo. I've seen stuff y'all don't ever wanna see. Oh, yeah, I got plenty of stories that I can share. When do I get to attend a meeting?"

"How about next week?" I said.

"Next week it is, then," he said. I was touched by his humility and willingness to support us. There was almost a sadness about him. I couldn't wait to hear some of his war stories, but I had one more announcement to make. "Okay, before we leave. Next week we will talk about our dreams and goals and how to reach them. So bring some goals with you," I said, packing up my stuff.

As we left the hotel, we made sure to walk past the rude desk clerk and smile and say our good-byes. He had not ruined our day. He couldn't. What we were doing was bigger than him. We had done it. Meeting one was out of the way. UNEEC was official.

We got back into the van and headed home. Back to chores. Back to reality. Back to the same challenges. But even though there were harsh realities waiting for us in the 'hood, we felt equipped to deal with them. That's how powerful UNEEC was already. We had arrived at the Ramada Inn as fifteen little people, yet we were returning home as fifteen little businesspeople.

Mr. Perry dropped us all off at the exact location he'd picked us up. When I walked into our apartment my brothers, sister and mother greeted me with the usual, "How was it?" They didn't want to ask too many questions just in case things hadn't gone as planned. But for the rest of the weekend, I was a motor-mouth, nonstop chatter. They were probably ecstatic when I hit the pillow that Sunday night.

It was Monday morning at school before most of the UNEEC members saw one another again. One of the boys who had gone with us on Saturday started ridiculing the club. "Man, you looked like a fool on Saturday," he said to us. We all looked at him as he laughed alone. "You're not gonna start no businesses. Rich people start businesses."

On cue, we left him standing by himself. So who was the joke on? In just one weekend, our daring group had made one decision. We weren't going to give in to the jokes and the negative things people were going to say to or about us. Andre had told me something when I was about five years old that I never forgot. He said, "If we can work hard enough to buy a car, then we can drive out of here to a new life."

Saturday was there again before we knew it. And so was Mr. Perry, on time at ten o'clock sharp. We were all there. Even Mr. Negative, who we'd left laughing by himself earlier that week, was standing right alongside us.

And there was something different about the van this week. It had two extra passengers. They were Mr. Perry's two sons. I didn't know why he'd invited them, although I did remember him saying that he wished his boys had listened to him years ago. All of the kids greeted the young men. One of them spoke up, "Our dad wants us here to hear him speaking to you all. He said we would learn a few things about him that he never had time to stop and tell us years ago when he was working like a dog." His words sounded familiar. Reminded me of my mother. I often wondered about all the stories she could share, given all of the experiences she'd had. I'm sure there were lots of things that she'd endured she'd never share with her children.

Something told me we should have asked for a box of Kleenex for this meeting because Mr. Perry seemed like the kind of guy who could easily have you in tears or stitches. And this was one day I didn't care if my friends saw me crying. When we'd finished our pizza, Mr. Perry stood and started his speech. He had grown up during segregation. Many men of his generation had quit school to go to work to help support their families. "Get your education," he said. "And all education ain't in books. You can learn a lot just by watching, talking to people."

Mr. Perry had been an excellent student in grade school. He said he loved learning. "We didn't have the same opportunities as the white children. Our books were used, torn. You had to fight not to feel like you were less than them," he said with a tear in his eye. "That's why I get so upset when I see our people dropping out of school to sell drugs or run the streets. I think to myself, *Don't they know that people died so they could have the right to a good education?*"

Mr. Perry went on to talk about the importance of strong role models. He said that it's impossible to improve if your only guide is yourself. By now, there was hardly a dry eye in the room. Mr. Perry's genuine, heartfelt words had cut to the core. He'd shown us how fortunate we were to be starting something like UNEEC. "I know you are too young to know how big UNEEC is, but what you're doing is gonna change your lives. I wish we'd had something like this when I was coming up," he said.

As we boarded the shuttle bus, our minds were still on Mr. Perry's speech. He'd closed by asking us a question. "You kids like to play games?" Yes, we said. "Well, life is no game. You can't play games with your life. You take care of business, and let other people play games, ya hear?" We all nodded yes. Mr. Perry was like E. F. Hutton. When he talked, you listened.

Mr. Perry was a serial chatterer, so although his formal keynote had ended, he continued to break us off with his wisdom. "Hard times and challenges never end. Your mothers and fathers may be struggling to keep roofs over your heads and to feed you. That's their challenge. You're about to be business owners and that means other types of challenges, ya hear?"

Challenge was a big word, but we understood what he was saying because Mr. Perry had a way of speaking that shot straight through your heart. He continued as we sat motionless, riveted by his smooth delivery and conviction. "Just remember, don't get too big for your britches. And be sure to do your homework and put school first," he said. We started to clap. He interrupted us, "One more thing . . . stick together."

> *People seldom improve when they have no other model but themselves to copy.*
> —Olivia Goldsmith

We started to clap again, but not too loudly because we figured Mr. Perry would have "one more thing." We were right.

"Okay, I promise, this is the last thing this old man's gonna say before he drives you home," he said. We laughed. Yeah, right. "Right now you are just little people. The outside world doesn't think you're all that important. But let me tell you how important you are as a group. Individually, you're important to your families, to your mamas and daddies."

We had no idea where this story was going. "When it gets cold here in Chicago, we call it a 'hawk,' right? Well, each one of those little snowflakes are not that important until they stick together with all the other little snowflakes." His voice became loud and thunderous. "Boy! That's when that hawk hits ya!!!" He laughed. "Now let's go. I gotta get you home."

REAL POINTS: The Beginnings of Success

Success isn't something that happens overnight; it's a process. You have to nurture it along with continuous care, and the best way to do this is to have the right people working with you. Not for you, with you.

1. **Have a plan and stick to it.** If you try to revise on the fly, you'll just get yourself into more trouble. Trust yourself enough to see your idea to fruition.
2. **A business isn't just about money; it's about the pride of ownership.** That is true of everything in life: your personal feelings are just as important as the material reward. Remember that there is more than one way to measure everything.
3. **There are those who will try to knock you down.** They may come from the outside, like the employees at the hotel, or they may come from inside, like the member of UNEEC who laughed at us. They may even come from deep inside your own doubts and fears. Enthusiasm is infectious, but so are negativity and self-limiting thought patterns. Which will you catch?
4. **Mentors are vital.** Keep looking until you find someone you respect and trust in your area of interest, then ask, ask, ask them everything. Even more important, listen to their answers.
5. **It's important to listen, but it's more important to listen to the right people.** Three people tried to drag me down; I ignored their criticism. Two people wanted to lift me up; I took their love and respect to heart.
6. **A good idea is nothing without the will to make it happen.** You don't have to think up every good idea. You simply need to learn how to put those ideas into practice.
7. **Never be afraid to take what others are offering you, but always give them proper credit.** And also pay them back

threefold in kindness and admiration. You are not owed anything; every helping hand is a gift.

8. **If you are the boss, you have to be the leader.** Don't look for someone else to do your job or get you out of an awkward decision—including your mentor. The responsibility is yours.

9. **Keep your word.** Success is a house of cards, which one foolish act can knock down. This is especially true when you are just starting out. The loss of one loyal friend or one key contact can destroy all your efforts. There is no opportunity worth the risk, and there is no excuse for not meeting your obligations.

Reallionaire Affirmation:

◆

*I can dream alone, build alone and
strive alone, but true success always requires
the help and support of others.*

Reallionaire Exercise:
Build an All-Star Mentoring Team

This week, you are charged with putting together a powerful, dynamic group of people who are going to support you on your reallionaire journey. I suggest starting with a core group of three. But to get to the three, you're going to brainstorm and come up with nine. Why so many? Because it's a lot easier to reduce from a large group than it is to come up with three guaranteed selections.

First, let's be clear about the definition of a mentor. Write down your definition.

A mentor is: _____

_____

_____

_____

Now, I want you to pick up the phone and call one of your mentors (or a trusted friend or colleague) and ask his or her definition. Just ask the person to share with you, but don't reveal your definition. Now write his or her definition down.

_____

_____

_____

What did you find? You probably didn't come up with the same definition, right? That's because there are as many definitions of mentors floating around the universe as there are varieties of potato chips. The key is to develop a mentoring relationship that both people can agree upon. In other words, if you think a mentor is supposed to give you business leads, but your mentor is under the impression that she's supposed to simply chat with you about business strategy, there could be problems. So get clear beforehand.

Write down what you'd like, in an ideal world, from a mentor.

_____

_____

_____

Now make a list of nine potential mentors.

1. _____
2. _____
3. _____
4. _____
5. _____
6. _____
7. _____
8,
9. _____

Over the next seven days, make contact with these nine people, sharing your business goals or dreams and asking for their support. Keep in mind that you have an ideal-world wish list, so be honest when you approach your potential mentors. Good fortune!

Seize Every Opportunity

**how I learned that opportunities are everywhere,
even in your biggest problems and setbacks**

Remember that show, *Kids Say the Darndest Things?* That show must have been named after me because somehow I was always putting my foot in my mouth. Oh, not in a bad way at all. But I was always asking the question most adults hated: "Why?"

I'd grown up with a mother who was very much from the "do as I say, not as I do" school of thought. And if you asked "why," it was sure to be met with "because I said so." That's just how she was raised. Children didn't talk back to grown folks. And they certainly didn't question them!

So my "whys" were always met with a mixture of contempt and curiosity. On one hand my mother wanted me to be inquisitive. On the other hand, she wanted me to take my rightful place in the hierarchy and simply follow the rules.

I was an "out of the box" thinker. It wasn't that I wanted to challenge my mom and other grown-ups. I was genuinely curious about the world, my surroundings and how things worked.

And more important, my head was full of positive thoughts of what was to come. Once I started UNEEC, this little voice was always going off in my head, saying, *Way to go, Farrah. You are really making moves instead of just dreaming.*

A goal is a dream with a date on it.

—Unknown

And now the pictures in my head were even more vivid, more colorful. I used to ask myself, *When I grow up, who do I want to be like?* Now, the little voice answered, *You can't be like anyone else. You're Farrah.*

I was like a young child sitting in the driver's seat of a brand-new sports car. Unfortunately, I didn't know how to drive. And worse, I couldn't even reach the pedals! I felt a blend of excitement and anxiety. There's usually one person a child could go to for help in that situation. Someone to help him or her feel safe in the world. For me, it was Mom.

"I have a stomachache," I told her one night as I laid my head on her chest.

She squeezed me tightly. "A stomachache? You don't look sick." She stroked my head gently. "I think you just need your mommy."

We both laughed. Mom was right. Whatever was wrong in my world would be made better by some quality time with her. I grinned from ear to ear, but Mom didn't smile back. Instead, she turned away. Her spirit changed from happy to sad. I thought maybe I was sick, but she didn't want to scare me. Did I look that bad?

"What's wrong?" I asked.

"You're fine, Farrah. It's probably just your gut telling you that things are about to change," she said. "You have a classic case of a nervous stomach."

"So I won't have to take any medicine?"

"No, sweetheart."

"Good." I felt better already. But Mom's expression remained sullen. "What's wrong then?"

She took a deep breath. "We have to move in a few days."

I pulled away from her, shocked. "What? Why?"

"We're going to get evicted," she said, trying to keep her voice from cracking. Now I was sick for sure. Not only was I sick, I was also angry. I wasn't angry at my mother, but I was mad at something.

"Why, Mom? We don't have enough to pay the rent?"

"No, baby, we don't. I spent the rent money preparing for the meeting where you met Roi Tauer. I have about forty dollars to my name, that's it."

"But . . ." I couldn't believe my ears.

"I had to pay the printer quite a bit of money to produce the presentations. All the materials had to be first-class and high quality. First-class isn't cheap. I had to pay for the conference room. I had to pay for the coffee, the donuts, sugar, cream, cups and napkins."

"But I thought you helped businesses make money."

"That's only if they choose me to be their consultant. They didn't choose me, Farrah."

I didn't understand what was happening. I just knew that I didn't want to ever see my mom wear that expression again. I started to tear up so she tried to console me. "What I had hoped for didn't happen. But you gained a mentor, and you learned a valuable lesson: don't be so desperate that you put all your eggs in one basket." She forced a smile. "You have to be a juggler and a hustler, sweetheart. I was hustling in the last meeting, Farrah. Hustling to prove that I was the most qualified person for the job."

"Why do you think you didn't get the contract?"

My mom paused for a second as if she wanted to choose her words carefully. She was not the type to mince words, but she was always a thoughtful communicator. She wanted to teach us well. She'd say, "You have to live with the consequences of your actions *and* your words, so choose them carefully."

"I thought you did a good job, Mama. Why didn't they pick you?"

"My gut feeling tells me they didn't know I had a permanent suntan until they walked into the room. I'd gotten the meeting based on a telephone conference with them. I'd never met them," she said.

My mom then explained that she had invited Roi Tauer to the presentation in the hope that his presence and credentials might soothe any ruffled feathers. She thought that her association with such a well-known and well-respected businessman would win her points with the potential client, even if she was black. "Not everyone you meet will accept you based on the content of your character and qualifications, Farrah. That's just the way it is."

I didn't fail, I was rejected. There's a difference, and you have to learn to deal with both.

—Mom

"But that's not right," I said. "They can't turn you down just because you're black."

"No, it's not right, baby, but there's one thing all of your mentors will tell you. If you're going to be an entrepreneur, you'll have to grow thick skin," she said. "Son, I didn't fail, I was rejected. There's a difference, and you have to learn to deal with both. But I'm an upperdog, not an underdog. I pulled myself up from my bootstraps to make it as a businesswoman. And I'll get another shot."

That night, as Mom tucked me into her bed, she said something I'll never forget. "Dream big, my little golden child. You can do and be anything you want." Then she planted a kiss on my cheek and left the room.

"Love you," I said as I watched her walk toward the doorway.

"Not as much as I love you," she said as she turned off the light and shut the door. That conversation sent me into orbit. I had a flurry of thoughts centering on eviction notices, racism and injustice. I couldn't tell what I was feeling most. Anger over the fact that my mom had lost a job because she wasn't white, or scared because I didn't know where we were going to live if we got evicted.

The next morning I couldn't get my mind off of the conversation. As I brushed my teeth, I couldn't help but be slapped with the reality that the person who bought the toothpaste, toothbrushes and every other commodity in our home had only forty dollars to her name. I looked around at the soap, towels, bathroom tissue and shampoo. Mom was responsible for providing us with all of that.

We affectionately called Mom the "miracle worker," but I wondered how she was going to save us this time. Did my brothers and sisters know what was going on? Did they know we were about to be kicked out of our home? I wasn't going to be the one to tell them. I was keeping my mouth shut.

The next twenty-four hours were gloomy at best. There wasn't a lot of chatter in my house that day. I spent most of the day just watching Mom. She worked around the house. Did laundry, washed dishes, cooked whatever food was in the cupboard. Occasionally, I'd catch a glimpse of her crying, though not often. Crying, like sleeping, wasn't something we saw very much from Mom.

As the oldest in her family, she was accustomed to serving and giving, not receiving or taking. So I knew she wasn't going to ask for anyone's help. But that didn't mean I couldn't ask for her, right? At least that's what I thought.

When Mom had gone to her room to lie down, I called Roi Tauer and told him that we were being evicted. Answers always seemed to come easily for Roi, so I thought he would be able to help my family. I had no idea that perhaps I would be crossing a line by calling him. To me, I was just a kid who wanted desperately to help ease his mom's pain. I thought I was doing a good thing. But after I told Roi about our situation, he sat on the other end of the phone silently. "Roi? Are you there?"

"Yes, Farrah, I'm here," he said.

"What do you think?" I asked.

"Listen to me, Farrah. I know you called me because of the business relationship we established through your mother, but you don't know me well enough to discuss your mother's or your family's business with me," he said. "I am certain she will not be very pleased."

Now I was the silent one. I thought that if you could trust someone with business secrets, you could probably trust them with personal information as well. "Yes, sir, I understand."

"This can be our secret, okay?" he said.

"Yes, sir, but what are we going to do? She said we're gonna be evicted."

"Farrah, have you ever seen your mom give up when things got tough?"

"No, sir."

"I didn't think so. You know, you don't have to have money to be a successful businessperson. You don't need a college degree. You just need a lot of common sense backed up by a willingness to work hard. Your mom has a lot of common sense, a great work ethic, and she works without ever complaining, right?"

"Yes, sir."

"I'm your new mentor, but you've got the best mentor in the world living under the same roof with you. Your mother believes in herself, and she'll pull through this situation. You've gotta have faith in her."

I was slightly baffled by Roi's comments. Here he was talking about confidence, faith and common sense while I was sitting on the phone wondering if we were going to have to sleep on the streets. My family had been evicted before, and we had had to live in our car until we could get another apartment.

What I really wanted was for Roi to tell me that everything was going to be fine. Maybe secretly I was hoping Roi would give us some money so we wouldn't be thrown out of our apartment. But after he reminded me that life sometimes serves food you may not like, he made another suggestion:

"Let's meet tomorrow. I'll call your mom later on, to ask for permission. While you're with me, she can get some breathing room, and you can get some exercise."

"What kind of exercise?" I asked.

"You'll see," he said.

Why did grown-ups love that phrase so much?

Jonathan took me to meet Roi the next day. We both wanted to get out of the house, and I wanted to talk his ear off because I was still excited about UNEEC. Kids have a wonderful way of bouncing back from seemingly tragic situations. I'd convinced myself that moving wasn't going to be too bad. I'd still see my friends in UNEEC since I'd hooked us up with free transportation every

Saturday. Plus, if we moved, I'd meet new friends and maybe get more members.

Jonathan and I were happy to be out together—but for different reasons. He wanted to talk to girls, and I wanted to talk business. When we arrived at Roi's high-rise condominium I told my brother, "This is where people who make money—a lot of money—live. I bet they aren't getting evicted."

Jonathan answered, "I told Mom that one day we're going to live in a neighborhood just like this. I'm going to own one of these buildings."

"I told Mom that I was going to retire her!" I shot back. We were always hearing professional athletes talking about retiring their parents, and that sounded like a great thing to me.

We buzzed Roi's apartment on the intercom. He met us coming off the elevator just as we were waiting for an elevator to take us up. "Let's go," he said. "The class has already started."

I knew Roi well enough not to ask what classes he was taking us to. As he'd taught me, silence can be a virtue. Shortly after we left his building we arrived at a martial arts school. Karate? I didn't understand, and I didn't want to go inside.

"Let's sit in on the class for a second," Roi said as we reluctantly followed him inside. For about an hour we did nothing but watch the instructor teach and interact with about a dozen students. When Roi had seen enough, we left.

Roi took us to our bus stop and said good-bye. Jonathan and I looked at one another. What had just happened? Roi had said all of three words to us during the class and even fewer after it was over.

We arrived back in our 'hood just in time to see Mom crossing the street. The closer we got to her, the more apparent it was that she was smiling.

"How are my babies?" she said.

"Hey Mama, where've you been?" She said nothing. Finally, she answered. "I'll tell once we get inside."

Once we were all inside she called my sister from the kitchen to meet us in the living room. We all sat in front of her, wondering why she'd gone from crying the previous day to smiling. "We don't have to move. Not yet anyway," she said.

We looked around at each other. "Why, what happened?"

"I had to do something that I pray you never will. I had to hold my nose while I drank dirty water," she said.

We all said the same thing. "Drank dirty water?! You drank dirty water, Mama?"

"No, I didn't drink dirty water. . . . That was a figure of speech. It means that I did something I didn't want to do. Something that was really hard to do."

Kiki sat up straight. "What did you *do*?"

"I signed up for public assistance."

"We have to go to the grocery store with food stamps?" That was Jonathan's question.

"What doesn't kill you will make you stronger, Jonathan," Mom shot back. "I just told you I had to hold my nose while I drank dirty water. You think that was easy for me? I did something that would have otherwise killed me, but we've got money to pay the rent and we're gonna have food to eat."

"Were you embarrassed?" That was Kiki's question.

"About what? About having to admit I'm not superwoman? All my family members have just enough to keep them from getting evicted. I would never burden them by asking for money they don't have," Mom said.

I was confused again. I'd always seen my mom giving to others, but I couldn't remember anyone giving her anything. "Why is it that no one ever gives you anything, Mama?" That was my question.

"Sweetheart, nothing's further from the truth! I may not receive money from some of the people I help, but I receive in other ways. Remember, whatever you send out comes back to you."

Kiki, Jonathan and I sat there for a few more minutes. For Mom, it was done. She'd done what she had to do to take care of her family. But she wasn't the one who was going to have to march down to the store with food stamps.

Even though we lived in the projects, there was this illusion that you weren't poor until your family had to rely on public assistance. Now we were in another class, and we were not happy about it at all. We knew that everyone in the neighborhood store was going to see us as poor.

Sometime you have to do things you don't want to do, but that's part of life. Accept your decision and build on it into the future.

That night I tossed and turned for hours. I couldn't get Mom's dirty-water analogy out of my head. The thought made me sick to my stomach. The idea that Mom had to ask total strangers for help didn't settle well with me. It was like we were begging. The next morning, I didn't ask any questions because I didn't want her to know what I was thinking. I wondered how many of my friends' moms were on welfare. How many of them were ashamed about being on public assistance? I needed to ask them how they felt about it. I needed to talk to someone about this new situation. But I thought back to what Roi had said about family secrets. I decided our welfare story had to remain in the family.

Like Brother, Like Son

"Tomorrow never dies," my brother Andre used to say, by which he meant there was always hope because you always had another day to pursue your dream. The oldest of five children, Andre truly believed he was destined for greatness. A cross between Billy Dee Williams and Colin Powell, he had it all: looks, intelligence and charm. And since he was so much older than the rest of us, he reveled in his role as surrogate father. He took great pleasure and pride in telling us how we should do things. He'd always say, "Now, you don't have to do it this way, but I'm just telling you what I would do." We weren't stupid; he meant you should do it his way.

Andre had endless dreams. He liked quoting Ralph Waldo Emerson, who once said that the world is all gates, all opportunities, strings of tension waiting to be struck. Andre was about to play a mighty tune. Watching Mom pursue her many entrepreneurial ventures fueled his own ambition, and one day he decided to enter an essay contest for an all-expenses-paid trip to Japan. His confidence must have faltered, though, because he never sent the letter. One day Mom came across the completed essay. She was so impressed by it that she mailed it in to the contest judges. She figured even if he didn't win the contest, he'd have a running start on writing an executive summary for his own future business.

When she told him what she'd done, I think he felt a blend of surprise and joy. Surprise that she thought it was good enough to actually submit; joy because he could see how excited she was about the possibility of him going to Japan.

"You really think I can win, Mama?" he asked her one day.

"Nope . . . I don't think you can win, Andre," Mom responded. Andre was baffled.

"Then why did you send it in?"

"You asked me if I thought you could win. . . . I don't. I *know* you can," she said.

Andre smiled like a kid who'd just gotten his first bicycle. I was only four at the time, but I can still see his boyish expression as she hugged him and told him how proud she was.

About a month later we all marched down to the nearby Kinko's copy center. Andre's notification letter had arrived. He'd been chosen. It was a proud day in the Gray household the day when we all went to Kinko's for Andre's passport photos. He would be leaving within the next three months on an all-expenses-paid trip to Tokyo as a delegate with the Young Professional Committee, promoting mutual understanding and friendship between the people of Japan and young American entrepreneurs.

> *Knowing is not enough; we must apply. Willing is not enough; we must do.*
> —Bruce Lee

Andre became the first in our family to travel out of the country and the only African American selected by the Japan-American Society to participate in the Century of the Pacific Conference delegation. My mother and grandmother bankrolled Andre for new luggage, two new discount suits, shirts and ties, a briefcase, and Japanese language tapes so he could learn basic Japanese grammar and expressions.

For a kid who didn't have the physical presence of a father, Andre was more than just "big bro." He'd become my confidant, the positive role model that every young black boy needs in his life. Mom had explained that his leaving was a good thing, and I believed her, but I was also a little sad because it meant I wouldn't get to see him for a while.

One night while he packed he noticed my long face. "Get over here, lil' man," he said. "What I'm about to do, you can do too."

"But I don't want you to go," I said. "Who's gonna talk to me at night before I go to sleep?"

"Mama. Jonathan. Alex. Maybe Kiki if you're nice to her," he said, laughing. "Okay, maybe not Kiki."

"Not the same," I said, looking away.

"I know, but I'll call ya and I'll write you and I'll teach you some new words in Japanese when I come home. It'll be okay. This is a real good opportunity for me. You know how Mama's always talking about starting your own business one day?" I nodded yes. "Well, I'm going to learn how the Japanese do business, and I'm going to share some of the stuff that we Americans do. Maybe you can visit me."

> *The world is all gates,*
> *all opportunities, strings*
> *of tension waiting*
> *to be struck.*
>
> —Ralph Waldo Emerson

I perked up. "Is Bruce Lee gonna be there?"

Andre let out a loud laugh. "Bruce Lee lives in China, not Japan."

"Oh," I said. "Is that near Japan?"

Andre kept laughing. "Come here, boy," he said, hugging me. "You're gonna be all right. I bet you'll see me before you know it."

Soon the time came for Andre to go on his voyage. We boarded the train and headed to Chicago's O'Hare Airport. It was the first time either one of us had gone so far from home. Mom held back the tears as we all stood at the gate waving good-bye to her first-born. Our train ride back home was long and lonely without Andre. The silence in the apartment was deafening. We all went to our respective rooms. No one said a word. For the first time in my life I was speechless, which I'm sure came as a shock to everyone else.

But the time flew by, and before we knew it Andre was on his way back home. Once he was home, we looked at his three photo albums. Each picture showing Andre having the time of his life. He'd visited the Tokyo Stock Exchange and even met with Prime Minister Takeshita Noboru. Of course, the day he got home the first thing he wanted us to do was, you guessed it, go to a sushi bar. Mom said, "We'll go, but we ain't eating no raw fish, you can forget that!"

Later that night, before he could even unpack, Mom called a family meeting. "I've made arrangements for Andre to move," she said. What? Move where? We'd never known Mom to drink but she wasn't making any sense. Hadn't Andre just gotten home? After we regained our composure she explained that while he was away she'd contacted a very reputable family in the Washington, D.C., area asking if Andre could visit them to put his business plan into effect. *What business plan?*

Andre finally caught on to what Mom was talking about. He answered for her. "My Protocol Couriers essay that won in the delegation contest!" I was puzzled; there were too many unfamiliar words in that sentence for me to know what was going on. Protocol? Couriers? Delegation?

Andre's idea was simple. Protocol Couriers would hire foreign students attending college in the United States as international couriers. The students would take time-critical business packages to their home country. These would be students who knew the ropes of international travel, such as how to clear customs and navigate their home turf. They would get to briefly visit their families in-between class sessions and during the turnaround or round-trip deliveries. Mom saw the trip to Washington, D.C., as Andre's rite of passage into business. She just had a hunch about this program, and besides, she explained, being in the D.C. environment with an upper-middle-class family would serve him well. Two weeks later we were off to Chicago O'Hare Airport again!

Within a few weeks, Andre had his basic business tools in hand—his new company business card and flyer bearing the address and phone line on the switchboard of a recognized medium-sized African American law firm. He was an in-house courier to a law firm my mother had worked with in her days as a lobbyist at the Capitol, but in his spare time he traveled to all the area college and university campuses to meet with the various student groups representing the foreign students on campus.

Various campuses suggested that Andre find out more about the Association of Collegiate Entrepreneurs (ACE). Although he hadn't attended college, his stable of couriers offered many different business concepts from an international point of view. So Andre joined ACE to network with young and ambitious entrepreneurs and encourage them to engage in business enterprises all over the world. This was a job for which he was very well suited.

During his off time he attended Japanese language classes, and he also started spending time with Japanese students wherever he could find them. He wanted to stay sharp with the language. He met very receptive Japanese students who wrote letters on his behalf to possible sponsors for a move back to Japan. Mom was unaware of this. He had the whole thing planned. With those letters he sent copies of the photographs from his delegation trip, which made him an easy sell to prospective sponsors. Who wouldn't be impressed by a photo of Andre and the prime minister? He used to say that his plan was bulletproof. The only thing he lacked was a knowledge of golf and his mama's permission to return to Japan.

When he returned to Chicago, he had all of his ducks in a row. He'd show Mom that he was responsible and capable of making it

alone in a foreign country. "I've turned over my courier business to
the son of an attorney I know," he explained. "I can do this, Mama."

Mom knew in her heart that he could succeed, but the thought
of him living indefinitely in a far, far away place was a lot for her to
swallow. She'd always told us to dream big and wide and that's
exactly what Andre was doing. How could Mom say no?

She didn't.

Andre had hooked up with a sponsor named Kenji Yamauchi.
He was in his midthirties and the department head of the golf
course construction division of Yamauchi Engineering, his father's
engineering firm. He saw Andre's potential to generate business for
the U.S.–based clients in his division. When Andre arrived back in
Japan, Kenji met my brother at the Narita airport to welcome him
and take him to his hotel.

Soon Andre was introduced to Myrna Vargas, a multilingual
interpreter who'd been born and raised in Mexico and who was flu-
ent in both Japanese languages, as well as Spanish and French.
Myrna and my brother came from similar backgrounds, and they
both shared the same primary goal: to make money to send back
home to their families. The two started a company with the assistance and guidance of Andre's sponsor. Within a month they
launched the Export Now Trade Delegation in the Minato-ku business district in Tokyo.

A UNEEC Success Story

While Andre was thriving in Japan, UNEEC was doing well
back home. With support from our community mentors and sponsors, we'd started various businesses. One of our sponsors gave us
one hundred dollars to fund a lemonade stand venture. We made

cookies a la Mrs. Fields and sold them at churches in the neighborhood. This was a thriving market because back in those days there
was a church and a liquor store on every street corner, much like
Starbucks today. Benjamin Franklin said he that waits on fortune is
never sure of dinner. We were accustomed to this kind of uncer-
tainty. All of us had had many nights without food, but more important, we realized that UNEEC afforded us a variety of vehicles for
making money. We designed UNEEC T-shirts and sold them as fundraisers to grow the business. Later we created a gift-card collection
that was a big hit at beauty shops, churches and other local businesses.

The thing I loved about UNEEC is that we were a temporary
employment agency for kids. We could take on all kinds of jobs,
such as helping older folks take their groceries home, cleaning,
mowing lawns, sweeping and cooking. There was hardly anything
we couldn't do. We were a finely tuned machine.

We had been advised to keep our structure simple. Not to com-
plicate it with bureaucracy, a word none of us was familiar with.
But we agreed. We didn't have any officers. I was the liaison between the adults and UNEEC, which meant that I conducted the
business of telling our sponsors what we needed and how the businesses were faring. Roi helped us open a bank account, and whatever money we had left over after paying our bills—like copies and
gas for parents who carpooled kids to events—we split evenly
among the now fourteen members of UNEEC.

After UNEEC had been running for about three months, Roi
and I began discussing a spin-off of UNEEC's concept. He suggested dividing it into two new entities, one a "for profit" and the
other a "nonprofit."

I thought long and hard for a new name that would be distinct,
memorable and easy to pronounce! Roi came up with N.E.W., New

Entrepreneur Wonders, which was a great name with one flaw. It was so similar to UNEEC that I told Roi we should come up with a way to make it stand out more. Plus, the name didn't specify that it would be a business for tween- and teenpreneurs. With a little brainstorming we settled on a math-science style name—NE^{2}W (New Early Entrepreneur Wonders).

I told Roi that I didn't want to rush anything. I wanted to start an organization that would have staying power. Grandma was famous for saying, "Baby, if you don't make up the bed right at the top, it won't fit at the bottom." In other words, plan well, and don't let your plans get ahead of your ability to make them happen.

We kept the structure simple to avoid bureacracy. We didn't have officers because I wanted to start a company that would last.

I was doing just that. Rather than spending all of my UNEEC salary on candy and video games, like some club members, I gave my share to "Miss Savings." Kiki wouldn't let me spend the money on anything that wasn't business-related. Sometimes, collectively, the UNEEC members would agree to finance a trip to the movies, but we understood that these monies were to be taken out of our company stash. And, of course, I began using that money to help my mom—although she wouldn't be needing my help for long!

Happy Days Are Here Again

I turned cartwheels and moon-walked a few yards when I heard that Roi was going to be returning to Chicago from China. He had opened an Ideators Think Tank office in China, and he was coming home to make some new connections. His return signaled changing winds in both my mother's and my future business's direction. He introduced Mom to a young lawyer, Fiona Wong, the first Chinese to be licensed to practice law in the United States. Although she lived in America with her U.S.–born husband, Fiona was the daughter of the head of the military in the northern region of China. Fiona's government ties kept her on the search for joint venture partnerships. Before coming to the United States, she was manager of a state-owned import-export company for several years. She was excited about meeting Mom because Roi had extended such a high recommendation.

The two women found they had only one major difference between them, and that was their cultural backgrounds. Otherwise, they mirrored each other in their thinking and approach to business. They started a joint venture named Municipal Bond Finance Partnership, whose principal service was matching Chinese and American businesses and creating business prospects for wealthy Chinese seeking investor visas in the United States.

My mother set up a lobbying office in conjunction with the law firm my brother worked with in Washington, D.C. Fiona established another office in New York. She managed the day-to-day operations while my mother became the traveling partner.

With new business came the money to finally say farewell to food stamps. The new job also meant that we'd be moving into a three-bedroom apartment in a downtown Chicago high-rise apartment building with a doorman and all types of conveniences. I felt like George Jefferson and Weezy. We were movin' on up to the east side. We'd finally gotten a piece of the pie!

When you grow up poor, you don't own many prized possessions so there's no anxiety about how to pack your belongings. So as we prepared to leave our apartment, I had no thoughts of breaking precious heirlooms or how certain items might travel. We were poor, so we didn't have much. In fact, it was actually customary for us to leave old furniture behind whenever we moved. It was simply cheaper to purchase basic furniture that fit our new environment rather than figuring out a way to rent a U-Haul or pay someone to help us move.

Moving meant making several trips from our old apartment to the new one, which gave me a chance to see how different your life can be with just one choice. My mom had put herself in a position to change her life, and as a result she attracted a great business opportunity. Her persistence had resulted in a higher quality of life for our family, and I, for one, was thrilled.

As I unpacked my bags in my new bedroom, I looked out of the window with renewed hope for my future. I agreed with Greek orator Demosthenes who said that small opportunities are often the beginnings of great enterprises. It was exciting to be moving to a place where I could walk three feet without bumping into someone else in the same room. Plus, the new place had an indoor swimming pool, restaurants, security and amenities that rivaled a five-star hotel. We were in heaven!

But as we settled into the confines of our new abode, certain realities set in. Mom was going to be traveling back and forth to New York. She'd be gone at least three to four days each week. Andre was about to return to Japan. Our monthly living expenses had just quadrupled, so even though Mom was making more money, most of it was going to our plush, new living quarters. There wasn't really room to hire a babysitter, and besides, I wasn't a baby! Still, the main question around the dinner table was always, "What are we going to do with Farrah?" It was a question that wouldn't be answered immediately.

But Roi also brought with him a bit of bad news. According to him, Andre's business, Export Now Trade Delegation, was up against a competitor. He explained that rarely have there ever been two major powers in this business in Asia. Japan's economy was on the downturn, and China was becoming the Pacific Rim country of choice for trade. He explained the yin and yang circumstances that would ultimately shut down Andre's business.

Talk doesn't cook the rice.
—Chinese proverb

The global economic and business climate had changed, just as Andre was flying high. Within no time, he was back living with us after having such an exciting time in the Pacific Rim. But he was about to get an unexpected knock on his door. A former business acquaintance of Andre's sponsor in Tokyo was expanding his business consultancy service to London, and they wanted to chat with Andre about overseeing those operations. Andre was a natural candidate to host a two-way trade mission from Japan to London and London to Japan. He had firsthand cross-cultural communication skills and understood Japanese business etiquette and protocol.

The first time he'd gone to Japan, Andre's letters always mentioned that "relationships and loyalty are very important factors when conducting business in Japan." Your word is your bond over there, he said. It's not like the way we toss that phrase around in the States. He was about to see both relationships and loyalty come through when he needed them most. My brother's dream to return to Japan had come true. Within weeks he would be boarding a JAL (Japan Airlines) flight for Tokyo to begin working again.

Our family was maturing. And without the constant pressure of eviction and hunger, we were able to relax and enjoy life a bit more. Together, we explored downtown Chicago with different eyes.

Kiki's window shopping ignited her desire to attend school for fashion design. Fashion design was a perfect fit. Kiki was pretty, petite, creative, stylish, artistic and had already filled notebooks with her own fashion illustrations. She was anxious to attend the local fashion school in the Merchandise Mart, which was within walking distance from our apartment. Jonathan was a loner, following the beat of his own drum. Alex's asthma problems were mounting, so Grandma took him to live with her in Phoenix, Arizona, where the air was drier. And I was trying to work out the logistics of running UNEEC from my new neighborhood. Even with all of the excitement of the move and the new neighborhood, I was getting restless. I missed those familiar faces and places back in the 'hood. I had no one to play with or talk to. No Roi, who had gone back to China. No Mom, at least for three to four days out of the week.

Soon after he got back from China, I decided to confide in my big brother. I told Andre that I didn't think UNEEC was going to last much longer. Parents were "tripping," as we say, trying to manipulate the club for their own gain. Andre told me not to worry, that failure was a part of being a success.

I frowned. "That doesn't make sense."

"You don't do something just to succeed," he said. "You do things because they are in your heart to do them. But even though you follow your heart, there are still no guarantees, old soul."

> *Small opportunities are often the beginnings of great enterprises.*
>
> —Demosthenes

I was starting to understand all of the concepts that Roi, Andre and Mom had been harping on for the past four years, when I was too, too young to grasp them. Andre told me he was going to ask Mom if he could take me to Japan with him for his six-week trip to start his new job. "But let me ask her," he said.

"Don't go being a motormouth!" He knew me well.

Andre explained the grand plan. There would be many advantages to me living in Tokyo with him. He would sell Mom on how it would be an education for us both. I would be learning about a new culture and getting a degree in business from the school of hard knocks. Mom would no longer have to worry about how I was being cared for at home while she was away on business. The plan sounded good to me. And to Mom. She said yes.

The next day we went to Kinko's for passport photos. Brimming with excitement and high hopes, I prepared for my new excursion to a place where the people spoke Japanese and ate sushi. That's when it hit me like a ton of bricks. *I can't speak Japanese! And I hate raw fish!* I thought. Within a few hours, I got cold feet. I announced that I wasn't going anywhere! I was staying home.

Andre explained that people from America lived and worked in Japan. He assured me there were all sorts of activities for English-speaking foreigners and their families. Besides, he explained, "When I'm not in a meeting, you will be with me all of the time. And if you don't like living with me, I will bring you back home." That was my introduction to win-win relationships. Andre had made me an offer I couldn't refuse— and even had a built-in "out" clause. I was ready for my new life.

> *He is poor who does not feel content.*
> —Japanese proverb

The flight to Japan was about ten hours long. It was too long for an eight-year-old to sit still in a suit. But I was excited, and Andre had promised that I would love my new home away from home. We hadn't even landed, but I was already missing Mom, Jonathan, Kiki and Alex. To occupy my time, I flipped through some magazines and read the dictionary on the plane. I can't remember the movies they showed, but I know I watched them because I was bored to tears. I think that's when I decided that a private jet was somewhere in my future.

From the airport we boarded a train, which was like riding a roller-coaster on the ground. Andre was my personal tour guide. His business associates made sure I experienced Japanese cultural activities such as Kabuki theatre, a tea ceremony, Buddhist temples and castles, plus plenty of duty-free shopping. The sushi? Well, I still couldn't stomach raw fish, but I ate a lot of tempura shrimp and chicken!

I missed my normal surroundings, but I can't say I missed school. Why? Because I was in school. I was enrolled in a new world of education that committed me to lifelong learning on an ongoing basis, a classroom that provided me with hands-on experience. The lessons I learned through UNEEC felt like kindergarten compared to what I was about to absorb in Japan. The Japanese ran their businesses and personal lives like warriors—with precision, execution, discipline and perfection.

As dynamic as Tokyo was, it was also ultraconservative when it came to business. I was struck by the politeness of Japan's corporate warriors. I was particularly keyed in to how they interacted with Andre. He made it easy to do business with him. He could speak their language. He ate their food. He dressed, walked, talked and conducted business in the same way they did.

In only six weeks, Andre taught me a great lesson in adaptability. Now it was time for me to head home. On the flight home he asked some very important questions. "Do you have a greater sense of who you are after being in Japan?" he asked. He explained that our mother had raised us to be independent thinkers who believed that poor, ordinary people could achieve great things. "Anything is possible, Farrah. Nobody's guaranteed a great start, but we can all influence our finish."

My mind raced back to everything Mom had taught me about business. She insisted that we pay attention to everything around us. She instructed us to study and read everything that crossed our paths, whether it was a business card, leaflet, flyer, newspaper, book, magazine, people or whatever. Andre had been a fantastic role model.

Once back in our Chicago apartment, I began to put my plan in motion. First, I had a different take on the "look" of success. I had been mesmerized by the Japanese businessmen in dark suits carrying expensive briefcases. I'd have to upgrade my lunchbox briefcase to a real one. But as impressed as I was with how they dressed and carried themselves, I also had to remind myself that they were men, just like my brother and me. As Mom used to say, "They put their pants on one leg at a time just like the rest of us."

After deciding where I wanted to store all my Japanese souvenirs, I ran across the UNEEC file box where I kept all my important business papers. Staring at me was a photocopy of a poem given to all of the members of UNEEC by a former Tuskegee University college student. It was written by Edgar Guest and had been recited by Dr. George Washington Carver during his commencement address at Selma University in Selma, Alabama, on May 27, 1942. It's called "Equipment," and I think these few lines sum up more than anything I've ever read the UNEEC spirit:

> *Figure it out for yourself, my lad,*
> *You've all that the greatest of men have had,*
> *Two arms, two hands, two legs, two eyes*
> *And a brain to use if you would be wise.*
> *With this equipment they all began,*
> *so start for the top and say, "I can."*

REAL POINTS: Your First Setback

You're going to experience problems on your road to success; that's life. Learning to deal with adversity and keep a cool head is the most important skill you will ever acquire.

1 **You are going to suffer setbacks.** Guaranteed. The greatest basketball player in the world misses thousands of shots, the greatest baseball hitter strikes out. Trying to avoid failure at all costs is not only a waste of time and money, it keeps you from pressing forward for success. Preparing for setbacks is worth every effort.

2 **There is a difference between failing and being rejected.** All problems are not your fault—and racism is only one of a thousand examples. Analyze every situation so you can understand it and learn from it.

3. **When times are tough, do what you have to do.** My mother didn't want to take welfare, but she did it for her family. She was building a bridge to a better future. Be proud, but don't let pride stand in the way of things you really have to do. There's no shame is having a realistic outlook on life.

4. **Your first business may fail, but that doesn't mean you're a failure.** My mother and brother both failed in business. As you'll soon see, so did I—more than once. But we all bounced back because we kept a winner's attitude and kept moving forward. Even when you fail—and you will at least once—you have to continue to believe.

5. **Relationships and loyalty are the bedrock of success.** They will see you through the tough times.

6. **Don't do things just to succeed.** If you have the burning fire in your heart, you can find a way through any storm.

7. **Invest in people, not opportunities.** The right friends or business

associates will stand by you in times of trouble because they believe in and care about your ultimate success. The same is true in reverse. If you're not willing to see someone through the tough times and continue to believe in them, then you shouldn't be invested in them.

REALLIONAIRE AFFIRMATION

◆

When things are at their worst, I am at my strongest.

Reallionaire Exercise:
Seize Every Opportunity

How many opportunities walk right past our doors every single day? How many times have you gone to a conference, heard a speaker in your field and let that person walk out of the building without making an introduction? That's not seizing, that's snoozing! And to paraphrase the old Chinese proverb, "Talk doesn't cook the rice." You gotta turn up the heat if you expect to cook!

Part of seizing opportunities involves charting a reasonable course for your success. You may wonder why I waited until Step Four to have you write down your goals. There's a method to my madness. We must all get in touch with the "inside" stuff that keeps us from realizing our dreams. That's what we did in Steps One through Three. Unless that process takes place, you will never get a sniff of your goals.

By now you should have a more crystallized view of who you are and what you want. Now you can begin to capture those on paper. There are four areas to nurture in order to become a reallionaire: spiritual, emotional, physical and mental. I'll give you a head start by sharing from my log.

Farrah's Goals

Spiritual: To spend at least twenty minutes a day in prayer or meditation

Emotional: To become more aware of how my triggers affect my employees

Physical: To engage in some form of physical activity (outside the office) each day

Mental: To recognize when I'm overworking and take some time off before it takes a toll on my body and mind

Now, it's your turn. Write three goals for each area.

Spiritual

1. _____
2. _____
3. _____

Emotional

1. _____
2. _____
3. _____

Physical

1. _____
2. _____
3. _____

Mental

1. _____
2. _____
3. _____

Now I want you to create a success ladder for each area. Chart your progress over the next twelve weeks, recording how you are doing with each step.

Go with the Flow . . .
But Know Where You Want to Go

how I learned to stop trying to beat the system and start loving life

My most prized possession growing up—besides my business cards—was my library card. Mom always said that a library card is a poor kid's best friend, and the older I got, the more I understood why she believed that. Education reigned in our house. We were encouraged to learn—from books, from newspapers, from speakers—as much as we could. My mother read the dictionary four times a week when she was young because they didn't have many other books in her house. Through the power of words, she was able to visit places in her mind. My mother always believed that knowledge and education could get you out of any situation.

But knowledge and education were two things I didn't have to fall back on as a nine-year-old trying to run a business club. UNEEC had honed my leadership skills and taught me never to fear rejection. I was becoming a salesman, a negotiator and a philanthropist. I had learned the power of working with kids and how important this was to business and community leaders. Everybody was willing to help the kids . . . at least at first.

As I said, most adults love working to make a positive change in the lives of kids—especially kids from the ghetto. I was selling community pride and recycling community dollars—that was the thrust of my sales pitch whenever I'd call a prospective speaker.

"Yes, this is Farrah Gray, I'm the spokesperson for UNEEC, Urban Neighborhood Economic Enterprise Club. We're a group of young people ages seven to twelve who are working toward creating our own businesses and making a positive impact on the world." *Bam!* Most people became intrigued just after hearing that!

As my presentation and speaking skills continued to sharpen I set out to impress and convince my listening audience to invest money and contribute the products and services we needed to launch our businesses. I made it clear that we were looking for investors. I'd finally learned what that word meant and, more important, how useful it was when talking to people in positions of power. UNEEC was attracting three primary types of support: investors, mentors and earth angels who would share their wisdom and give us much-needed advice as we built our ladder of success.

I was selling more than just "help the kids." We were like-minded youngsters who were making sincere efforts to distance ourselves from the urban blight and the everyday dramas and traumas in our communities. We were trying to distance ourselves from situations that were more than ready to rob us of the true opportunity to develop our natural potential. Some adults were more comfortable calling their contributions donations, but to us every single bit of capital, time and energy was an investment in our future. You'd have to be a Scrooge not to support the premises under which we operated.

We opened a bank account at South Shore Bank, where we were only allowed to withdraw money with the permission of the branch manager. The bank statements were mailed to my address, and I had photocopies made for everyone to take home to their parents. This process ran smoothly for the first year with outside support, guidance and cash injections from local businesses. We were excited that our enterprises were generating enough rev-

I was selling more than just "help the kids." We were like-minded youngsters making sincere efforts to distance ourselves from the urban blight and the everyday dramas and traumas in our communities. We were trying to distance ourselves from situations that were more than ready to rob us of the true opportunity to develop our natural potential.

enues for us to treat our families to dinner on Sundays after church. We were no longer wearing clothes that had been handed down or bought from thrift stores. Suddenly, going to the movies wasn't an occasional treat but a regular form of entertainment. But the greatest perk of being rookie entrepreneurs was personal pride. We were routinely recognized as community role models, and we were occasionally featured in the newspapers and on television.

I was feeling proud of how it had all developed. My dreams were taking shape. I was learning new things and making money. Things were going fairly well, and I didn't expect the bubble to burst anytime soon. Most eight-year-olds know nothing about contingency plans, and I was no different. But Roi had prepared me for potential peaks and valleys. And I was about to encounter a ditch the size of the Grand Canyon.

Although the kids in the club had managed to keep their focus on the team concept, their parents had started to make things difficult for us. When we started, all of the adults were super-supportive. They were excited to see young boys and girls cooperating and working in the spirit of unity. Within a blink of an eye, that all changed.

In a little over a year, greed had reared its ugly head. UNEEC was doing well, getting lots of attention and, more important, a fair amount of money from the business community. At the height of our growth, certain parents began plotting to pull their children out of UNEEC to start their own version of business clubs with, you guessed it, their child at the helm. We later discovered that those same parents were pushing their own personal agendas and didn't really have their children's best interest at heart.

Things were getting to be pretty rough, and I couldn't seek Roi's counsel because he had flown to China on an extended business trip. Roi would understand what I was feeling, and I desperately needed his support and guidance. But he wasn't there, so I had to go it alone. Andre gave me the

The greatest reward of being a rookie entrepreneur was personal pride.

perspective to see beyond the moment, but it was my mother who pulled me through the rough spot. I'm sure she saw UNEEC unraveling but she remained optimistic and supportive. She was a sounding board who encouraged me to listen to my own intuition. Although Mom is known for her strong opinions, I'm grateful that she engaged me in a discussion about the future of UNEEC rather than telling me what I should do.

At eight years old, I faced an incredibly difficult decision. Should UNEEC continue or be dissolved? I was the founder, and this decision rested squarely on my tiny shoulders. I had started this club with friends and now those friendships were being tested. I knew that if we continued the way we were, things would get uglier and uglier. They were already out of hand. People were telephoning my house and asking my mother strange questions, such as, "Why is Farrah the leader?" It was pathetic.

After a week of listening to discontented parents issuing threats and demands by the pound, I made a decision. I called our book-keeper, who was a real estate broker and tax preparer who donated his time to maintain our local bank account. I asked him to close the bank account and distribute an equal share to all the members. We had made more than one hundred thousand dollars in our year in business, but after the dust settled each member got around fif-teen hundred dollars. A measly fifteen hundred dollars. We could have probably cashed out at $1.5 million had we been allowed to develop our businesses and keep greedy parents at bay. I never under-stood how grown folks could be so selfish. It didn't make sense. With one phone call, UNEEC had been put to sleep.

New Beginnings

After returning from Japan and closing down UNEEC, my top priority became school. After all, I was only nine years old, and after UNEEC and my six-week stay in Japan I felt as if I had gained wis-dom beyond my years. But even with all of the fun and adventure of my international travels, I was looking forward to attending school full-time. It would be a nice change of pace. I'd finally get to be around people my own age. I was becoming quite a sports fan and thought that I might even get the opportunity to go out for basketball or football, since I was growing so fast.

Unfortunately, the school serving the area where I lived was not within walking distance, and there was no school bus. Our building was brimming with young, on-the-go, single professionals or young couples with non-school-age children. The other parents in this upscale, high-rise area sent their children to private school because the local public school was also attended by children from Cabrini Green, the notorious housing project. We couldn't afford private school, and public school was beginning to look like more trouble than it was worth—especially since I'd have to take two buses to get there.

Kiki was the most logical choice for helping me get to school. While I was away in Japan, she had qualified for a scholarship to attend a few classes in fashion design and pattern-making at a local school in the Merchandise Mart. "If I've gotta take Farrah to school, I'll be late for school, and if I'm late, I could lose my scholarship," she announced one night at dinner.

That left Mom, who by this time had become a full-fledged workaholic, a behavior she'd learned not only from being the oldest in her family but also from raising her children single-handedly. She wouldn't be able to see me off to school. She reminded me that she wasn't getting any younger and that's why she had to throw herself completely into this new partnership, to have some kind of nest egg to keep us from going back. Back where? The projects? Poverty? Hunger? Leaky toilets and roaches?

Eventually Kiki came up with a solution. She had met a few Loyola University graduate students who were earning part-time money tutoring kids. The university was only seven blocks away from where we lived. Mom and Kiki researched the Illinois home school rules and discovered that I was two years older than the minimum age requirement. Mom's résumé proved she could earn a degree based on her real-world life experience, so the parent-teacher qualification was not an issue. Creating a suitable environment wasn't an issue either because, as long as I could remember, our apartment had been her convertible office. In a one-mile radius there were three universities, two colleges and the main Chicago Public Library, giving us a large pool of potential tutors and plenty of books to choose from.

Mom and I walked to each university placement center to post our part-time opportunity. Within two days we'd received eleven telephone inquiries—all from international students. We scheduled the appointments and invited the students to meet us at a restaurant near our apartment. I already knew the manager of the restaurant because I had checked the place out and handed him my business card right after I returned from Japan. He didn't believe that I'd actually lived in Japan for a short while, until I showed him some of my souvenirs, including my passport and old boarding passes from my round-trip airline ticket on JAL.

> *I may not amount to much, but at least I am unique.*
> —Jean-Jacques Rousseau

Mom let me be the lead interviewer, so it became my own little business meeting. After all, I was the one who'd be spending hours with the chosen applicant. One by one we met all of the students. I can still remember the look on each student's face when they saw us in the restaurant. One by one, they'd entered the doors and looked around for what I'm sure was a white family. I know this because we sat there and watched as each of them scanned the place, never looking our way—even though we'd told them there would be three of us.

After the initial eleven interviews, we had five callbacks. One female in particular stood out during her interview. Henda, twenty-five, was the daughter of a career diplomat. Her mother was a Paris-born documentary film producer of African descent who spoke six languages fluently: English, French, Italian, Spanish, Portuguese and Russian. Her stride resembled a runway model's, and she had a great sense of humor. She didn't need to work, and she didn't need the money. Her interest was in doing something constructive with a family because she was getting homesick for family. If she weren't chosen she was going to volunteer her time at the Chicago Boys & Girls Club.

The night after we met Henda I told my mom I liked her. "I want to learn to speak two languages like Andre," I said. My brother had taught himself two Japanese dialects all on his own. I was eager to prove that I was a player too! Mom and Kiki liked Henda too. We all agreed. We'd offer her the job. The next morning Mom called her and made it official.

Henda never told me outright, but I believe she saw our family as her extended family. I was the little brother she didn't have, and she took a deep interest in my learning more about other cultures and their languages.

She became more than a tutor to me; she became a friend to my family, introducing Kiki to other students studying art and fashion design at Loyola University. Our connection with Henda was instrumental in opening up the path for Kiki to realize her dream of going to the fashion capital of the world, Paris. Henda's father helped Kiki get selected as one of a fifty-member cultural exchange student group to study the French language, culture, fashion, fine arts and photography in Paris—all on scholarship.

I had a regular five-day-a-week school regime. Henda tutored me three days around her college schedule. The other two days were for Mom and Kiki. After a few weeks I was breezing through my new grade-level courses. I was improving in all areas of study, and I was eager to get NE^{2}W going.

"I can't wait to start my new business," I told Henda one day.

She looked at me like I had a horn growing out of my head. "Why would you want to start your own business when there are so many great companies to work for?" she replied.

I looked at her like she had a horn growing out of her head! I couldn't believe my ears. She grew up with a father who worked as a Foreign Service employee and a mother who worked in a non-governmental organization affiliated with the United Nations. Her university studies in public administration, she explained, were to prepare her for some type of international government-related assignment. She had zero appreciation for self-employment, and the American version of entrepreneurship baffled her.

Sure, she was tutoring me in the necessary modules of elementary education, but that wasn't so I could go and slave away in a nine-to-five for somebody else. Was she crazy? I was making plans to make a job for myself. Instead of becoming a company executive, I would manage my own business. Her reaction both surprised and disappointed me. After that conversation, I knew Henda's days as my tutor were pretty much numbered.

She had become close enough to my family to stop by on weekends for dinner. What she saw during those gatherings further clouded her perception of entrepreneurship. She couldn't understand why my family was so gung ho about launching our own enterprises when we could barely afford to live where we were living.

She'd heard of Mom's Chinese partner, Fiona, and knew that my brother Andre was in London finalizing the trade and business promotion mission between professionals in Tokyo and London. Even though Mom spoke about her "partnership" with Fiona, Henda somehow believed Mom "worked" for Fiona, and Andre was employed by some big international company. In other words, she was under the impression they were mere employees. In an attempt to convince her of my family's stand on owning our own businesses, I pulled out all my photos taken while in Tokyo and the souvenirs in my file box, items that showed Andre as an equal in his business dealings. She was still a nonbeliever.

Mom was known to say, "Only a fool would work himself to death for someone else," and I couldn't have agreed more. But Henda refused to see us as entrepreneurs, which would have been fine had she not been so vocal about it. "I don't understand how you can think about starting a business when you are barely keeping your head above water as it is," she once said. I fumed when I heard that. I didn't care how bad things were; nobody had the right to limit our aspirations. That's when a light came on.

Henda had bought into the hype. She was accustomed to seeing black folks portrayed a certain way in the media, and she'd fallen for those depictions hook, line and sinker. She'd heard about Cabrini Green and the Robert Taylor project's violence, gang activity and drug dealing. It was a staple on the nightly local news. Yet Henda was not visiting me inside a housing authority high-rise. Her tutoring was taking place in a nice, clean, security-guarded high-rise building where she was greeted in the lobby by a genial doorman. She was not walking into a place where she needed to clutch her purse or look over her shoulder every five seconds. So I couldn't understand why she wanted to hold on to those stereotypes of African Americans. I was frustrated and I needed to talk to someone. I tried to tell Jonathan about it, but he was too busy talking about his girlfriend of the week. I couldn't get a word in edgewise.

Alex and I didn't talk much since he'd moved in with Grandma in Phoenix. Mom was rarely home, and Kiki wore an invisible "Do Not Disturb" sign around her neck, so I didn't bother her too much. I was starting to hate the fact that we'd ever gotten me a tutor. Even though Henda was an excellent teacher, her beliefs got in the way of my learning. Deep down I wanted Mom to do more of my home schooling.

Unfortunately, by then Mom had convinced herself that she had to bring home the bacon, eggs and toast for her family, even if it meant neglecting herself. "I'm teleparenting you so you won't have to worry about anything later on," she once said. Her statement, though innocent, actually planted the seed for a future business venture of mine, which I'll tell you about later.

What grown folks call depression, kids call sadness, and I was sad during this time of my life. No one at home was really listening to me. Correction, they were listening, but I don't think they were hearing me. I called the one person who was always willing to listen to my endless rants: Grandma. After I'd repeated myself a few times she asked, "Would you like to know what I think?" I told her I'd love to hear her thoughts. "Can you handle the truth even if it's not what you want to hear?"

I knew that Grandma wasn't big on placating feelings. She gave it to you straight, but she never forced her opinions on anybody. I braced myself for the medicine. "Your mama has to let your tutor go. She sounds like a very smart and intellectual student, but she's not the right teacher for you, baby," she said.

I smiled into the phone. Grandma and I were kindred spirits. "Henda's a nice girl, but she wasn't raised to be an independent thinker like you and your sister and brothers," Grandma continued. "She's global in her travels but narrow in her thinking."

Grandma was right on the money. Henda's world had always consisted of butlers, maids and drivers. She grew up well bred and well fed. Her goal was to go to college, get married and have the appropriate number of children. She'd grown up being driven in diplomatic vehicles to and from private school. She spoke multiple languages and mingled with other privileged children.

Grandma told me that when Mom was in the fifth grade her homeroom teacher took exception to her being well behaved and well mannered. "My children went to school knowing that they deserved a good education," she said. Grandma shopped at the better thrift shops to buy good-quality clothes so that her kids went to school cleaned and pressed every day. "Your mama's teacher took exception to the way she carried herself. She had a lot of pride and confidence."

According to Grandma, the teacher treated Mom like the Cinderella of the class. Before, during and after homeroom she would demand that Mom pick up behind everyone else. Grandma started to laugh as she continued the story. "One day your mama came home and warned me that she was going to be sent to the principal's office because she had had enough," she said.

Mom kept her word. A few days later the school called Grandma to request a meeting. "When I walked into the room, the homeroom teacher was surprised. 'Oh, you're her mother,' the teacher said, her voice dripping with sarcasm." Before the teacher could speak, Grandma said, "I came to tell you that if you can't treat my daughter respectfully, please ignore her."

The teacher was dumbfounded. "What do you mean? Your daughter cheats on her homework. That is why she has to clean my homeroom as a form of punishment."

"My daughter doesn't have to cheat to get good grades," Grandma told her.

The teacher's reply sent Grandma through the roof. "There is no way your daughter can get A's on her homework and tests without cheating," she said. "You're on welfare and the father is in prison. There's no way she's doing this well on her own."

Grandma refrained from slapping Mom's teacher. She simply reiterated what she said when she walked into the office. "If you cannot respect my daughter, please ignore her." And with those words, she left the office.

I could feel Grandma's temperature rise as she recalled the story. "Farrah, what you have shared with me about your tutor reminded me of what your mother experienced. Sometimes teachers have negative perceptions of the children sitting in their classrooms, and instead of encouraging them, they sabotage their hopes. You can't let that happen to you," she said.

Over the next few days I thought long and hard about Grandma's comments. How could

> *There is only one success— to be able to spend your life in your own way.*
> —Christopher Morley

I allow someone who knew nothing about me to come into my home and squash my dreams? I couldn't. I wouldn't.

My mind was made up. I would speak to Mom after I spoke openly with Henda about what I thought would be best for me. To my surprise, she agreed. We were no longer a good match for each other. I had challenged her core beliefs, which she admitted had caused her to resent me. She suggested that she stay in contact with my family to be something other than my tutor. She offered to screen potential tutors. "And I'll be sure to tell them that they are being paid to provide tutoring, not advice about what you're going to do with your future," she said. Finally, Henda and I were agreeing on something.

Henda's departure left my family with the old recurring question, "What do we do with Farrah?" There were no college or university students calling about filling the vacancy left by Henda, and I was quite happy about that. Now, I'd have time to get some of my new business endeavors up and running. My self-esteem was now off-limits to potential detractors, and no trespassing would be allowed!

My experience with Henda had reaffirmed two things: I wasn't born with a silver spoon in my mouth, and success wasn't going to come me on a silver platter. I would have to work to overcome other people's expectations. I was fine with that, because as legendary soul singer James Brown was famous for saying, "I don't want nobody to give me nothing. Open up the door, I'll get it myself."

The Most Important Decision of My Life

I was always the kind of kid who questioned most things around me. *Why did most television anchormen and women wear the same outfit? Why were all of the presidents of the United States white men? Could clouds be touched, and if so, did they feel like cotton?* These were the kinds of questions that roamed around in my brain on most days. So naturally I questioned the words that came out of the mouths of adults. One axiom in particular puzzled me for the longest time. "April showers bring May flowers." What was that? I think there was even a song about those showers and flowers. I later interpreted it to mean "What hurts can also help." I was ten years old when I figured that one out.

In this case, the April showers—losing my tutor and not being able to get to school—came with a familiar May flower—my brother Andre, who invited me to live with him in London. He was there on a business promotion mission for six months. His duties included finalizing export deals with U.K.-based small and medium-sized businesses interested in expanding their operations into the Japanese market.

Living in London meant many challenges for a young boy. Chief among them was the painful price of missing Mom. After all, I was the baby of the family, and I was very attached to my mom. It was hard for me to think about what life would be like being so far away from her, but I still had one saving grace: my enterprising spirit. I still had an appetite for entrepreneurship, but my dream of forming another entrepreneur club any time soon was fading fast. I lay in my bed one night thinking back on my short life and how much Mom had sacrificed to make sure we had food to eat and a place to stay.

Somehow it felt like Mom was about to reap her just rewards for all of those years of struggling. I was happy for her and proud of her. I only wished we didn't have to live so far apart. Finally, the dreaded day arrived. We were all going to different locations. Jonathan was headed to Phoenix to live with Grandma. Alex had already moved there earlier in the year. Kiki and I were going to London. Mom was staying in Chicago, although she was rarely there because her job required so much travel. Mom had planned our departure times just hours apart on the same day so we could travel to the airport together to save money. Plus, she wanted to be able to say good-bye to all of her children.

I can still remember the sadness I felt as we all stepped onto the elevator at our apartment. I can still see the tears beginning to well up in Mom's eyes. I remember that because Mom rarely cried. In fact, I can't remember ever seeing her shed many tears when I was young. She didn't want us to worry about her. But on this day, it was too difficult for her to hide her emotions. We were all going to different parts of the world. And it hit us all like a ton of potatoes.

The same elevator we'd all taken on a more joyous occasion a few months earlier was now the transportation for a more somber event. We could all sense it was our last elevator ride to and from our apartment. But what was next? When would we see each other again and under what circumstances?

As we rode to the airport in the taxi, I was reminded of the excitement I felt when we moved into our new neighborhood. My mind flashed back to all of the tourist attractions I'd planned on visiting in downtown Chicago, including the movies in the big Water Tower indoor high-rise shopping mall near where Oprah Winfrey and other rich people lived.

Now I had to give up my dream of summer fun with my brothers. Once more, I'd be going to the other side of the world. I was already missing Mom and was hurting for her, knowing that soon she'd have to watch her children leave. I wondered if the sacrifices were necessary. But Mom always said the only thing that enabled her to whistle while she worked twenty hours a day was the joy she felt in being able to provide for us.

Soon it was our turn to board our plane. After the kisses, hugs and tears, Mom gave me and Kiki some warm parting words, "I love you. More importantly, I trust that you will land on the positive side of any changes and challenges you face."

It was true. Once we all left each other, our individual and collective worlds would change. The physical changes would be obvious. The next time we'd see each other, Jonathan and I would be taller. Alex and Jonathan would be flexing the growing muscles in their arms. Kiki would be a maturing young woman. Mom might have a few gray hairs. Change. It was inevitable, just as Mom had said all those years. There wasn't anything I could do to stop the changes taking place, so my new motto was simply "Go with the flow."

As soon as the plane took flight, Kiki pulled out her tote bag and reached for two paperback books: the Berlitz self-teacher in French and a French phrase book and dictionary. Our cousin, Briscoe, taught himself to speak French fluently. He gave Kiki

If you can't accept losing, you can't win.

—Vince Lombardi

some pointers on how to learn on your own. Kiki's a quiet bird who rarely talks about what's on her mind, but you always know she is in deep thought by the profound comments she makes. Like the time she explained that sometimes when you come from humble beginnings you never make plans to accomplish anything or be anywhere at a certain time because of the basic challenges you face getting even the most basic tasks accomplished. She started this flight with one final suggestion, "Instead of listening to the conversations of the other passengers, you might want to spend some time exploring who you are. Who is Farrah? What does Farrah want? Does Farrah have the talents, abilities and aspirations to achieve his dreams in life? What do Farrah's dreams consist of? Are they achievable or unrealistic?" So much for watching the in-flight movie and drinking soda after soda!

According to Kiki it was time for me to acquire a little knowledge of self. I had dreams of becoming that twenty-first-century CEO and forming New Early Entrepreneur Wonders (NE^{2}W), but first things first. I had to find out who I was and what I was really about. Without knowing that, I would have difficulty in figuring out whatever I truly wanted to become in this lifetime. I had experienced respectable success as a kid by forming UNEEC. I was proud of that accomplishment. But Kiki explained that by really knowing myself

I'd be able to renew and reinvent myself for every change and challenge I would face in my life. In other words, through serious soul-searching I would come to know what I was made of.

I made a number of important decisions on that flight. I decided, once and for all, that I really and truly was going to be a businessman. I decided that my attitude would always be positive and that I would never do anything I didn't believe in just to earn a dollar. I knew that everything I touched would not turn to gold, but I wasn't afraid to go for my dreams. Legendary football coach Vince Lombardi told his teams that if they couldn't stand losing, they'd never truly understand how to win. I decided that I would give back to both my family and the community because they had always given to me. And most importantly, I realized what my business needed to be about. It needed to be about what I knew. And in this case, that meant products for kids and teens. In hindsight, this last decision was the smartest and most important one I have ever made.

Most importantly, I realized what my business needed to be about. It needed to be about what I knew. And in this case, that meant products for kids and teens. In hindsight, this last decision was the smartest and most important one I have ever made.

Hours later, and only minutes before our plane landed at Heathrow Airport, Kiki asked me how the trip had been.

"It was cool," I said.

"I meant inside your head! Not the airplane ride."

That was Kiki. Always thinking. I was grateful to her. Sometimes it takes people half a lifetime to discover themselves, but in my case, it was a plane ride from Chicago to London. Kiki had helped me shave off thirty years of potential wandering in the wilderness.

A Budding Samurai

When we arrived in London, Andre met us at the gate. He was looking as sharp and strong as ever. "Can't believe you're here," he said. "Maybe one day we'll all be together again."

It was obvious we were in another part of the world. The airport design, the signs, the people, and the outfits and uniforms were nothing that I had ever seen before. In the Tokyo Narita airport almost all the people were Japanese and Asian. But in the Heathrow airport I saw every member of the global family represented. There were dozens of foreign languages being spoken.

Once we were outside the airport the taxicabs looked like big black boxes on wheels, like something out of a James Bond movie. The weather, rainy and muggy, reminded me of Chicago in the fall, but it was summertime in London. There was no sunshine, and it was cloudy and chilly. Once inside the taxicab I heard Andre say, "Our flat is located . . ."

My face contorted. "Flat? What's a flat?"

"An apartment, Farrah," he answered.

I remember thinking that was a strange thing to call an apartment. And that was only the beginning. "What are those circles in the middle of streets?"

"Those are roundabouts," he said.

"Roundabouts? What's a roundabout doing in the middle of a major street intersection?"

Upon arriving at the three-story red brick building, the driver asked if we needed help up the lift. "What's a . . . ?"

But before I could finish the question Andre answered, "An elevator. I see you haven't changed. Still asking a million questions," he said laughing. "That's good."

Thankfully, I was familiar with the dominant language of the British-English. That was a switch from Japan. Another big adjustment came at my brother's flat. He directed me down a narrow hallway to a dimly lit bedroom. "How do you like your own bedroom?" My eyes were the size of egg yolks. I had not expected to have my own room. I'd grown accustomed to sharing a bedroom with at least one other person. I was in shock. The room was fully equipped with my own television, desk, chair and big tourist magazines. But that wasn't all. In the corner, just waiting for me to break it in, was a brand-new black briefcase. Maybe that dream of becoming the twenty-first-century CEO wouldn't be in the freezer for too long.

I was nine years old and about to live in my third country in five years. The journey from the projects to the high rise to London hadn't always been rosy, but I can say that those years were preparing me for personal and professional success. And most important, the journey was laying the foundation for what has become my reallionaire success plan. Part of that plan involves adapting to change. There had been a lot of change in my short life, and things were just getting started.

As I walked around my new home, checking out the furniture and fixtures, I remembered thinking back to a joke I'd heard one passenger tell another on the way to London. "How many psychiatrists does it take to change a lightbulb?" he'd asked. "Only one, but the lightbulb has to want to change!"

The female influence in our immediate family unit can be traced back several generations. Their extraordinary values, work ethic and principles impacted generations to follow. My mom and grandma believed, and taught us, that if you don't make your bed right at the top, the sheet will not fit at the bottom. They always spoke their minds and were not given to retractions or recanting their opinions. Vocal and vibrant, Mom commanded us to be the best at everything.

Dr. Martin Luther King Jr. was known to have said, "If a person sweeps streets for a living, he should sweep them as Michelangelo painted, as Beethoven composed and as Shakespeare wrote." Mom and Grandma felt the same way. So did Andre, who was given the task of being my surrogate father. He took me under his wing and taught me everything he knew about life as a young black man. His exposure to the world, as well as our family's seemingly Bedouin tendencies to always seek more prosperous environments, would whet my appetite for future travels.

As demanding as his job was, Andre always made an effort to spend quality time with me every day. His Japanese employer's office sat in the heart of the global business center, Trafalgar Square, which was very accessible to museums, cinema screens, Piccadilly Circus and restaurants with cuisines from every country in the world. We often traveled on the underground, a transportation mode similar to New York and Chicago's subway and train system. The daily trek on the underground allowed me to look into the faces and observe a wider range of people than I'd ever seen in real life or on television.

Andre had also introduced me to less (at least on the surface) business-oriented interests, such as sports. His natural athleticism seemed to rub off when we went to a diamond or basketball court, which means he took all the credit when I excelled and assumed no fault when I stunk up the place.

Most important, though, Andre was my very first exposure to martial arts. He started taking karate classes with our cousin when they were very young. I remembered seeing pictures in a family photo album with Andre in his *gi*, the uniform jacket and pants

> *Fast as the wind; quiet as the forest; aggressive as fire; and immovable as a mountain.*
>
> —Samurai battle slogan

worn by martial artists. *Gi* also refers to the fancy jacket, nice pants and white shirts the Japanese wear after business hours at the sushi bar or tea cere-monies—a nice metaphor for his dual role as mentor and business-man. A samurai battle banner hung in his bedroom that read, "Fast as the wind; quiet as the forest; aggressive as fire; and immovable as a mountain." That's what I wanted to be when I grew up.

In London, the martial arts culture was as diversified as the city itself. Twice a week, we sat in on different schools, or *dojos,* to help me decide what style would best fit my temperament. One inter-esting martial form was called *capoeira.* Its origin can be traced to Angola, where my tutor Henda was born and raised before attend-ing Loyola University in Chicago. Another martial art is jujitsu, which is very similar to karate. One day during an interview with a jujitsu master, I noticed that he kept referring to my *ki.* I had never heard this word so finally I interrupted him and said, "Excuse me, what exactly is *ki*?"

He smiled warmly and told me that *ki* in Japan was a process of cultivating an extraordinary form of personal power. In the English language the equivalent definitions are inner strength, energy, life force, aura, spirit and vitality. This definition somehow reminded me of my sister and took me back to the flight over to London when she had urged me to stop wasting time watching and listening to other passengers on the plane and to look within myself to find myself.

Whenever Kiki spoke, her words were always deeply rooted in wisdom and wrapped in a lighthearted, positive spirit. Like my mother and grandmother, she's always exuded a strong healthy sense of self with no touch of ego. I hope to get there one day. If you spend ten minutes with her, you'll feel the warmth in her heart. What's inside of her seems to just ooze out. I've always loved that about her. She impressed upon me the importance of being authentic, the necessity of keeping it real. Most important, she was teaching me how to learn from the inside out.

When I told Andre the story about the jujitsu interview, he laughed. "Farrah, you never knew why mother named Kiki, did you?"

I told him I didn't have clue. He leaned back on the sofa and flashed a smile wider than the Atlantic Ocean. "When Mama was three months pregnant and I was three years old, I told her that she was carrying my baby sister."

"How did you know that?" I asked.

"I could feel her energy and spirit. Some things you just know," he said.

What he told me next amazed me then and still amazes me to this day. "In her fifth month, I told Mom that the baby wanted me to tell her something."

"The baby told you this?" I couldn't believe my ears.

"She said she wanted to be called Kiki."

I smiled. He nodded his head. "That's where she got her name?"

"Yep. She was Kiki before she was born."

Those kinds of family stories fueled my spirit. My first teachers and best friends were my brothers and sister. They were also my first imprints of love. I meet people throughout my travels, especially youth, who aren't sure if their parents love them. Whenever I hear this, it breaks my heart because I knew I was loved because of the way I was treated and taught. I've since learned that what I had in my home was truly special. It wasn't happening everywhere.

What was happening in my life at the time was this unfolding of my young manhood. Andre was ready for me to make some decisions, but I explained to him that I wasn't ready to choose a martial art, philosophy or discipline. First I had to stop and reflect on the real experiences that were beginning to shape my thinking. My first priority was to observe and understand the importance of being rooted in the reality of all things that connected me to both my family and culture.

Second, I wanted to read more about the samurai spirit, tai chi, Zen, Taoism, Buddhism and Confucianism, all Eastern philosophies I'd become acquainted with during my stint in Japan.

Third, I needed to identify those ingredients that would cultivate my spirituality.

I began to spend many hours in my bedroom reading, writing and thinking. There would be days that I would lie in bed as quiet as the eye of the hurricane. This had become my routine, but it was about to be disrupted . . . in a good way, by my cousin, Bris. I'd heard a lot about Bris, but unfortunately, the first time I'd met him was at the funeral of my great-grandmother, who's still very much with us in spirit.

Growing up, Andre, Kiki and Bris were called "The Trio," the first three grandchildren on my mother's side of the family. They were pretty much inseparable. Bris was an extremely sickly child who suffered from asthma and severe allergies. He was an avid reader and artist who would doodle for hours with his pen and notepad. Bris said he remembered me as a toddler being curious and insightful, which led him to nickname me the "little one-hundred-year-old man."

During his stay in London, he and Andre stayed up for hours talking. I was too young to understand every aspect of the conversation, but I still absorbed quite a bit. Let's just say that my ears went to bed full.

Bris was a fourth-degree black belt. His mother had enrolled him in classes for strengthening exercise. Over the years he not only mastered martial arts, he also took command of his physical health. Instead of succumbing to his frailties, he turned inward and learned to strengthen his spirit. He became a voracious reader and a student of life. Bris had a commanding presence but was still a gentle giant who always began speaking by saying "in my humble opinion." Then he would proceed to break you down with his extensive vocabulary and thought processes. My mother used to say that whenever Bris was around, she always had a dictionary nearby. "You just never know what he's going to say," she'd say, laughing. "I wanna make sure I can follow the conversation."

Bris was very cool when we gave him a hard time about his ency-clopedic rants, and his visits always left me richer and fuller with an inherent understanding of the natural duality that exists in life. He helped me see that, in the words of one of my favorite sayings, "Nothing too good or too bad lasts too long." In a very short time, I understood the bond that he'd developed with Kiki and Andre because now I was a part of their special connection. To this day, I call him my fourth brother.

Before Bris continued in his travels, Andre showed him around London. This included some sightseeing tours and a black tie char-ity event with some of Andre's business acquaintances. At the event, Andre was introduced to a group of young, business-savvy Brits who were scouting out a promising partner to join their team. Their plans were to establish an independent record label. My brother's experience bridged three worlds—the United States, Japan and the United Kingdom. Soon, Andre was caught up in a whirlwind of "get-acquainted" meetings that eventually ended in a meeting with heavyweight boxing champion Lennox Lewis and his younger brother, Dennis.

Andre taught me that relationships aren't built in a day. Successful people are known to toil into the wee hours while their competitors are copping Z's. And even though nothing came of that initial meeting with Lewis, their paths would cross again a year later at Lewis's contract signing with his new boxing trainer Emmanuel Steward, the premier trainer in the sport. Mr. Steward masterminded Lewis's title up until his retirement in February 2004.

Whenever he had an important meeting, Andre would say to me, "You'll be there, but you won't be there." This meant that he'd seat me at a nearby table so that I could eat while he was conducting business. One night I'd gone to the restroom and noticed an empty phone booth directly outside the restaurant front door. With my prepaid calling card in my pocket I decided it was time to reach out and touch Mom, even though she was six hours behind us. It was nice to know that when I called her, she was also thinking of me.

A musician must make music, an artist must paint, a poet must write if he is to be ultimately at peace with himself. What one can be, one must be.

—Abraham Maslow

I wasn't homesick for Chicago, just a young boy missing his mama. I'd been gone from the table where Andre had seated me for more than twenty minutes. It had been a few days since I'd spoken to Mom, and I didn't want to let her go. I couldn't. I was rattling on about my life, completely unaware that Andre and his friends had been scouring the restaurant looking for me. Mom sounded like business was going well, but I could tell that she really missed her children. "It's so quiet around here," she said. Sometimes silence is more deafening than noise.

It wasn't until Mom asked, "Where's Andre?" that I realized where I was and that he probably thought someone had abducted me. I'd sunken so deep into the red phone booth that Andre almost didn't see me when he walked by. Frantically, he swung the door open, wearing an expression of panic and relief. The phone booth incident highlighted how much time we all had been away from each other. It confirmed that even though our family bond was tight, we'd also been stretched to the limits. Were we sacrificing family for the sake of business?

That incident in the phone booth led indirectly to a successful business a few years later. As I said before, I'd decided to focus on businesses I understood, and my experience in London taught me that long-distance calls could be a lifesaver for kids away from their parents, whether it was themselves or their parents on the road. Long-distance rates were outrageous back then, and some families didn't even have long-distance service on their phones. It was clear to me that we needed a calling card that made it easy for kids to contact their parents. Remember, this was 1994, and calling cards hadn't yet hit big in America—but they were everywhere in London! That's why a little worldly perspective can go a long way.

I developed a partnership with Stephen LaChapelle, an executive at a telecommunications company called WorldTel. I met Stephen through one of Andre's business acquaintances. After

The heights by great men reached and kept were not attained by sudden flight, but they, while their companions slept, were toiling upward in the night.

—Henry Wadsworth Longfellow

talking with him about my niche marketing ideas—a business way to say kids' products—we came up with a product called Kidztel, which offered young people prepaid calling cards on key chains and chain necklaces so they could call from a pay phone or another person's home in case of emergency.

Kidztel phone cards were ultimately sold nationwide as community and school fundraisers, but one of my favorite Kidztel stories is out of this world. In 1947, aliens were suspected to have crashed in Roswell, New Mexico. With Stephen's son, I became the cofounder of the Roswell Alien Life Form (R.A.L.F.) Kids Club.

Stephen wanted to promote unity among the races, so he featured me with his son as the faces of the fiftieth anniversary celebration of the Roswell event. We decided to join forces to market a product called the UFO Museum Calling Card, targeted to teens and tweens. We used the Roswell event as the backdrop—more like centerpiece—for the calling card promotion. I appeared on the cover of the July 2 *Roswell Daily Record* inflating a fifteen-foot alien to open the Roswell UFO Encounter six-day festival. Now, I didn't see any UFOs, but that doesn't mean the experience didn't help change my life. This one-day event resulted in sales of more than fifty thousand calling cards during the July Fourth weekend.

In March 1995, Andre was extended an invitation to attend a boxing match in Bristol, England. A young light-heavyweight Norwegian boxer named Ole Klemetsen was being trained in Detroit at the Kronk Gym founded by Emmanuel Steward. Mr. Steward and his entourage invited Andre and the rest of our family to join them for dinner before the match. Someone thought it would be cute to ask me, the ten-year-old, for a prediction.

"Who do you think'll win it, Farrah?"

I replied quickly, "Whoever's fighting Ole."

No sooner than the words flew out of my mouth could you hear a pin drop on cotton. The room became silent, and all eyes were on me. Andre almost swallowed his tie. But of course, I was my grandmother's child, so I didn't back down. Instead I repeated myself.

My boldness intrigued Mr. Steward, who asked "Why do you think my fighter will be knocked out, young man?"

"Your fighter will be jet lagged," I said. "Your opponent has been training in Bristol for a week."

"Hmmm. Interesting observation," he said, rubbing his face. "I hope you're wrong." Everyone laughed except Mr. Steward, who simply stared at me. I had gained his respect by standing my ground, even though his fighter eventually won the match. Afterward, he invited me to his meetings, including the signing of Lennox Lewis to a ten-year contract.

Mr. Steward lived in Detroit, where some of the boxing greats had trained at his Kronk Gym. The day before he was scheduled to return to Detroit, he asked if he could spend the night at our flat. We were happy to oblige him. We made greasy-spoon fried chicken, mashed potatoes, spinach spiked with vinegar, potato salad and skillet-fried cornbread. The food was good, but the conversation was even better. Here I was, not even a decade old, and I was sitting at the feet of a master. He talked about being born in Bottom Creek, West Virginia, the firstborn child of a coal miner.

At eight years old he received a pair of boxing gloves as a Christmas present. No one ever thought those boxing gloves would begin a journey to fame, fortune and a historical legacy. When he was eleven years old, his mother moved to Detroit with his two younger sisters. He worked odd jobs to contribute to the family income. He delivered newspapers in the evenings and on weekends assisted with groceries for locals at the supermarket. He would also mow lawns, rake leaves and do odd jobs to earn extra money for his family. Before he was legal age to drive he had already earned enough money to buy his own automobile.

I was fascinated by his journey, but Mr. Steward paid me the greatest compliment when he asked if I would give up my room for him. He said he wanted to be able to say that he slept in the home, in the bed, of one of our country's greatest leaders. I was humbled by his prediction. Once again, fate had intervened and put me in the path of a great man, affirming my decision to go with the flow in life.

My time in London had allowed me to witness a full spectrum of life's beauty. I had come full circle in my search to discover myself. The yin and the yang were in harmony, and I had truly begun to live life from the inside out. I had learned to be true to myself, and I had recognized the value of a real-world outlook, even in its most unforgiving terms. This may not seem like a lot—after all, I hadn't made a million dollars while in London—but I think it was probably the most important time of my life. You can't be truly successful until you truly know yourself, and by going with the flow and following where life took me, I learned not only who I was, but where I really wanted to go.

And then, in May 1995, my mother suffered a major heart attack. She was only forty-six years old, but she had finally pushed the envelope too far. She was physically spent. For the next six years, she remained on heart medication; instead of being our guide, she now needed our helping hands. Andre, Kiki and I rushed back to Chicago to be by Mom's side.

Mom's health issues thrust me from a time of learning into a champion athlete's mode. I was spiritually, physically, mentally and morally fit, in a get-ready, get-set, go stance, waiting for the baton to lead our team to victory.

REAL POINTS: Reassessing Your Life
from a More Mature Perspective

Very few people know exactly what they want and exactly how to get it the first time around. Take the time to assess your situation once your feet are wet.

1. **Take a second look at your plan.** Earlier I recommended sticking with your plan no matter what. That's the only way to get over the first few hurdles. But guess what, there are thousands more hurdles to jump. Once your plan has been tested by both success and failure, go over it in detail and change it where necessary. At the very least, reassess your plan every year; there's no use taking a winding path or hitting dead ends when there's always a straight road to your destination.

2. **Don't be afraid to pull the plug.** You don't need any extra baggage, especially dead weight. Don't stick with something out of loyalty or fear. If an honest assessment says it's time to pull the plug, pull it now. Delay will only cost you in the end.

3. **Going with the flow doesn't mean accepting everything life throws at you.** It means that you fight the battles worth fighting and you acknowledge that every battle will not result in victory. Even in defeat, reallionaires walk away with valuable lessons.

4. **People want different things, and that's okay, but it's often still better to part ways.** Henda and I had different ideas about life and different goals for the future. That doesn't make either of us bad, but it did mean we shouldn't work together. Part ways with people who don't share your values—even if they're very good at their jobs. You can remain friends, but you shouldn't work together.

5. **Evaluate yourself.** Is your goal still the right one for you? If so, stick with it no matter what, but remember there is more than one way to get to the Promised Land.

6. **Be ready to change.** If not your attitude or your dreams, then your surroundings.

7. **Be outspoken and stand by your convictions.** You may be outnumbered, but that doesn't mean you're wrong. Even if you are proven wrong in the end, people will appreciate and admire the strength of your convictions.

8. **Know your customer.** How did I know the calling card idea would work? Because I knew kids wanted and needed it. When you know your customer, the opportunities are all around you. I've said it before, and I'll say it again, because this is important: pursue what you love and know your market.

REALLIONAIRE AFFIRMATION

◆

I am honest with myself about what is working, what is failing, where I am and where I need to go. I have the courage to make decisions based on the facts instead of fighting the tide.

Reallionaire Exercise:
Turn Lemons into Lemonade . . .

Today, we're going to make lemonade. Here's how the exercise goes. First, on a separate sheet of paper, write down all the ingredients you need to make lemonade. If you're making gourmet lemonade, feel free to add more ingredients. I'll give you the first one . . . lemons.

Next, write down the directions for actually making the lemonade. Again, the first one is . . . cut ten lemons and squeeze the juice into a pitcher.

Now, I want you to take a real "lemon" from your life and make lemonade with it. What event or circumstance is currently, or was recently, causing you to be sour?

Write it down.

_____

_____

_____

Now, let's take this lemon and turn it into lemonade. Using the identical exercise above, write down the ingredients you need to turn this sour event into a sweet sensation.

Now give yourself directions for turning the situation into lemonade. Write down the steps you need to take to turn that negative into a plus. Now go out there and do it!

STEP **6**

Be Emotionally Prepared to Handle Failure

how my biggest disappointment turned into
a life-changing opportunity because I took
responsibility and moved forward

From the outside looking in, our family appeared to have received
a serious blow when Mom suffered her heart attack. We were all
deeply concerned about her health and speedy recovery. We'd
turned a blind eye to her years of working too much. Now we realized that what had happened to her hadn't only happened to her. It
had happened to all of us.

And it could happen to all of us. Mom had worked herself nearly
to death before the age of fifty, and I could see the tendencies for us
all to become workaholics if we weren't careful.

Every family develops it own lifestyle, habits and patterns, and
our family was no exception. The root principles of love, truth,
honor and honest communication were interwoven into our family
fabric, but so was a work ethic that could lead to burnout. As my
cousin Bris would say, "in my humble opinion" someone needed to
communicate to Mom that her counterproductive behavior had

put her health and well-being at risk. It's hard to tell your mom that her choices haven't been in her best interest, especially when you know her heart was in the right place. But Mom had told us that she never wanted to be "the last to know" of any situation with her children. In other words, she didn't want to find out something about one of her children from someone else. And she never wanted us to avoid giving her tough love if she were ever in danger. We had gotten to this point.

The news of her heart attack sent shockwaves through our close-knit family. Our mother, our first teacher and example, had gone against one life law she'd taught her children: take care of your health first and foremost.

Like most women of her generation, particularly black women, Mom had chosen to take care of everyone else but had neglected herself. Anytime someone suggested that she slow down or take it easy, she rejected it. "I'm fine, I'm fine," she'd say. And we'd accept that answer until the next time she appeared to be suffering. I don't know what we expected. Mom was simply doing what women of her time did. They ran on. If they got tired, they kept running. If they got weary, they kept running. She'd grown up seeing women who had incredible strength and stamina—women who, like her, never took a day off.

As the eldest of four children, she'd learned to be responsible and caring. Those behaviors had carried over into her life as a mother of five. For years she had shouldered the responsibility of mother and surrogate father to me and my siblings. I don't think she expected that it would catch up with her. We were so used to seeing her work and work, we didn't know what to do when she wasn't working!

Mom's condition appeared to take a toll on Kiki and Andre, who struggled with how to approach her. "You know how she can be," I heard Andre tell Kiki one night after Mom had gone to bed. "She's stubborn." I stood at the doorway listening to their conversation, fully aware of what they were saying. Someone needed to have a little chat with Mighty Mom. I was the baby of the family, but somewhere in my heart I felt she'd listen to me. Grandma even agreed to cosign the deal. It was not going to be easy, that was for sure. Mom was famous for reminding us that she was only four generations removed from slavery and that complaining was not in her vocabulary.

Sleep didn't come easy for me that night, but the next morning I mustered up the strength to approach Mom. The rest of the family was either at school or work, which gave me the perfect opportunity to talk to her. I knocked on her bedroom door. "Who's there?" she asked.

"Me."

"Me who?" she said, laughing.

"Me!"

"Oh, *that* me. Come on in."

I entered the stillness of her room, her music playing softly in the background. She was reading a book. "How are you feeling?" I asked.

"Pretty good. Be back to work in no time," she said, smiling. *Perfect*, I thought. *She's going to toss me out of here on my butt like a bouncer.*

"Mama?" I said.

"Yeah, baby."

"Can I talk to you about something?"

"You can talk to me about anything. You know that."

That was exactly what I wanted to hear. Maybe I wouldn't get bounced. I sat on the side of her bed and cleared my throat.

"I was thinking. . . ."

"That's good. I like hearing that," she said.

"I was thinking that maybe since you had a heart attack, a big one, that maybe you shouldn't work . . . so much, right now, you know." The words weren't flowing like butter the way they had when I practiced in the mirror, but I wasn't going to let up.

Mom peered through me. "I see," she said.

"I want you to be here when I get big, and if you have another heart attack, you might not be here," I said, tearing up.

Mom's book was resting on her lap. She moved it aside and pulled me closer to her. "I'm not gonna have another heart attack, Farrah."

"You might. You might if you keep working so much," I said as she rubbed my back. "Why can't you just work one job? Why do you have to travel so much? Why . . . ?"

"I don't," she said. I was shocked. "You're right, I don't have to work that much. . . . I just don't know how not to."

Mom pulled my face toward hers. "Farrah, I've worked all of my life. Even when I was your age, I worked. We never had enough food. We were always trying to make ends meet. I swore that my family would never have to live like that."

"But you're gonna die," I said. I could barely get those words out.

Mom must have seen the sheer terror in my eyes because something changed. We exchanged a long stare. It was the kind where no words are necessary. You just know what the other person is thinking and feeling. Mom took a deep breath and let out a heavy sigh. "Okay, okay, Farrah," she said, consoling me. "I understand. Mama will do better."

Arrangements were made for an apartment in Scottsdale, Arizona, so she could be within driving distance of Grandma and my brothers Alex and Jonathan. They didn't fly into the Windy City with Grandma to pick up Mom because they were attending school, but we were in constant phone contact with them.

Andre was able to sublet our Chicago apartment. Kiki and I sold some of our household items to folks in the building. Shortly after Mom was released from the hospital we were efficiently packed and ready to head toward the airport. It was a déjà vu moment. I left with Mom and Grandma for Phoenix. Kiki and Andre were going back to London. What a difference twenty-four months had made.

The sun shined brilliantly the day we landed at the Sky Harbor International airport in Phoenix. It had been so long since I'd seen the sun peek from behind the clouds that I'd forgotten what it looked like. Living in London will do that to you. As we deplaned, I saw two chocolate-covered bookends waiting for us at the gate. If I didn't know better, I would have thought they were two college basketball players.

Jonathan and Alex had grown several inches. They had facial hair and muscles to boot. I guess I looked a little different too, because they kept saying, "Man, look at you!" We hugged and

No one can make you feel inferior without your permission.
—Eleanor Roosevelt

high-fived for several minutes before heading out of the airport. There was a lot of chatter on the way from the airport to the new apartment.

The apartment in Scottsdale was roomy, and there was an outdoor Olympic-size swimming pool with a backdrop of the most magnificent mountains I'd ever seen. A high-rise scene in Chicago could never rival the spectacular view of the sun setting behind those mountains. It felt like the ideal place for us to heal physically and emotionally. Plus, it was the optimal environment for Mom to learn how to love herself again. Peaceful, tranquil, perfect.

As you know by now, my mom was a 24/7/365 working woman. She rarely took days off, and she almost never slept. She wasn't used to being cared for; she was most com-fortable in the caregiver role. But now I had settled into the role of Mom's pri-mary caregiver. I did everything around the house. Chores, cooking, cleaning, you name it. I was Mr. Mom. And I loved it. It was an honor to serve my mother. She had given her life for my

Mom was simply doing what women of her time did. They ran on. If they got tired, they kept running. If they got weary, they kept running.

siblings and me. What I was doing for her wasn't a burden; it was a privilege. I enjoyed watching her sleep like a normal person.

Meanwhile, Andre and Kiki were making plans to return to the United States. Their deep concern for Mom wouldn't allow them to continue with business as usual. Andre called the apartment on a regular basis, saying that he and Kiki were cooking up a plan to get back to the States. I knew that if anyone could make it happen, Andre could. Two months later, Andre the rainmaker struck again. He negotiated a job that would take him and Kiki to Las Vegas, Nevada. The state of Nevada was one of a few places in the world that foreign corporations incorporated to conduct business in America. He'd simply shifted his contracts to another international city. Now my big brother and sister were only a short, one-hour flight away from me and the rest of the family.

The same company that had leased us our Scottsdale apartment also leased a two-bedroom apartment to Andre and Kiki, just two blocks from the Las Vegas Strip and five minutes from McCarran Airport. Nine years later, Andre and Kiki still live in Vegas. Andre is a mortgage agent, and his wife is a real estate agent. Kiki is a single, certified sports-fitness trainer. After graduation from high school, Jonathan enrolled in a college just outside Chicago. Mom, Grandma and Alex still reside in Phoenix, commuting regularly to visit family in Las Vegas.

Cha-Ching City

Las Vegas was all that! Andre flew me in from Phoenix for a heavyweight boxing match at the MGM. Special boxing excursion trips to Las Vegas for Brits were offered at great prices. Many of Andre's friends from London were flying into Vegas, and he wanted me to hang out with them. According to boxing legend, the sport was said to have originated in Britain. At the boxing match where I met Emmanuel Steward in Bristol, England, the fans in the audience reminded me of a group of kindergarten kids in the classroom without a teacher. They were loud and obnoxious. The ringside seat holders in the United States were in for a treat. On the surface London appeared to be a conservative city. But go to a football (soccer) game or watch a Parliament meeting (congressional session) on television, and you will realize you got it all wrong.

Vegas fascinated me. The lights, glitz and glamor left little for my imagination. A kid could run wild with all of the stimulation. That's probably why no one under twenty-one years of age can walk through a casino unless accompanied by an adult. So what did kids and teenagers do when they came to Las Vegas with their parents? They went to expensive shows that were geared toward their parents. While in London I had come up with another kid-friendly business idea. On cold, rainy days, I spent a lot of time playing video games, but I didn't have all the games I wanted. What about a rental service of video games for kids stuck inside on rainy days?

In Vegas, I saw how this germ of an idea could come to fruition.

My idea was perfect. Video game rentals for hotel rooms; the ideal solution for bored kids stuck in their hotel rooms while their parents went to see Tom Jones or Siegfried and Roy. This may not seem like such a breakthrough idea now, with video game rentals featured in every Ramada Inn this side of Timbuktu, but in 1995 there was nobody on this scheme. It was all mine.

As Andre showed me around the Strip, my mind was turning like a windmill. I was never short on ideas, but I have to admit, this one had me hyped. UNEEC had been a great experience, and it had allowed me to get my feet wet, but back then I didn't feel like I was quite an entrepreneur—yet. I was still working on it. But since the UNEEC days I'd grown considerably as a critical thinker. My conversations with Mom, Roi and Andre had helped me to mature as a businessman.

I learned that the first thing you have to do after you hatch a new idea is research. I didn't tell anyone about my idea; I simply took notes and watched everything around me. I told Andre I needed to make some business calls but "don't worry, most of them are local." By now, I was a master cold-caller and completely unfazed by rejection. I made a target list of companies to call and found two wholesale distributors in Northern California to order Sega and Nintendo set boxes and game cartridges from in large quantities. To my utter surprise neither of them asked the popular question, "How old are you, kid?"

Maybe my voice was a little deeper, but the reception from businesses made me feel good. Things were moving at a nice pace. The demand for youth-centered entertainment was obvious, but I still did my due diligence and asked every teen and tween who'd talk to me if they'd be interested in hanging out in the hotel room instead of hanging out with their parents at a boring Vegas show. They all said yes. I did "man on the street" interviews on every major intersection of the strip. Andre thought I'd lost my mind, especially since I wasn't yet revealing what I was asking these kids. "I'll tell ya later," I told him.

I set out to find two things during my visit in Vegas: books on doing business in Vegas and a mentor. Roi Tauer had taught me that the best thing to do before you start a business is to find a mentor. Kiki and Andre needed to know the inner workings of doing business in Nevada. So we went to the bookstore and bought four books: *Getting Established in Las Vegas—The Inside Scoop, A Guide to Starting a Business in Las Vegas, Incorporating in Nevada Without a Lawyer* and *Starting & Operating a Business in Nevada.*

It was time to reveal my big business idea. Andre, Kiki and I sat down at one of the many outrageously cheap all-you-can-eat buffets and played catch-up for about fifteen minutes. They asked me the golden question, "Is Mama behaving?" We all knew what that meant. Was she doing what she'd agreed to do: take it easy? "For the most part," I answered. "You know Mom. She can't sit still for longer than a minute."

I was momentarily distracted by the size of the lobster on Andre's plate. "I've never seen anything that big. Do they feed them steroids?"

Andre took a bite. "In Vegas? Probably," he said. "So, what's this top-secret mission you couldn't tell us earlier?"

"You want to start another UNEEC?" Kiki asked.

"Nope," I said. "It's bigger."

I looked around the room to make sure no one could hear me. Then I leaned in and whispered. "A video game rental service for hotels."

Andre and Kiki stopped chewing. "That's a great idea," Andre said.

"Is anybody doing it already?" Kiki asked.

"Nope. That's why I'm whispering. It's a wide-open market, and I'm just the bruthah to break it open."

Kiki and Andre looked at one another. "Congratulations on another one, bro'," Andre said as he high-fived me.

"What about piracy?" Kiki asked.

I nearly swallowed my shrimp whole. "Pira—who?"

"Piracy," Kiki repeated. "What if someone steals the idea from you?" Steal the idea? I never thought about that. I hate to think negative, but you've always got to cover all your bases in business. Always consider all the ways your idea can go wrong. Piracy was definitely a possibility, but what could I do to prevent it?

I began to talk the idea through with everyone in the family. I had tons of questions and what-if scenarios. What if I partnered with a publicly traded, cash-rich property owner? Most of the hotels on the strip were not currently doing anything to cater to children; they were just straight gaming establishments. But once they had the idea, why would they need me? They'd just do it themselves. What if I targeted some of the smaller hotels and motels? Same problem, but maybe even worse—little guys are always looking for an advantage, and sometimes out of desperation they'll burn you faster than the corporations. Better to get my feet wet and get the money early, before anyone else caught on.

I hate to think negative, but you've always got to cover all your bases in business. Always consider all the ways your idea can go wrong before putting your plan into action.

I settled on a video game delivery service. You don't expect to order pizza and have it delivered to your hotel room. The hotels won't allow it because it's a direct competitor. But with my new gig I would not be competing with their food service. There were no services offered to kids in the hotel rooms because Vegas at that time was not considered a family-oriented destination. It was perfect. The bells were sounding in my head. This was a good idea. Now all I had to do was figure out how to execute the plan.

Andre knew that I would need the seed money, so he contacted a friend in London, Chris Leigh. Andre put me on the phone, and Chris was impressed. The market potential was huge. We'd never have to pay for advertising because basically we would have a built-in audience of bored kids stuck in their hotel rooms. Millions were being spent on advertising by the hotels and Las Vegas Convention & Visitors Association to keep more than 30 million people every year coming to Sin City. Chris had heard plenty. He was sold. My idea appealed to the kid in him (my secret weapon), and it made good business sense. He gave Andre a sizable check for seed money.

At that point, I though the idea was foolproof . . . and that's probably exactly the reason I acted like a fool. Here's a tough lesson to learn, but an important one: in business, never assume the money is banked until it's in the bank.

Soon after I came up with my idea, a young man in his early thirties became interested in dating Kiki. I can't quite remember how she told us she met him, but before I could say "blackjack" he was pursuing my sister like there was no tomorrow. From the start there was something about him that wasn't quite right. I couldn't put my finger on it. I thought maybe I was being a little overprotective of Kiki, so I gave the guy a break.

One night John (not his real name) came by to pick her up to take her to dinner. After the introduction I asked to see his driver's license. He thought my question a little odd, but he agreed. I checked it out and told him, "I'll be keeping it until my sister

_____

Never assume a plan is foolproof. That's a guarantee that you will start to act like a fool.

returns safely." Yes, I asked for his driver's license, and yes, I was going to keep it until he brought Kiki home. Andre was in Phoenix visiting Mom so technically I was the surrogate big brother that day, even though I was only ten!

I hung around in the living room like a fly at a family reunion. I'm sure I was bugging the hell outta the guy. "So, Farrah, I hear you're an entrepreneur? Your sister says you've got another big idea cooking."

"You heard right," I said.

"That's cool," he said. "What businesses have you started?"

I told him about UNEEC and how much fun it had been to be in control of my destiny. He asked a few more questions, mainly about my new idea. I gave him the broad strokes and off they went.

When he brought Kiki home later that night I was still awake. I had been watching the clock for a few hours. He sat on the sofa in our living room, looking around. "Here's your license," I said.

"Thanks," he said. "Say, tell me more about that idea you have," he said.

I was excited that he had taken an interest in my idea so I spilled a few more beans. "Right now we basically have no competitors. No hotels are really catering to kids," I said.

The next day he called and offered us tickets to attend a live, casino simulcast of a television and radio show called *Backstage Live*. It was an interview show that highlighted celebrities and entertainers. I learned that this guy was a casino employee, which is why he had no problem capturing the vision of my idea. Whenever he'd call my sister on the phone he'd say, "So what's Farrah up to?" or "Let me talk to Farrah for a second."

Once on the phone, he'd ask a million questions about the video service, saying that he was really impressed with me. "Farrah, you're really a smart kid, you're going to go far in life. . . . Uh, how's your business plan coming with the video game service?"

After that first date, John put on what's called in basketball terminology "a full court press," which meant he was relentless. His efforts to try to impress my sister went into full gear. One night when he came over to our house he made me an offer. "I'd like to be a partner and investor in your video business," he said. "I think we'd make great business partners." I was wide-eyed and bushy-tailed so I agreed. "Cool!"

He appeared to be a big shot in the business. "I'd like to have you and Farrah as my guests at an upcoming show," he told Kiki. "I get special seats." I learned later that he'd been given the tickets by the show's cohost. This was one of my early introductions to the art of schmoozing and lying. There is no such thing as a free lunch. Or breakfast or dinner, for that matter. Someone always pays a price.

And boy, was I about to pay dearly. A few days later he came to the house, where we had our first real business meeting. He told me he would be the salesman for our newly formed business corporation. "I'll make all of the sales calls," he said, "since I know a lot of the hotel owners." I was ecstatic. Here I was with a partner who was already in the casino business, and he wanted to be in business with me? How lucky was I?

Kiki and I created a killer marketing presentation. We spent thousands of dollars on the usual expenses associated with launching a new enterprise: incorporation fees, business licenses and

> *To accept ourselves as we are means to value our imperfections as much as our perfections.*
>
> —Sandra Bierig

permits, plus an entire image campaign, which meant hiring a graphic artist to design the logo and marketing materials. The printing costs alone were enough to feed a small country for a day.

The letterhead, business cards and brochures were four-color and glossy, printed on the best paper because Mom had taught us that presentation was everything. "If you want to be taken seriously," she'd say, "then you have to look like a serious player."

Since I wasn't old enough to sign business documents, Andre signed on my behalf. He then handed my new partner approximately one hundred business folders with our presentations contained inside. I was convinced this innovative video rental business was about to put me among the business elite. I was half right.

For a while I was seeing John almost every night. We'd go over the business plan. He made suggestions for strengthening it. It seemed like a business marriage made in Vegas. He'd visit my sister and we'd talk about our plan for blanketing the hotels with our new service. He was becoming more familiar with my plan, but as he became more familiar, I heard from him less. He wouldn't return calls. His visits became less frequent. I would call him on the phone, and he'd always say, "I'm just leaving a meeting with XYZ Hotel. They loved it."

When I'd ask to see copies of contracts or meeting notes, he always had an excuse. And because Kiki was no longer interested in him, there was no guarantee that he'd ever show up at the house again. Pretty soon, my calls went unanswered and ol' John was a ghost. The writing was on the wall. My business partner had gone MIA. When I finally got him on the phone, he told that he would be moving out of the town because of a family emergency. I later found out he was moving to Henderson, an upscale community just outside of Vegas.

If you want to be taken seriously, you have to look like a serious player. Your letterhead, business cards and brochures all must be top-notch.

One day I decided to go into a few casinos to see if my suspicions were on target. I started seeing the V-cards (promotional items) on hotel buffet tables inviting parents to order a video game setbox for their rooms to keep their kids entertained. That sucker had stolen my idea. Correction: I gave it to him.

A few weeks later, when I was flying back to Las Vegas from Phoenix with Jonathan and Alex, we saw him picking up a girl-friend in his new convertible Mercedes Benz.

I felt horrible for a lot of reasons. First, someone who pretended to be a decent guy had betrayed me. Second, someone else was capitalizing on an incredible business opportunity that I created. And last but certainly not least, I'd let Chris, Andre's buddy, down in a big way. I'd lost all of his seed money.

They say that sometimes the things we need the most are sitting right in front of us. I had been reading book after book during my stay in London, but I never picked up the two books on Andre's shelf that probably could have helped me the most. I had judged them both by their covers. They looked older than I was with their yellowing pages and crinkled covers. Yet staring me straight in the face was *Winning Through Intimidation* and *Looking Out for #1*. They should have been my companion study guides to the martial arts and spiritual self-help books I had been reading.

I was in the tank, but who could I blame? No one. He hadn't

held a gun to my head or forced me to go into business with him. He'd done what tons of people do every single day: pretend to be someone they're not. It was a powerful and painful lesson for me. Now every time I check into a hotel, I think about the million-dollar idea that I let slip right through my fingers.

Five Minutes till Air

I knew getting them to go with me would be a long shot, but I thought I'd try it anyway. Jonathan and Alex wanted to walk the Strip to check out the scores of girls who were walking by the big hotels on any given day. I wanted to go see the antique car collection. It was a free attraction. Perfect for three teenage boys who didn't have any money anyway.

I used a business tactic. I created a win-win situation. I told them there would be plenty of girls to check out where I was taking them, and there would be cool cars. I was right. It must be in our DNA for boys to love cars, because my brothers lit up like Christmas trees when we walked into the venue. After all, who wouldn't be interested in seeing the cars owned by rich and famous celebrities? While my brothers drooled over the antique cars, I noticed a camera crew was setting up in the Duesenberg Room for the show *Backstage Live,* broadcast before a live audience. I left my brothers and headed toward the Duesenberg Room.

Backstage Live featured celebrities who lived in Las Vegas or owned their second or third home there. It was commonplace to see megastars like Bruce Willis or Mike Tyson being interviewed. On this day it was Michael Jackson. Yes, *the* Michael Jackson and not a Michael Jackson impersonator. Vegas is world famous for its impersonators from the long-running *Legends in Concert* show. Somehow I made my way near the stage, where I got to meet his father, Joe, and his brother Jermaine.

Ms. Ross, the producer of the show and the department head of marketing and advertising for the Imperial Palace, took an interest in me and asked my name. Little did she know that I was an average nine-going-on-ten kid who'd already lived an extraordinary life. Whenever someone asked me what I enjoyed doing, I told them about my business successes, my goals, my dreams. Sometimes they didn't believe me. Other times, they thought I was just blowing smoke. Finally my grandmother pulled me aside. "Sweetie, don't tell people your business or where you've been, because you're a black child and they won't believe you. Keep your business to yourself, okay?" I never forgot that.

So when the producer asked me what had brought me to *Backstage Live* that day, I gave her a plain vanilla answer. "I'm interested in starting a business in Vegas one day," I said. Perhaps her motherly instinct sensed something in my *ki* that intrigued her.

She invited me up to the restaurant for a free meal with Jonathan and Alex, who chose to sit at another table because they never had any interest in what interested me. As Ms. Ross and I began to eat our dinner, her cohost, Gary Campbell, joined us. He told us all about the show and how he was looking to branch out to do some innovative things. I loved hearing people say that. Those words were music to my ears. I knew that I wanted to have my own talk show one day, and Gary sounded like he might be just the mentor to help me get there. I got his phone number and asked if I could call him. "Any time," he said. "I like to see young men taking the bull by the horns."

After a few follow-up calls—remember that you'll never go anywhere if you don't make the calls—Ms. Ross and Mr. Campbell decided that I would be a novel attraction and addition to their cohost lineup. "Do you have any interest in broadcasting, Farrah?" Were they kidding? "One of my dreams is to host my own talk show," I said.

"Now, this is an unpaid job, but you'll get some great experience," Ms. Ross said. "And you'll get free dinner passes, too." Free food and a chance to be on the air? I was there.

It sounded great to me, but I knew I'd have to get buy-in from the rest of the family. I couldn't leave Mom alone in Phoenix. I couldn't live with Kiki and Andre again either, as they were both starting their own families. But no one wanted me to miss out on the opportunity. They knew my wounds were still healing from the video services deal, so they thought this might be a good opportunity to get me back in the game. And the fact that *Backstage Live* was the very show John had taken me to when he was stealing my idea made it all the more sweet.

I called Mom. I needed her touch. She always knew just what to say without saying too much. I told her how disappointed I was that Mr. Don Juan had stolen my video games rental services idea. I was trying to regroup, but I didn't want to be too hasty.

"Go for it, baby," Mom said. "You always said you could make lemonade outta lemons."

I laughed. "And package, market and sell it," I said.

"That's what I'm talking 'bout," Mom shot back.

"And don't forget the profits, baby," I said.

After that conversation, it was a done deal. I would be one of the cohosts for *Backstage Live,* twice a month. I'd get to hobnob with some of the world's most famous celebrities. I'd get to interview them and ask them all the questions I'd always wanted to ask from my living room. It was pure irony. A kid from the 'hood cohosting

Backstage Live with Connie Ross and Gary Campbell at the Grand Salon of The Auto Collections, known as "the most expensive studio in the world."

The first order of business was my attire. I had to look good for my first appearance! For my birthday, Andre had ordered my first tailor-made suit from one of the world's most famous department stores, Harrod's in Knightsbridge, which produces special clothing items and accessories for the Royals in London. When I was dressed in that white-cuffed shirt with very British, very conservative red tie and a pin-striped suit, I felt like royalty.

My first day on the job was an out-of-body experience. It was totally surreal. Sitting in my chair with headsets that almost covered my entire face, I knew my life was on an upward turn. I didn't have to pinch myself. I knew it was really happening as I looked out into the audience to see Andre, Jonathan, Alex and Kiki smiling with pride that their "little man" was in the big leagues "representin'."

As I sat there preparing to go on the air, I thanked Mr. Thief/Don Juan and felt sorry for him at the same time. He didn't have a clue that he didn't have a clue. It is an undeniable, universal law that we reap what we sow; we get what we give to the world. I knew that he would eventually be "rewarded" for his dastardly deeds.

During the first year I cohosted my fifteen-minute segment of *Backstage Live* it reached over 12 million listeners and viewers every Saturday night. And that "unpaid" gig soon turned into a very lucrative speaking career. I received speaking engagement requests from various statewide and national youth conferences, including HBCU (Historical Black Colleges and Universities) and churches of every denomination around the country. That first year, I earned more than fifty thousand dollars from speaking engagement honorariums to help support my family. I was commanding between five hundred and five thousand dollars an appearance. I was on cloud nine!

The word spread, and soon I was being offered ten thousand dollars for national keynote lectures. Requests were pouring in from all over the country: New York, Texas, Florida, Washington, D.C. . . . even Nebraska! Why would they offer me so much money? The organizations were mandated by their mission and corporate sponsors to bring in a "superstar" young role model to impact the lives of the youth they were serving. Three years earlier my family was being evicted, and now people were paying me ten G's to share my story? Only in America!

I was leading by the example of focusing on the inside, which was resulting in my becoming rich on the outside. I was showing people that you can start at ground zero, create an investment club raising six figures, become a national talk show cohost in the entertainment capital of the world and make it to the top—all before the age of twelve! I was showing every poor kid in the country that you don't have to sell drugs to make a living. You don't have to go to prison to be somebody. All you have to do is find your purpose and ignite your passion.

The greatest warrior is the one who conquers himself.

—Samurai saying

But I wasn't even close to the apex of my mountain. There was an additional step I had to take to become rich on the inside. I had to adopt the wisdom of the samurai, who said, "The greatest warrior is the one who conquers himself," and Mahatma Gandhi, who said, "The weak can never forgive. Forgiveness is the attribute of the strong."

I had learned some important lessons. I had learned that I couldn't blame people for the things that didn't go right in my life. I played a part in things going wrong. I learned from that pain, and

I had to learn to forgive. If I didn't forgive, I'd never reach my full potential. So I acknowledged there had been deep hurt caused by the wrong actions of a few motivated by greed. First came the parents who wanted to withdraw their children from our first entrepreneurial club to start their own. And second came the smiling casino employee who offered to become my partner and then stole my idea. They'd have to answer for their actions, but I had to assume responsibility for my contribution.

I found perfect harmony by dedicating my whole existence to becoming rich from the inside out. I wanted to start early building my legacy as a business and social entrepreneur "doing well and doing good." I created the Farrah Gray Foundation with a 10 percent youth tax that was committed to giving back to the community and other young entrepreneurs like myself.

Ten percent of my speaking engagement earnings were deposited into the foundation to support youth-related, community-based organizations and after-school programs. My sincere hope is that I will be blessed to hear the many success stories from youth all over the country. And who knows, maybe I'll become a stakeholder in the next UNEEC. I don't believe in investing in projects; I invest in people, in the human soul. If the stars align, I could even be instrumental in launching the career of the next Bill Gates, Oprah Winfrey, Russell Simmons or Sean "P. Diddy" Combs.

I don't believe in investing in projects; I invest in people, in the human soul.

In fact, I am looking forward to a reunion of the original UNEEC members. I can't wait to reminisce on all of the twists and turns our lives have taken since we left our old stomping grounds. As the old folks used to say, "What a time that will be."

Is There a Speaker in the House?

How does a kid who grew up on the south side of Chicago end up shaking hands with the president of the United States? How does a young man who once lived in a car with his family get invited to spend Christmas at the White House? How does this same kid mingle with affluent CEOs of *Fortune* 500 companies and make it onto *Black Enterprise*'s cover before the age of sixteen?

It all started with a set of core values: honesty, integrity and hard work. From there I began to understand the importance of ethics, positive intentions and drawing strength from the knowledge that I am a good person. Beyond that, I've taken pride in celebrating my humble food-stamps-to-finance journey. Some people don't like to talk about being poor. I don't mind. It keeps me grounded in reality. And I never forget what it felt like to be an elite member of the "have nots." I don't dwell on it, but I certainly never forget it.

I'm a fisherman. And in order to become a fisherman, you have to be taught to fish. Nobody just goes to the ocean, casts a net and catches a boatload of fish. It doesn't happen that way. We have to be taught to fish, and I had good teachers. I had a supportive home life. I came from the womb of a woman who possesses a heart as big and tender as you will ever find.

She taught me that you never know who's watching or listening. So when people walk up to me with genuine words of encourage-ment after a speaking engagement, I know that I've earned their respect and admiration. That's something I never take for granted. I use a lot of my mom's and grandma's anecdotes in my speeches. They have such colorful language and wisdom that sometimes I walk around with a notepad and pen in hand because I know they're gonna say something memorable.

Grandma told me, "Once you qualify, people can justify."
I'd never heard this one. "What did you just say?"
"Once you qualify, people can justify," she repeated.
"Okay, Grandma, break it down for me," I said.

That's when she told me that once you show someone you are worthy of their support, they can justify recommending you on a personal or professional level without being embarrassed or regretting making an introduction to someone in their circle of influence.

> *Once you qualify,*
> *people can justify.*
> —Grandma

I guess my qualifications were rising because within a span of two years I was invited to some of the country's most exclusive and prestigious events. My keynote addresses have been heard in inner-city high school gymnasiums and *Fortune* 100 boardrooms. When I hear comments such as, "Farrah is a powerful role model for the children of society," it moves me to tears because I know how important it is for all of us to have people we can look up to. I'm grateful that I can be a vessel for other youngsters. At nineteen, I have been truly blessed with myriad experiences—extensive travel, cross-cultural interaction and business exchanges that most people never get the benefit of experiencing. I have become qualified to be justified, just as Grandma told me I would be.

She also taught me the importance of being "one of them" and never "above them." That lesson was critical to my development as a businessman and speaker. This attitude makes me popular with teenagers because I position myself as one of them. In the universe there are no "big I's" and "little u's." When I look out into the sea of teenagers in an audience, I see myself in them, and I give them the message I would want to hear; therefore, my message is more likely to be received. People feel sincerity. It can't be manufactured.

I don't remember the exact date, but I was very young when I made the decision to make a difference in the world. I talked it over with my family, and not surprisingly, they encouraged me not only to dream big, but to do it right. I vowed to only work on things that would help make a difference. That commitment could extend to business, as it did with UNEEC or a nonprofit organization like the Farrah Gray Foundation, which supports two fundamental ideals: economic and social entrepreneurship.

> *We poison our lives with fear of burglary and shipwreck and . . . the house is never burgled, and the ship never goes down.*
>
> —Jean Anouilh

To support the Foundation, I accepted every speaking engagement I could squeeze into my schedule between tutors and spending time with my mother. Every week I was speaking in elementary schools, churches, companies . . . you name it. I did morning assemblies, brown bags and banquets. I accepted all invitations because I was serious about making an immediate difference, and I wanted to touch as many lives as possible.

For a while it felt like I was on a marathon speaking tour. I was rarely at home. Some days I'd deliver three or four speeches. I was on a mission! It was an ambitious endeavor; I had a blazing fire in my belly.

This passion led me to finally launch New Early Entrepreneur Wonders (NE^{2}W), the organization I discussed with Roi Tauer right after we launched UNEEC. He encouraged me to be patient, and he strongly urged me to accept any and all appropriate speaking engagements, even for free where necessary. This would not only improve my speaking experience, it would also improve my "q" (my media quotient), which would give me more name recognition when it came time to approach the "pockets" for NE^{2}W. He reminded me of my first selling days when I was selling the concept of UNEEC to the hotel owner. "You got that guy to give you a free meeting room with all the free pizza and soda you kids could eat. That's pretty good selling!" he said.

Roi taught me the value of the "elevator pitch," or articulating your point in a sentence. They both emphasized one key point: stakeholders invest in people first and ideas second. People invest in other people based on their worthiness. I have seen wealthy-looking people walk past a homeless person holding out a cup. The homeless person was deemed as having no value. A person wants to receive some sense of mutual benefit when giving. I never fail to give whatever money I have my pocket or briefcase to any homeless person because one cannot judge a person by their current conditions, as if their circumstances dictate the content of their character. The mere fact that I could have just donated the money to buy a hot meal filled me with joy. Because my family and I had been evicted, maybe I am a little sensitive to their plights. But I would never sit in judgment, period!

At one point I was invited to the Chicago headquarters of the Rainbow/PUSH Coalition by Axel Adams, then chief of staff, to work on setting up a youth business expo. While there I saw a hand-painted portrait of a black child crying. The message engraved on the picture frame was the statement "Weeping endureth for the night and joy cometh in the morning!"

Perfect your "elevator pitch." You've got to be able to articulate your point in one sentence or you'll never get anywhere in business.

I understand weeping. And I understand joy. I don't know how anyone survives by keeping it all inside. Roi had told me that the darkest night is just before the day. He said that having the "right intentions" is fine, but you also have to go out there and "get the experience" to make your life better. Roi also talked to me about healthy competition. Don't look at the other guy as your prime competitor—seek to outdo yourself. Steward Johnson echoed Roi's sentiments when he said that our business in life is not to get ahead of others but to get ahead of ourselves—to break our own records.

Part of getting the experience was sharing my message through my speeches, my foundation and my businesses. The more I spread my message, the more accolades and exposure came my way. It was incredible. Being a cohost on *Backstage Live* provided a steady stream of leads for speaking engagements, but it didn't stop there. My publicity machine was just kicking into high gear.

The first in a string of major network media interviews started with the Las Vegas NBC television affiliate. The manager, Mr. Campbell, set the stage for me to be interviewed during one of the most watched programs in television history—the 1996 Olympic Games in Atlanta, Georgia.

It was off the hook! A full ten-minute, one-on-one interview with my main man at my side—my brother Andre. I'd done a lot of speaking, but you have to remember, I was only eleven years old in the summer of 1996, so having Andre there was a safety measure, just to keep the conversation flowing. They thought he'd be the seasoned media personality. It turns out he was nervous and I wasn't.

That same afternoon I was interviewed on NBC's FM radio station. That's when I discovered the power of radio. As I sat there discussing my life and my triumphs, more than seventy calls flooded the switchboard. People chimed in with praise and encouragement. Plus I picked up additional business opportunities. It was great.

Sometimes when you grow up in an impoverished environment, it's easy to wonder if you really have anything to offer the world.

But after my television and radio interviews, I was convinced that I wasn't broke and I didn't need fixing. To my surprise I was as comfortable, fluid and at home in the media setting as I was on the podium.

After those two media hits, my life literally changed . . . again. Parents started calling, asking me to give them advice concerning their own children. Assistants from various churches called to ask me to speak to their congregrations. I was booked even more solid than before, and after about a year and a half I'd logged more than two hundred thousand air miles. Although I'd made the commitment to speak for free, offers were pouring in with high-priced honorariums. I couldn't believe it. Somebody wanted to pay me thousands of dollars just to share my life story.

I was overwhelmed by what was happening, mainly because I could see how my story was affecting other young people. The great thing about being a speaker is that when I connect with my peers they can see in me all they can be. My message, then and now, remains the same. I encourage young people to sidestep all of the pitfalls and senseless distractions that can rob them of their natural potential and inevitable greatness.

As much as things change, they have a tendency to remain the same. Many of the young people who hear me speak come from backgrounds just like mine or worse. This fact alone gives me immediate "street credibility." They can relate to me. They can see themselves in my stories.

I realize that growing up a black male in a single-parent household makes me an instant member of the underestimated. So it's my mission to knock down those walls and send a message to anyone who's ever doubted himself or herself that they can do it—whatever it is. It's natural for people to see me now and think that

> *Our business in life is not to get ahead of others but to get ahead of ourselves—to break our own records, to outstrip our yesterdays by our today, to do our work with more force than ever before.*
>
> —Steward B. Johnson

I was born with a silver spoon in my mouth, so sometimes I have to tell them, "Don't let the suit and tie fool you." I'm proud of my accomplishments, but I feel the most pride that I was able to overcome such long odds to get where I am today.

It bothers me that sometimes people make the assumption that my achievements are the result of being born into the "right" family, by which they mean an affluent or famous lineage. Sometimes people will ask me, "Now, whose son are you?" As if one can only become successful if they have a foot up on the rest of the competition. Believe it or not, some folks also believe that successes is a by-product of luck. Nothing can be further from the truth. Most people have achieved their successes through sheer determination and hard work. Sure, it's easier to get to the mountaintop if you've got someone giving you a hand, but you still have to do the climbing. The workload still belongs to you. Never rely on hookups, introductions, free passes or special privileges. We receive in direct proportion to how much we give.

I've been blessed with a tremendous opportunity to add value to the lives of others. I believe that's what makes every single human being's story so amazing. My story, though similar to a lot of other rags-to-riches tales, is still uniquely mine. There are no exact duplicates of my life. And guess what? That means you also have something special to give to the world. I accepted my gifts a long time ago, and I've been flowing ever since. What about you? Will you cheat the world of your brilliance? Will you hide your light under a bushel? Or will you embrace your talents and contribute to this great world of ours?

Let Me "Edutain" You!

I think back to my first visit to the Chicago headquarters of the Rainbow/PUSH Coalition. I'd gone for an educational conference. I kept running into paintings and portraits with profound sayings underneath them. I've already told you about the "weeping endureth for a night" one, but another one that left an imprint on my heart was a simple mural that read: "Nobody makes a greater mistake than he who did nothing because he could only do a little." Statesman Edmund Burke said that as he studied the theory and practice of British politics.

No one knew the gravity of those words better than I did. I've always wanted to do something that would change the world. I still do. That's why I never take for granted the impact my words might have on someone who hears me speak or share in a radio interview—even if only five people are listening! Maybe reading this book right now is changing your life. I hope in some tiny way it is. Because even though it may only be a small shift, it could lead to humongous changes. If it does, I hope you'll let me know.

> *Nobody makes a greater mistake than he who did nothing because he could only do a little.*
> —Edmund Burke

If I'd waited until I made a million dollars to start thinking about what was happening with young people in America, surely I would have missed hundreds of opportunities to share my story. Who knows what lives have been changed through your message, your example or your life? I, for one, didn't realize how important my work was until a young person came up to me after a speech and said, "I came here tonight with a friend and, I'd had every intention of going home and taking my life."

My knees almost buckled when I heard that. For about three seconds I literally couldn't breathe. "But when I heard that you and your family had slept in a car and that you went days without food," this young man said, "I knew I could do it too." That's when I knew that what I was doing was more than relevant; it was necessary.

"Hang in there," Roi used to say. "Before a man eats, he must sweat." In other words, there can be no rewards without work. My work was just beginning. For the longest time I didn't call myself a speaker; I was a businessman who flew around the country sharing his story. After cohosting *Backstage Live* for nearly two years, I'd racked up a lot of frequent flyer miles. None of those engagements had been the result of a booking agency. There was never a thought to contact a speaker's bureau to represent me. I was fortunate enough to have people zero in on my love for reaching out to young people. Somehow I was touching their lives during a time when the general consensus was that this demographic wanted nothing more than cell phones, designer clothes and drugs.

The requests were pouring in. My grandma, who was my bookkeeper and assistant on some days, fielded more than twenty requests a month. As I said before, I never intended to go into the business of public speaking, but I begin to see the beauty and the responsibility of being a public figure, a celebrity of sorts. I wasn't a singer, actor or athlete. I didn't have a record deal, movie contract or signing bonus to join a sports team. I was just a regular guy.

My secret? I truly wanted to share the story of my personal and professional trials and triumphs. That's it. It was a charge I took very seriously. I wanted to touch the hearts and minds of my peers. No one taught me to speak, although I do think there's a great deal of value in learning speaking techniques. I simply spoke from my heart.

One of my favorite speech openings involves a series of questions. "Have you ever heard of me? Have you ever heard one of my songs playing on the radio? Have you seen me in any television commercials? Any cameo parts in a movie? Have you seen me dunking on Shaquille O'Neal in the NBA? If the emcee had not just introduced me, would you even know my name?" Of course, the answer to each of these questions is always no.

But it is my final question that typically results in a hush over the crowd. "So how in the world did I get here to speak in front of you?" The answer is the same reason you're reading this book right now. "Because I have a story to tell. It's my story. No one else can tell it the way I can. No one else has lived it because it's mine. Then I tell them that they too have a story, that there's something great and unique within each of them. I don't know what it is, but I know it's there. We all have it. That means you too."

As I say those words, I can see lights flickering in the eyes of nearly every person in the audience. Many of them have had their pilot lights blown out by life, abusive loved ones, unforgiving circumstances and even media messages. "But I am here," I say, "to light your candle."

I tell my audiences they can call me a motivational speaker. They can call me an entrepreneur. But the name I prefer to be called is one given to me by my grandma. She calls me an "edutainer." Part educator, part entertainer. I can't imagine being a lecturer. It reeks of seriousness. I am serious, yes, but I'm not as serious as most people think I am. Part of that's my fault. I wear suits. I use big words. I listen intently when people talk to me. I can see why people have said, "He's so serious," or as one Hollywood studio executive said, "He's almost too polished." Imagine that. Ever heard a jeweler say of a diamond, "It's too polished"? I don't think so. It is what it is. And whatever it is adds to its beauty. Remember that.

I don't defend my seriousness. As I said, I *am* quite serious about business, but I also like to keep it real. I like to be playful, down to earth and a straight-up teenager. But when I address an audience what's most important to me is that those under the sound of my voice know there is no separation between us. I am them, and they are me. Right before I take the microphone, I always think about a favorite samurai maxim:

Victory goes to the one who has not thought of himself.

—Samurai saying

"Victory goes to the one who has not thought of himself." My focus from behind the podium is simple: this moment is about them, not me. That's my best advice on anything you want to do well in life.

A Personal Chat

After every speaking engagement, I sit in the middle of the room fielding questions from audience members. I'm always fascinated by the questions complete strangers are willing to ask. Personal things such as "How big is your house?" or "How much money do you have in the bank?" The number-one question is about my parents. Who are they and where are they now? What do they do?

Sometimes the questions are a bit harder to answer. "How did you get to be so smart? Why do you carry a briefcase? Do you have a girlfriend? Do you have to always wear a suit? Do people call you 'Mister'?"

People are astounded when I tell them that basically I'm still a kid. Strip away the millions, the first-class flights and dinners at the White House, and I'm just like any other nineteen-year-old male. I love to have fun and joke around. I like hip-hop music and hip-hop gear. I like to keep it casual. They really trip out when I tell them the mall is still the place I go to get a few girls' phone numbers and that nothing gives me greater joy than playing video games and beating one of my brothers—which I do on a regular basis, by the way.

More important, I show them my humanity. I have insecurities and doubts just like everyone else. One of the hardest things about being "on stage" is how people respond to you after a performance. At many of my appearances or speaking engagements, sponsors arrange for an after-party. Sometimes people stand around watching me, waiting to see if I have any rhythm! That's hard because I want them to be themselves and forget about me. By the way, if you're wondering, I *do* have rhythm—or so I'm told!

Without a doubt, the best part about being called a role model is the opportunity to connect with other people who desperately need inspiration. My challenges pale in comparison to what a lot of young people have to endure while growing up. What's harder than not having food to eat or a place to live? Lots. How about not having the love of a mother? That's a pain I'm glad I didn't have to grow up with. How about not knowing your father? That's an agony no one should have to endure.

It's amazing how many young people feel unloved inside their own homes. I'm thankful to have had a loving mother and siblings. My travels have made me realize how fortunate I was to have been born into my family. Like Mom always said, "Poor ain't permanent." I never forgot that.

Even though my family was there for me, I try to impress upon young people the need to love themselves even when they feel the world doesn't want them. This is a message that we need to hear over and over. Sometimes I got phone numbers from young people at my events, just so I could call them and offer a word of encouragement.

Because the Farrah Gray Foundation is a 501(c)3 nonprofit corporation, certain expenses were paid for and deducted as part of our overhead. But even if they had not been a part of my general operating expenses, I would have gladly paid for these calls out of my own pocket. They were that important.

The conversations with teens often center on the usual banter— the opposite sex, their parents, school, and drugs and other negative elements. While I wanted to validate their experiences, I knew that I would be doing them a disservice if I allowed them to wear the "victim badge." I couldn't stand that. We have to play the hand we're dealt. We don't have to accept the circumstances, but we must accept our beginnings and then decide on our ends. I have always believed, and put into action, my faith that we carve our own statue. We write the lyrics to our own song, and we paint our own picture based on our innate talents. We are our own Picassos, painting our lives, stroke by stroke. Decision by decision.

Our choices don't define us permanently, but they certainly provide insight into where we are in that moment in our lives. I'm reminded of the story of Hetty Green, "the Witch of Wall Street" who was the world's richest woman in the early 1900s. She inherited her wealth from her father's real-estate business but had an unhealthy personality and mindset toward her blessings. Mrs. Green loaned the City of New York 4.5 million dollars in cold, hard cash, but when her son became ill she refused to pay for a doctor to treat his injury.

After two years without treatment, her son's leg had to be amputated. His mother, the richest woman in the world, who had amassed a real-estate dynasty that included two square miles of choice property in Chicago, along with several skyscrapers, wouldn't pony up for her son's medical bills. Truly void of love and compassion, she was bankrupt from the inside out. Money couldn't pay off the mess she made within her family. The moral of this story is that sometimes the richest parents don't always do the best by their children. Sometimes parents forget that love is the great equalizer. All the money, riches and prestige in the world will never be able to do what an ounce of genuine love and concern can do in a child's life. Never.

REAL POINTS: Dealing with Your Crisis

There will be at least one full-blown, all-out crisis in your life. How you deal with it will determine your ultimate success.

1. **Take care of yourself first, then take care of your loved ones.** This doesn't mean to abandon ship—if you're the captain, you stay until the crew is off. It does mean that you need to ensure that you will survive every catastrophe by planning ahead. For instance, don't feel bad if your partner is left with nothing because he didn't invest wisely when he had the chance. Simply congratulate yourself on not being in his shoes.

2. **Talk to people now if you have something to say.** You may not get a chance later. That's a regret you don't want to have.

3. **Before you begin, make sure you know all the drawbacks.** Plan for the negatives; don't just dream about the positives. I'm the type of person who hates to take a pessimistic view of things, but I've learned the hard way that you have to consider the worst to be the best.

4. **Analyze everyone.** Always remember: invest in people first, not ideas. I was blinded by fast talk and a lot of connections when I should have been checking out the person behind the boasting. Don't let this happen to you. We are all equipped with a sixth sense, a gut-level intuition that tells us when something's a little fishy. Don't ignore it. It's there to protect you.

5. **Sometimes the best next move isn't making the most money right away.** If you truly believe in the project, like I did with *Backstage Live*, find a way to make it work—even if there's no money in sight. Think in broad terms, plan long-term and believe in what you are doing.

6. **Forgive, but don't forget.** You have to forgive everyone who contributes to your personal crisis—especially yourself. But you

should never forget the lessons you learned in the moment of testing, for they are the most important of your life. And never, ever do business again with someone who has burned you in the past!

7. **Qualify to justify.** Give people a reason to support you. The best reasons are honesty, integrity, respect and a strong work ethic.

REALLIONAIRE AFFIRMATION

◆

I'm moving forward in a positive way, I'm honest with myself and others, and I'm eager—not willing but eager—to give back to those around me with no thought of my own reward.

Reallionaire Exercise:
Give Back and Pay It Forward

This exercise is all about contributing to your family, community and the world.

Every reallionaire knows that a big part of the wealth equation is philanthropy. That's why I accepted every engagement that came my way. That's why a portion of every speech I deliver goes to my foundation. I know that by giving, I am sure to be blessed. If service and philanthropy are not currently a part of your daily, weekly and yearly life, I encourage you to find ways to make it a part of your life. You will be instantly blessed.

Now, before you run out and give, we must first assess what we have to give.

What is wealth to me? _____

_____

_____

_____

What does it mean to give? _____

_____

_____

_____

What do I feel are my greatest gifts? _____

_____

_____

_____

_____

When is the last time I made a contribution to my family or community? Describe both. _____

_____

_____

_____

_____

_____

How did it feel to know that my contribution made a difference?

_____

_____

What do I care about most (teens, diseases, homeless animals, etc.)?

_____

_____

What is my idea of service? _____

_____

_____

My plan over the next thirty days is to contribute to my family, community and/or world in the following ways: _____

_____

_____

_____

Dedicate Your Time to What You Know

how my life in the kitchen turned into a million-dollar idea aimed at other people just like me

Superchef Emeril Lagasse ain't got nothing on me. Yep, ain't got nothing. Not now and not when I was five years old.

Long before 1997, the year I started a teen-oriented food company, I was always in the kitchen making a mess, trying to concoct something tasty for my family to eat. I didn't always succeed, but that never stopped me from trying. When you're poor, going to the grocery store usually means that you go looking to buy the basics. Without the basics you can't make the meal.

While growing up I heard tons of stories about how all of the grandchildren in our family would gather four to five times a year to help can fruit and vegetables. These products would then be passed on through to the immediate family. I had one aunt, I was told, who was the famous "from scratch" dinner-roll queen. My great-great-grandmother, a member of the first generation born out of slavery, got her nickname, "Ma Bird," because she turned her living room into a restaurant dining room that she opened to the public, selling fried chicken dinners to laborers getting off work. The back of her kitchen was transformed into two rooms. There was a laundry room where working men dropped off their laundry and then walked a few yards to the front door, took a seat and enjoyed "Ma Bird's Blue Plate Special" on red and white picnic tablecloths.

Back in those days, Grandma says, the kitchen was the laboratory where a struggling mother could come up with creative ideas to get her family through some hard times. Grandma made dishes from scratch. Everything from pancakes to preserves. I thank Grandma for planting the seed of invention and ingenuity because she gave me permission to experiment with food.

I was a foodie before the term was popular. I dabbled with every seasoning, powder and liquid in the cabinet. Sometimes I had to take special precautions to get my experiment just right because I didn't have the luxury of goofing up on a recipe and ruining ingredients. When we didn't have the ingredients to make pancakes, I made French toast. There were always plenty of old bread ends. I'd take the one or two eggs in the refrigerator, add a little milk and go to work. I learned how to make syrup by watching Grandma and was amazed at how easy it was. That's when I started thinking about developing a product for my people, by which I mean my age group.

Every kid on the block loved pancakes. I didn't know what grown-ups liked to eat, but I had the corner on the kids' market. So every time I entered the kitchen, I had one thing on my mind: creating a food product I could make for kids. The kids in my old neighborhood didn't have a lot of discretionary income, but I knew that if a kid begged long and hard enough, he could get his parent to pony up the money to buy something.

On Saturdays, after I'd watched way too many cartoons, I sometimes took out a sheet of paper and wrote down all of the businesses I could start. Not just enterprises but businesses I could start without stepping foot outside of our apartment. I knew I couldn't own a gas station. I knew I couldn't produce toilet paper or toothpaste. I kept coming back to cooking. I

Niche your way to riches. Conquer the world you know, no matter how small the market seems. There is big money in "small" ideas.

didn't know this at the time, but Mrs. Fields baked cookies in her own kitchen until her husband borrowed fifty thousand dollars to start her gourmet cookie franchise.

Mom divided food stamps between my siblings and me. She took what she needed to get the household necessities and then she gave us the rest, much like an allowance. I made my stamps go a long way. I bought strawberries, apples, oranges, sugar and ice cream. Okay, and a few candy bars, but mostly I used the food stamps to fund my culinary experiments. I focused on creating a good-tasting syrup.

I took the basic ingredients I'd seen Grandma use and added my own twist. I blended in small amounts of vanilla ice cream to give it a little kick. It tasted good to me, but I needed to try out the recipe on real consumers—my brothers and sister. I got a variety of responses from "ewwww" to "not bad" to "that's fly," which of course meant awesome. I was shooting for fly. I kept cooking, kept mixing ingredients, hoping that one day I'd get to serve my syrup to a national market.

Five years after I mixed my first batch of syrup, I was invited to attend a minority business awards dinner in Las Vegas. I was thirteen years old. The keynote speaker was a successful African

American businesswoman from Chicago who'd also produced syrup. We'll call her Linda.

I was riveted, completely glued to my seat as I watched Linda share her amazing and heart-wrenching story, which was very similar to Mom's upbringing. I watched her weave together the events of her life in such a way that we were all hypnotized. She had a bona fide rags-to-riches story. She too had learned her recipe from her great-grandmother. She had been a single mom, raising her daughters alone and basically making a way out of no way. After her divorce she'd gone on welfare until she landed a part-time job selling cosmetics at a department store. By day she showed women lipsticks and eyeliners, by night she experimented with her grandmother's syrup recipe. On her lunch break she sought out joint-venture opportunities.

Eventually her efforts paid off, and she launched her own food company, selling millions of dollars in orders of her syrup in bottles to regional grocery stores. She capitalized on her minority supplier status and sold syrup in bulk to restaurant chains through their diversity programs. I was listening to a real-life success story from someone who'd grown up in circumstances like mine.

After her speech, there were hordes of people standing around congratulating her. I stood in line and waited my turn. I had to meet this amazing woman. I was so proud and honored that when I finally got to the front of the line, I kissed her hand. I told her that I was planning to launch a food company to develop products for kids. "Wow!" she said. "Niche your way to riches, young man, that's a great idea."

She was impressed with my knowledge of the food business but became even more intrigued when I dropped the names of a few CEOs I knew in the food business. They were heavy hitters who'd promised to help me get my venture off the ground when I was ready. "How do you know him?" she asked.

"I met him at a food event in Chicago," I answered. I could tell she wanted to know more about my contacts.

"Here's my card," she said. "Call me, I'd love to help you in any way I can." I couldn't believe it. I was soaring.

I've learned that when people ask you to call them, you should do just that, but I wanted to make sure I gave her time to get back and get settled. A few days later, I called. Her assistant answered the phone and put me right through to her. "Can you send me more information on you and your company?" she asked. I had plenty to send her because I had five and a half years of business experience already under my belt.

Remember, presentation is everything, and since that includes the timing of your presentation I sent my materials to her by next-day air. Once she opened the FedEx package she saw tons of newspaper clippings and magazine articles. I wasn't just some kid with a dream. I was someone who could clearly add value. She called me. "Very impressive, Farrah,"

> *If someone won't treat you right, they won't teach you right.*
> —Grandma

she said. "Why don't you pay me a visit the next time you're in Chicago?"

I didn't wait for an opportunity to present itself. "What's your schedule like next week?" I remember asking. I didn't want to wait any longer. I had a real-life potential mentor, and I wasn't about to let her slip away. She told me that she couldn't see me the next week but that the following week would work. As soon as I hung up the phone, I called United Airlines.

Her offices were located in a South Chicago suburb. When I got there I realized that she wasn't just an officer in the company. She owned it. She was the boss. Not only did she take me on an extensive tour of her corporate offices, she also showed me her plant. The place where the magic was made. "You can have the same thing," she said. "You're already on your way." I could hardly contain myself as she gave me samples of her products and promised to help me get my business off the ground. She was saying all the right things.

I left Chicago with a renewed sense of inspiration. I had a new mentor and surrogate mother. My first stop when I returned to Vegas was the library to research a few trade industry magazines and resource directories. There I found out about FMI. The Food Marketing Institute hosts an event every year that is the granddaddy of all conventions and conferences in the food marketing industry. Next I went to the bookstore to buy all the books I could find on starting a food manufacturing business.

There was never any doubt what I'd call my food company. I'd read somewhere the importance of using a derivative of your name in your company name and image (think Mrs. Fields and Famous Amos), so I went with Farr-Out Foods because I knew my products would be out of this world!

Then I began devising a business plan. My niche market was teens and tweens; my concept was great taste, crazy flavors and cool packaging. Within weeks, I was incorporated. In another month, I had created a knockout label and printed my business cards, letterhead and envelopes. I ordered subscriptions to trade industry magazines, and even more important, I read them. UNEEC had already been a member of the Chicagoland Chamber of Commerce, which meant that I could utilize their database and resources to help launch Farr-Out Foods. Now all I needed was a copacker.

A what?!

Linda had told me that I'd need a copacker for my products, a company that would be my partner. I'd come up with the recipes and they'd handle everything else, such as the assembly-line manufacturing, shipping and billing. "Go home and get your ducks in a row," she told me right before I left her office. "Then call me and we'll start the process together. I'll teach you everything you need to know." Was I dreaming? I had to pinch myself.

I knew that I could find a good copacker because the prospect of making cold calls didn't send me into panic mode. Remember, I was a champion cold caller—no fear, right? I was also a champion researcher—dot your i's, right? I was bouncing off the walls with excitement, but I put my enthusiasm on ice because I wanted to follow Linda's suggestion of allowing her to lead me through the process. "Call me next week," she'd said.

So I did. I called her the following week. Then the next. And again the next. I sent one fax after another with updates on my progress only to be told by her assistant, "She'll get back to you next week." In other words, don't call me, I'll call you.

I didn't sweat it. She was, after all, running a multimillion-dollar company. She'd get back with me as soon as she could, just as she'd said about seven times. Plus, I knew we would meet again at the Food Marketing Institute (FMI) convention held annually in Chicago. So I phoned her and told her I'd be attending the convention to meet some key people in the industry who'd indicated at the previous year's conference that they were open to hearing about my food product ideas.

She left me a voice mail inviting me to attend a private off-site convention party sponsored by Coca-Cola. She picked me up right outside of the McCormick convention center and we went to the Coca-Cola party together. There I made fast business friends. I was a hit, I have to say. I was networking with one goal in mind: to find food brokers, distribution outlets and supermarket chain buyers.

But when we arrived at Linda's table, I immediately found out what time it was. "This is Farrah Gray, my protégé," she said. "I'm going to show him the ropes." She had not invited me to sit at her table as a young entrepreneur starting his own food products company. She was treating me like a kid. Like window dressing.

After I caught my breath, I began to devise a way to make lemonade out of this fresh batch of lemons. After the reception, I told Linda I was going to walk the party alone. I was no stranger to networking or walking up to people to introduce myself. Let's be real, I stood out. There weren't many teenage African American boys roaming this industry event. In fact, many people struck up conversations with me before I had a chance to introduce myself.

One CEO in particular took me under his wing. His enthusiasm was genuine as he took me around to booths introducing his new business friend. We took photos and posed for the media all night. I'd made a fast friend, but as the night grew older, I knew that I needed to find Linda, my transportation to the event. I walked the entire building looking for her, asking mutual acquaintances if they'd seen her. Not lately, they all said.

I walked the area again, thinking that maybe we had missed one another. When I arrived back at the venue entrance I was faced with a sobering reality. Linda had left me. She had packed up her things and taken off without so much as a good-bye. Now I'd have to figure out how to get back to the convention hall where my brother Jonathan, who lived in Naperville, would collect me. I spotted a female photographer nearby who looked to be packing up to go home.

"Excuse me," I said. "My ride seems to have forgotten me."

She smiled. "Where ya going?"

"Back to the convention hall."

"Give me ten minutes, and I'll be happy to drop you off."

The next day, bright and early, I headed to Linda's exhibit space. She greeted passersby with that same smile I'd seen in Vegas months earlier. "Hi Linda, what happened last night?"

I expected her to say something like, "Oh, I'm sorry, I had an emergency and didn't want to interrupt you. You seemed to be networking pretty heavy." Instead she said, "Farrah, you traveled from Las Vegas to Chicago all on your own. Surely you could get where you needed to go without me." Those words would prove to be prophetic. She was right. I did know where to go without her. Straight ahead, letting no grass grow under my feet. I was about to be one heck of a rolling stone. "Good to see ya again, Farrah," she said. And with those words, she stuck a toothpick between her teeth and turned to someone else.

I was devastated but not defeated. And I hadn't seen the last of Linda. Later we would meet when I was serving my three-year term as the youngest member of the board of directors in the history of United Way. This time we met as competitors. Both of us were going for a food-service contract open to minority suppliers at the MGM Grand. I was acquainted with MGM's vice president of purchasing, a fellow United Way board member. This placed me on a very short list of vendors.

I'll never forget the day I received a phone call from her after she learned we were in the running for the same MGM contract. I accepted her call because Mom taught me never to run from a potentially difficult situation. Besides, I knew why she was calling, and I was looking forward to hearing her squirm at the thought of me beating her out for the MGM deal.

"I want you to bow out, Farrah. This contract is mine," she said. "You don't have the experience or the background to do this job." I sat on the other end of the phone very calmly. She was dead wrong. I would have never been a contender for the contract had it not been for my integrity and fortitude.

I had been dependent on a would-be mentor, but I soon found out that was not the role she wanted. Maybe that's why I set out to meet every single company that I could at FMI. I visited the exhibits of those who gave me business cards at the party the night before. I struck up conversations with them at their booths and told them that I would be calling them in the future. Roi had wisely warned me to expect disappointment and failure as a natural course of business dealings. Those words were etched in my brain.

The best thing that came out of the Linda situation was an introduction to Greg Calhoun, who at sixteen had bagged groceries at a Montgomery, Alabama, supermarket. He had worked his way up to management and ultimately acquired his former employer's supermarket. Greg Calhoun Enterprises was the largest black-owned supermarket company in Alabama. He was the only minority supermarket owner on the board of Food Marketing Institute. His company revenues at the time ranked his company on the *Black Enterprise* Top 100 Black Businesses in America list.

Mr. Calhoun embraced me like a son and proudly introduced me to Mike Wright of Supervalu, a publicly traded company with annual revenues of 20 billion dollars. He was the reigning chairman of the Food Marketing Institute. This same man boasted to Mr. Wright that he'd personally make sure Farr-Out Foods would become an exhibitor at next year's FMI convention. As excited as I was, I needed more proof. After all, I'd just dealt with disappointment. I didn't want to be set up for a similar situation.

Over the next few months Mr. Calhoun received my follow-up calls and directed me to two key executives of the company to work out the details of securing my exhibit space. I was excited. It appeared as though I was on my way in the food business. I wasn't. I made several phone calls to his office, calls that were systematically ignored. To make matters worse, the deadline for securing my exhibit space was drawing near. I never heard from him, but fate has a funny way of equalizing everything. We were seated at the same table at a minority business conference later that year. By this time, I'd inducted him into the Farrah Gray's Broken Promises Hall of Fame, a position I was soon to learn was probably unwarranted.

"I left several messages for you," I said.

"You did?"

"I never heard from those two men you referred me to."

"You didn't?"

When dealing with a corporation, you have to stay in front of the head man. That's hard to do, but it's the only way to win in a corporate environment.

This exchange went on for another few minutes, and it soon became clear that he had passed me on to underlings who had little knowledge of my situation and even less interest in dealing with me. That's the way it goes with large businesses, unfortunately. Even the best intentions (I'll give Mr. Calhoun the benefit of the doubt there) often get watered down or flat-out lost in the corporate structure. Once you're on the back burner, there's a good chance you'll be left to cool and eventually thrown out.

When dealing with a corporation, you have to stay in front of the head man. That's hard to do, but it's the only way to win in a corporate environment.

By now I'd had enough of grown-ups who didn't follow through. I was ready to strike out on my own, come what may. I did some additional research and found several copackers around the country. I sent them all letters and made follow-up phone calls, explaining that I had a product aimed at the teen and tween market. Out of about twenty-five queries, three of them returned my phone call. One of them was a company out of Batavia, Illinois.

They said, "Send us your formulation, we'll take a look at it." I was flying high again. I still didn't have exhibit space to debut my product at FMI, but I didn't care. My trusty sales manager, Steven Smith, and I flew into Chicago armed with Farr-Out Foods product flyers, business cards and product samples. We walked into the convention as if we were simply there as consumers from the general public. But when no one else was looking, we'd slide a product flyer and a sample down the exhibitor's throat.

Eventually, convention hall security caught wind of our shenanigans and chased us out of the building. The next time, we entered the building through a different door, knowing that we were taking a huge risk by coming back. But I had to get the word out about Farr-Out syrup.

> *You keep putting out good and good will come back around.*
>
> —Mom and Grandma

For a while we succeeded at our covert operation, even taking pictures at various exhibitor booths with potential buyers. We were quite the booth-to-booth salesmen. Many exhibitors asked my twenty-two-year-old, Idaho-bred sales manager if I worked for him, and he proudly confirmed that our business cards read correctly. "Farrah is the CEO of Farr-Out Foods, and I am the company sales manager, sir!"

By the midpoint of the day, I was thrilled that we hadn't been confined to a booth, but that we'd covered more ground and met more potential buyers and partners by being booth-to-booth sales-man. Our bootleg meet-and-greets had put us in front of some heavy hitters. We became familiar faces at the convention to the point that interested parties began looking for us. A group of women approached me asking if I had any orders. My response was simple: "I have orders." In reality, Farr-Out Foods had orders over one million dollars thanks to broker deals signed with Wal-Mart, Aldi Stores and all divisions of SuperValu. "And by the way," I said to the women, "I own the company. I'm not anyone's son or nephew in the business."

"I see," one of the women said.

"What Farr-Out Foods is seeking is a factory to finance the man-ufacturing of the lucrative orders in-hand," I said.

We found ourselves in a position similar to that of urban street outfitter, FUBU (For Us By Us), which secured a multimillion-dollar order from a major U.S. clothing chain but then had to seek a foreign partner to fulfill the order on the table. They seemed to accept my answer, but I don't think they believed that I was truly the CEO of the company.

> *He who has a why to live for can bear almost any how.*
> —Dr. Victor Frankel

Once I returned home to Las Vegas, I was invited to attend a small group meeting of select CEOs in the supermarket industry. Sitting in the room was a bevy of privately held and publicly traded company giants, which meant there was tons of *Wall Street Journal* lingo floating around. Major competitors were positioning them-selves collectively to compete with Wal-Mart, which was expanding to include in-store supermarkets. Albertson's, the parent company of a Midwest chain I was negotiating with, was closing hundreds of stores in twenty-five states, which reminded me that I had to find a factory to produce my original orders before pursuing more orders.

As if that wasn't enough to burden a young businessman's mind, when I returned to my office after the supermarket meeting, I found a business card on my desk from a barbecue restaurateur. I phoned the Texas headquarters listed on the business card. When we finally connected a few days later, I asked why this business card had been left on my desk. The man said that he was in the sauce business and thought we should meet the next time he was in Vegas. He said that he was interested in packaging and marketing the barbecue sauce that helped make his restaurants famous. He traveled frequently to Vegas because his partner had been setting up an airport fast-food franchise in one of the McCarran Airport terminals. I liked barbecue and thought it made sense for us to at least chat, given that we were in the same business.

Our first Las Vegas meeting had all the signs of a budding long-term business relationship. He shared his vision of marketing his private-recipe sauce. I agreed to give him my business plan and utilize my contacts to open doors for manufacturing, orders and nationwide distribution. On his second visit I met his wife, who confirmed how anxious her husband was to launch a new business with me. "I have to admit," she said. "I've never met anyone quite so young and so focused."

"Ever heard of Reginald Lewis?" I asked her. She hadn't. Reginald Lewis grew up in a Baltimore neighborhood similar to my Chicago neighborhood. Through passion, drive, perseverance and setting no limits, he opened a venture capital company and bought Beatrice International Foods for 985 million dollars, creating TLC Beatrice, the largest black-owned and black-managed snack food, beverage and grocery store conglomerate in the United States.

At its peak in 1996 (Lewis died in 1993), TLC Beatrice had sales of 2.2 billion dollars and was number 512 on the *Fortune* 1000 list of largest companies. I liked Lewis not only for his entrepreneurial prowess but also for his philanthropic commitment. His 1992 gift to Harvard Law School was the largest single donation the school had ever received. It created the Reginald F. Lewis Fund for International Study and Research. After his untimely death, his half-brother and former football player Jean S. Fugett took over the company. Lewis was one of the many success stories I told her about that day.

Before she departed Vegas, I gave her a paperback edition of the Reginald Lewis biography to read on the plane. A week later her husband suffered a heart attack. I quickly responded by sending them healthy eating cookbooks for men over forty, published by Cap Cure. Over the next few months, I continued to check in on him. His secretary told me that he was recuperating nicely and that he'd be back in the office soon.

One morning when I got into the office I called him, hoping to get him in person. "We're not going to move forward with working with you," he told me. "My son and I will take the information you provided and do it ourselves. We don't really see the need to collaborate with you." *Click.* End of story, close the book. I was starting to think I had a sign on my forehead that read "*Sucker,*" but Mom and Grandma assured me that I'd eventually attract good people. "You keep doing the right thing," Grandma said. "You keep putting out good and good will come back around." I couldn't wait for that day to come.

Learning from the Best

The Farr-Out Foods! Foodfulooza Strawberry Vanilla Syrup project launched as a direct-sale Web site offering youth-related nonprofit organizations and privately owned child-care centers a fundraising opportunity by buying wholesale and selling our products at retail. Looking to predecessors like Reginald Lewis and Paul Newman's Newman's Own food company, I became a community-conscious corporate citizen by donating 100 percent of our after-tax profits to grants for youth organizations. Farr-Out Foods became a classic example of cause marketing where the success of the product depended wholly upon its quality and philanthropic appeal, not its teenage founder.

What came next was both unplanned and unexpected. Within weeks after the site's launch, those two very inquisitive women I'd met on the FMI convention floor phoned to discuss a financially rewarding way to fulfill orders. "We've been watching you ever since we met you in Chicago," one of the women said. "Will you come to New York to meet with us and the chairman of our food company?"

I flew to Manhattan ready to hear a potential offer. What they had in mind wasn't exactly what I had in mind, but they made me an offer I couldn't refuse. An Israeli company, their strategy to enter into the American market was to buy small companies generating substantial revenues. I was small—so small I couldn't afford to finance the Farr-Out Foods' major orders without seeking out a factory. The owner was right. It would take me years to get my company in a position of leverage, so I listened very carefully to their buy-out offer.

While the negotiations rolled on, I continued racking up frequent flier miles with my speaking engagements. This kept me on the road meeting and greeting other potential stakeholders while I was experiencing "teething" problems with Farr-Out Foods. As a matter of fact, in the middle of our acquisition talks, we had to recall our first shipment because the pH balance in the formulation was incorrect and the product couldn't remain on the shelf for the mandated minimum of eighteen months.

Then we went to reorder labels and bottles only to find out that the original producer of the plastic syrup-bottle mold took the mold off the production line. It seemed there were rights for only a certain period of time to sell the excess bottles from the original mold. We couldn't afford to make our own mold, so we had to buy a new-style plastic bottle with a handle and recut our original labels to fit the new bottle. What a nightmare. Being out of the market pushed our shelving date back, but after we identified a new chemist and negotiated payment for a new formulation that would meet the contract standards, we were back in business.

By my fifteenth birthday we'd drafted a memorandum of understanding outlining the terms of the sale for $1.5 million. I was feeling on top of the world: successful, wealthy and honest with myself and my customers. Now if I could just convince the Department of Motor Vehicles to give me a driver's license, I'd be set!

REAL POINTS: Seizing the Big Opportunity

If we work hard, we will all get a chance to set our life on the road to long-term success. We may get more than one, but we will all get one chance—so be ready to recognize it and seize it.

1. **Build from what you know and love.** Your personal passion is the best guide to your future success. Do you love cooking? Reading? Football? Fly-fishing? Cosmetics? Those are all viable roads to become a reallionaire.

2. **Niche your way to success.** It's fine to start small, for even the mightiest tree was once a seed. Take the long view and dream big. No idea is too small. You can make a surprising amount of money from a very focused idea—even if others tell you there's no market!

3. **When you see an opportunity, leap on it.** Don't wait for things to get better, and don't play coy and hang back. You've got to run to your opportunities, or someone else will beat you to them.

4. **Don't rely on others; rely on yourself.** Mentors are important, but don't expect people to invest their time in you. Time is a gift many people can't afford to give. Seek advice, but always rely on yourself to get the job done.

5. **Always make your case to the leader.** Especially when dealing with large groups like corporations and schools, always go to the person at the top and stay in front of him or her for as long as you can. The second-in-command is only half as likely to help you as the commander of the ship.

6. **Creativity is essential.** If at first you don't succeed, try again another way. Just because it was your first idea doesn't necessarily mean it was your best idea.

7. **Network, network, network.** You can never know too many people in your chosen field. I was wrong four times about people in my food venture. Three times I thought people were going to help me, but they didn't. The people who ended up helping me were the very women I had almost dismissed.

8. **Keep putting out good.** It will come back to you tenfold in unexpected ways.

9. **Listen to every offer.** I had no interest in selling my food business, but I listened to the offer anyway. I kept an open mind, and I walked away with more than a million dollars in my pocket. Which leads me to a very important point . . .

10. **Be ready to accept the right deal.** Some people think that if someone is willing to give you a certain amount, someone else will give more. Don't fall into this trap. People who think this way rarely walk away winners.

REALLIONAIRE AFFIRMATION

◆

I believe in my market, my product and my contacts.
I know what I know. I know what I don't know.
And I know how to fill in the "in-betweens."

Reallionaire Exercise:
Know Your Audience

What product or service would you like to provide? Is it needed? Is someone already filling that need? Or have you identified a niche not yet exploited?

Get intimate with your customers or clients, find out what makes them tick, what they want. Here's an exercise that should help.

Write a five-hundred-word essay on your "target" customer. You want to know everything about him or her, what she drives or what he does in his spare time. This kind of market intimacy will give you a better chance of developing a product or refining a product that will keep the market satisfied. That's part one of the exercise.

Part two begins with your answer to this powerful question: "When people think of _____ (your product or service), do they think of me first, second, third or not at all?"

Now let's get specific with your particular product or service. What is it that you can do to fill this need differently or better than the next provider? Again, write a five-hundred-word essay on what makes your product or service unique *and uniquely desirable*.

Use these documents as the start of your market research. Don't toss them away. They hold critical information to give you a competitive edge.

Love Your Customer

how I learned that sincerity works, that giving back matters, and that you can't just respect your customers, you have to really care about them

Sit up straight. Brush your teeth. Don't talk to strangers. Smile. Do unto others. The list goes on and on. Since we took our first breath, people have been telling us what to do, haven't they? They meant well, but in the grand scheme of things, most of the advice people gave us growing up wasn't very useful. That's why I have a saying in my office: "Less is better—if less is good to begin with." I don't pretend to have all the answers, but I know what I know. In business you have to dot your i's, cross your t's, admit your mistakes and say "Thank you" if you want to get anywhere. Nobody wants to do business with someone who pays no attention to detail and isn't appreciative.

Stakeholders invest in people first and the idea second, as I've said. This premise is sometimes lost on entrepreneurs seeking seed capital. People invest in people based on their perceived worthiness. As I've already mentioned, I have seen wealthy individuals walk past a homeless person holding out a cup. Why? Because they felt that nobody should be given anything—and even more importantly, they didn't perceive that they'd be getting value in return.

Our world is caught up in the "you wash my back, I'll wash yours" syndrome. Some people feel it's foolish to give unless you're getting something in return. That's not true giving. That's conditional giving. I learned early in my life that the real gift is in the giving. Mom and Grandma taught me that.

My extensive travels resulted in many fortuitous meetings with business executives. I was suddenly thrust into a world known only to the elite. I was picked up by limousines and taken to United Red Carpet, American's Admiralty or Delta's Crown Room clubs, comfortable private lounges complete with VIP check-in and amenities. I must have been a sight, walking leisurely to my gate in a suit and tie and carrying a *Wall Street Journal* or a Japanese self-help book. I was also interesting fodder for the other first-class passengers. A man once told me on the way to New York, "Can't say I see many passengers like you up here." I remembered wondering what he meant by that. Was he referring to my age, race or both?

Eventually I was somewhat adopted by the flight attendants. They became my surrogate airline mothers who would look after me by waiting with me at the gate until the host sponsor representative met me. They would call the hotel to make sure I was checked in properly. Often, after the plane crew checked into their hotel rooms for their overnight stay, they would appear in my audience in uniform.

Life was good. I was seeing the world, meeting myriad people from all walks of life, and more good news was just around the corner. I became fond of the nightly business report on the local

PBS stations in the hotel rooms. This heightened my interest in the stock market, investing, venture capital and technology. But mostly I started studying the meals I was served on the planes. I got the strong urge to try my hand at preparing some of the unique meals I was served in flight and in the hotel. I made myself feel at home even when I was on the road. Instead of maid service I wanted to help clean the dishes and take the trash out, and I asked the room service attendants about the ingredients in the meals they delivered to me. I also learned the importance of physical and mental fitness on the road, where it can sometimes be lonely.

One of my favorite people is Emmanuel Steward, the famous boxing trainer Andre had introduced to me a while back. He taught me the importance of developing my body along with

I know what I know. In business you have to dot your i's, cross your t's, admit your mistakes and say "Thank you" if you want to get anywhere.

my mind. I have a daily training routine, which is never broken unless I'm ill. I do a minimum of one hundred to five hundred push-ups a day. My workout time is for more than building my physical body. It is also a time for me to regroup and get centered.

Being on the road gave me a chance to reflect on my life, the past and my future. My family was at a different crossroads at this time. I was traveling on my own across the country with little need for an escort. I was suddenly a breadwinner for the family. Since I still wasn't at the age where I could sign business documents, Andre would deposit my earnings, and I'd handle the management of my income and expenses. Grandma was the bookkeeper who'd pay for household and entertainment expenses. I can't tell you how good it felt to be able to provide for the two women who made me what I am today.

In the span of a few years, my life had done a complete 180.

I didn't realize it at the time, but I was becoming my mother. I know you're more accustomed to hearing women saying that about their moms, but it was true. I was becoming Mom. I was spending more time in the air than I was at home with my family. And if I wasn't on a plane, I was on the telephone making a deal. I had become accustomed to a certain lifestyle, but my travels left little time for me to bond with my family, who were all doing their own things.

Andre was setting up in Las Vegas, which demanded a lot of his time because he had to work within several time zones in the United Kingdom or Japan. Kiki had started studying to become a certified fitness trainer. My brother Jonathan had gone to Chicago, and Alex was still in Phoenix with Grandma.

Slowly but surely Mom gained her strength back. I sensed she would never be able to run as hard and fast as she used to. She was like a former heavyweight boxer. She still had that fire in her belly, which meant I always had to keep a watchful eye on her. I just knew that one day she'd walk into the room and announce her comeback, whether it compromised her health or not. Even on my travels, I called her several times a day.

I was enjoying my newfound freedom and earning power, but I missed my family. What kept me going was a liberal adaptation of one of Aesop's fables.

It seems that a fox spotted a rabbit and started chasing him around a field. The fox did everything in his power to track the rabbit but could never seem to catch him. The fox barked, thinking he could scare the rabbit into submission. He growled, thinking that maybe the rabbit would surrender. Finally, the rabbit was gone. Two people were watching the entire pursuit. One of the men shook his head in wonder. Then he said to his friend, "I wonder why the fox didn't catch him." His friend looked out into the distance as the rabbit disappeared from sight. "The fox," he said, "was chasing and running for fun. The rabbit was running for his life."

I'm the rabbit in this fable. I started running to provide for the health and financial well-being of my family at six years old. I was running for my *life*.

Everyone Is a VIP

"Are you ever nervous when you meet important people?" one teenager asked me after a speech. My answer floored her. "No, I'm not nervous meeting you right now."

She didn't quite understand. So she repeated her question. "I said are you ever nervous when you meet impor— . . ."

I smiled. She heard herself. "You are important," I said. "But yes, I'm sometimes nervous when I meet *famous* people."

Most of the time I'm comfortable, fluid and at home in all settings. Perhaps this comes from being exposed to so many different situations early in my life. After all, I don't know many seven-year-olds who attend weekly business meetings. Or maybe it was living in London and Japan that made me realize that no matter where you go, people are basically the same, so what's there to be intimidated about? Mom always said, "If you're too concerned with failing, what people think or making a mistake, you'll never do anything worthwhile."

I talk a lot about inspiring other folks, but it gets turned upside down every time I speak. I always meet amazing people—young and old. During one community-based speaking engagement in New York City I met a group of parents and students from all five boroughs (Manhattan, Brooklyn, the Bronx, Queens and Staten Island). I had been invited by their teachers to deliver a lunchtime keynote address. The fundraiser's goal was to bring in enough money to cover the last remaining expense for their upcoming four-day trip to Washington, D.C.

I was told that many of the students had never been to Greenwich Village, Times Square or Harlem. They all lived in their boroughs as cities inside a city, rarely venturing out. Traveling on Amtrak to the nation's capital would give them exposure and experience they might not have had otherwise. Only 5 percent of the families lived in homes of their own. The rest lived in the housing projects. As I looked around the meeting space, I felt at home. They'd set up tables to sell homemade pies, cakes and cookies. Students sang, read poetry, played instruments and performed dances.

I understood their plight. That's why this particular speaking engagement was so important to me. I could possibly play a part in helping these students dream in color.

As I got to the midpoint of my speech, I became tearful looking into the eyes of my audience. I was in my south side of Chicago . . . New York City. Those students and their parents were no different than my neighborhood friends and their parents. They were me, and I was them. No speaking engagement before this had reminded me of where I came from and to where I had returned. I knew exactly what I had to do. Those kids were *going* to Washington, D.C. As I closed my speech I announced I was donating my twenty-five-hundred-dollar honorarium to their travel fund, plus I was going to match my speaker's fee with another twenty-five hundred dollars from my foundation to help them meet their goal. The room erupted like a volcano. Kids were barking and hollering.

It was off the charts! My heart was filled with so much love and gratitude. I started barking too!

I remembered my promise at eight years old. I was going to make a difference. My intention was to help people, not just make money. If I was only motivated by money, people would see right through me. They'd think I was phony. That day in New York marked the day I became a stakeholder in something tangible and touchable. Because I was still a kid myself, when it was time for them to go on their trip, I joined them. And instead of flying directly to Washington, D.C. to meet them there, I returned to New York City so we all could meet at Penn Station to board the Amtrak train for our trip together.

I made several close friends that week. In fact, one day I received a call from a parent of a student who'd gone on that D.C. trip. She had an unusual question. "You mentioned having some airline passes," she said. "Can I pay you for two?"

Absolutely not, I told her. "I'll give you these passes." She said thank you, but just as she was about to hang up the phone she said, "See ya soon."

Her statement got my attention, but I hung up and didn't think much about it. Later that afternoon Mom started getting dressed to go out. "Ride with me to the airport," she said. I never asked her who we were picking up because the usual drill was going to Sky Harbor to pick up Kiki or Andre coming in from Las Vegas.

Mom and I walked through the airport like we had on many occasions before. I paid no attention to the flight monitor because we always went to the same area to greet them. I simply walked alongside Mom, whistling a happy tune. She stopped, so I stopped. To my surprise, I recognized two people at the gate— two people I'd met during the New York student-fundraiser and spent the week with on the trip to Washington, DC.

What were they doing in Phoenix? I still didn't have a clue that I didn't have a clue.

Mom was in on it! In fact, everyone in the family was in on the surprise. Their trip to Phoenix had been planned with help from my mother and grandmother. Danielle and her son, Philippe Jean-Jacques, were the chosen delegates representing the group in New York City to visit my family and make a special request.

Danielle Jean-Jacques was a mother of three, a motivational speaker, world-music radio personality and freelance writer who loved life. Philippe, her son, was eighteen months younger than me, so we had a lot of the same interests. He was eldest of three, with a brother nine years and a sister eleven years his junior. I offered him a few pointers to deal with his younger siblings since I had so much experience being one.

Danielle and Philippe had traveled to Phoenix not only to spend time with us but also to ask my family to consider allowing me to share my "free" time in New York between Danielle's family and Yaa-Asantewa Nzingha, who had been teaching school for twenty-plus years. Over dinner Danielle told Mom she wanted to make me a part of their "extended" family. "He needs a family on both coasts," she said, laughing.

I welcomed the opportunity to take charge of my life, but I was at a loss for words to express how much I was touched by their sincere offer to bring me into their family. "I would love to be a part of your family," I said to Danielle and Philippe. "Is it okay, Mama?" Mom nodded yes. "We'll need to get Danielle the necessary legal documents so she can make medical decisions when you're there."

Ten days later I was headed to New York for my first home-away-from-home visit. I split my time between Danielle's home—where

Danielle's mother, Rosette, immediately instructed me to call her "Grandma," which I still do to this very day—and Yaa-Asantewa Nzingha's home. Ms. Nzingha was my dedicated tutor, teaching me that I could do and be whatever I desired. I got to sit in on her classes and learn from her example. She allowed me to share my stories and experiences with her classes in the hope of inspiring them.

Engage, Empower, Eureka

R&B sensation Raymond Usher, known to his millions of adoring fans as simply Usher, became a successful entertainer on the national scene at the age of fourteen. And although I like his music and feel that he's a truly gifted brother, I was most touched by something he said in an interview many years ago when his star began to rise. A journalist asked him if he considered himself a dreamer. He became introspective and then answered, "Well, not really." The journalist appeared to be surprised. "I like to think of myself as a striver," he said.

> *Strivers achieve what dreamers believe.*
>
> —Usher

"A striver?" she asked.

"Yeah," he said. "Strivers achieve what dreamers believe."

Like many recording artists, especially soul and R&B singers, Usher grew up singing in the church where his mother was the choir director. At age thirteen, he entered a local talent show in his hometown of Atlanta, Georgia, where a record company executive spotted him. Soon afterwards he signed a recording contract that immediately launched him to the top of the charts. Usher's success was set in motion because he focused on striving, not just dreaming.

The question I ask myself before every speaking engagement is,

What can I say that will make the audience strive a little bit harder? I decided that actions speak louder than words. I would simply "show" them how striving had worked in my life. Everyone invariably asks me, "What's your secret?" My answer: "I put one foot in front of the other a little bit faster than most people." I started my entrepreneurial journey at age four, maybe even before.

I tell them that a loving family can do wonders for your dreams and aspirations. I know in my hearts of hearts that without their emotional support it would have been even more difficult to achieve what I've achieved. Could I have done it? Without a doubt, because I've always had a solid love of myself. Even when I didn't have shoes, I had much love for myself. Not the ego-driven, self-centered kind of love, but a deep, abiding love that doesn't depend on external factors to keep it going.

We come into this world alone, so why can't we love ourselves? We are the one person who lives inside our own hearts and minds. I made a decision way back when to love the little boy I looked at in the mirror every day when I brushed my teeth. I told that young little brother that I loved him.

It doesn't take a sociologist to figure out that many youths, especially urban youths, are not being showered with adulation and adoration. They are not being armed with the tools needed to give them a genuine chance of building a sense of dignity, self-worth, and emotional and psychological well-being. They're not being challenged to create their own destiny. I wanted to do more than fly in and deliver a one-hour speech followed by a thirty-minute question-and-answer period. How could I reach those who weren't on the invitation list?

How could I get the message across that our dreams can't wait?

It dawned on me that I wasn't striving as hard as I could myself.

I wasn't maximizing the platform I'd been given to engage and empower my peers. My goal was to shift the paradigm from "I can't" to "I will!"

If you have no confidence in self, you are twice defeated in the race of life. With confidence, you have succeeded even before you have begun.

—Marcus Garvey

For those of you who are still dreaming about owning or starting your own business, I encourage you to take a stroll around the downtown area where you live. Count the number of businesses you see, and know that the entrepreneurial dream is alive and well. You may think it requires a special quality to be able to start and run a deli, auto body shop, beauty salon or even a mobile car-washing unit, but in all likelihood those individuals are ordinary people with extraordinary drive. People like you and me.

Successful people intrigue me, and I never pass up a chance to find out what makes them tick or tock. I began studying the personality traits of highly successful people from all walks of life so I could emulate their successes in my own life. A public library card gave me access to study our country's greatest success stories. Reading about their trials, tribulations and triumphs inspired me to stay my course.

Eyes on the Prize

It was time to maximize my opportunities. I needed to reach more students. Not only did I want to reach them, I also wanted to get them on their entrepreneurial journeys. On one of my treks across the country, I began to inform audiences that I was beginning my search for twenty-first-century CEOs like myself to share the excitement of working together and developing our dreams into fields of opportunities. I was actually kicking off New Early Entrepreneur Wonders (NE^{2}W), one of my major life's goals for the past five years. All of my exposure to martial arts and Eastern philosophies had put me in contact with some truly wise sayings. One of my favorites was actually quoted by John F. Kennedy, who asked an audience, "Did you know that when written in Chinese, the word 'crisis' is composed of two characters? One represents danger, and the other represents opportunity."

I had become a thriving opportunist. I immediately began to recruit hundreds and thousands of budding young entrepreneurs. I was ready to enlist, engage, educate and empower them to seek nontraditional paths to becoming self-employed entrepreneurs. Living in New York City offered exposure to the worlds of finance, major corporations and advertising. My diverse experiences in Tokyo, London and Las Vegas helped me gear up to launch a very ambitious undertaking.

That's why I was so adamant about opening the NE^{2}W office in the right spot. Our office needed to be a haven where like minds could incubate ideas and benefit from each other's learning experiences. That office couldn't be in some remote location. It needed to be in New York City. It had to make a statement. It needed to say, "I'm here, and I'm serious." That could only be on one street. Wall Street.

NE^{2}W would set the standard for other venture capital firms. We would set out to find that diamond in the rough, not only to satisfy our financial but also our altruistic goals. I would instill in our young wonders the notion that "age ain't nothing but a number." You can always find a willing and trusted advisor to sign legal documents, get your business license and open up your bank account for you. Those are minor technicalities that should never get in a young person's way.

By the way, that "age ain't nothing but a number" mantra is for all of you "grown folks" out there too! Especially those who believe they're too old to get into the entrepreneur or reallionaire game. To you I leave a powerful axiom: never underestimate the *underestimated* in your own home, school, organization and church. They are the power brokers in the world.

That's why after I made NE^{2}W official it was time to head into the highways and byways to find warriors, kings and queens. I knew they wouldn't necessarily be studying in the best schools or colleges. Some of them were beating the pavements, trying to take care of their families. Some of them were fighting the temptations of the inner city. Some of them were simply waiting on someone to notice them.

> *When written in Chinese, the word "crisis" is composed of two characters. One represents danger, and the other represents opportunity.*
>
> —John F. Kennedy

So we launched a membership drive in every city where I was to speak. I felt like my forefathers and foremothers who had traveled thousands of miles during the '60s to register voters. It was such an exhilarating feeling; I still get chills when I think about our NE^{2}W campaign days, seeing those eager faces as they completed applications. I carried boxes of forms and ink pens in my suitcase to distribute to anyone with a pulse.

To me there were no differences among the faces in the crowd. If an adult said he wasn't interested in starting his own business, I handed him a card to pass along to his children, grandchildren or next-door neighbor's children. No one was getting away from me without being exposed to this great opportunity. I was evangelistic about helping others succeed. The motto that appeared on all of the NE^{2}W marketing materials was "Business courses through our veins."

My gut had been telling me that I had sufficient knowledge and knowhow to start NE^{2}W for years, but because of the UNEEC experience I'd hesitated. Still, my quest to see others succeed was greater than my fear of something not working out. I finally realized how crazy it was to let one isolated incident stop me from fulfilling my purpose here on earth—inspiring others to discover their unique success stories.

I didn't want to continue to be only one of a handful of role models for young people. I believe that being an entrepreneur is a very viable option for young people, as well as for older people who have let life interfere with their dreams. My message is for everyone, but especially the youngsters who don't have established programs in their communities. Sure, there is Junior Achievement (JA), the international nonprofit organization promoting entrepreneurship and business skills, but JA isn't offered at all schools. I don't think entrepreneurship should be relegated to a select few. It should be available to all. I want to be the giver of entrepreneurship so there are thousands of successful role models for young people to follow.

If you're fortunate to grow up or even hang out with people who are givers, you'll eventually observe something amazing. They also receive extreme joy from the act of receiving. I have been taught that it is as blessed to give as it is to receive. You may have heard that it is *more* blessed to give than it is to receive, but I think that creates a mindset that makes people uncomfortable with receiving. I believe it is important to honor both. Be a good giver and an equally good receiver.

There is a difference between receiving and taking. They are very different. There were those I had met who were takers; their only interest in me was seeing what they could get through our association. That's disappointing, but I never forgot what Grandma said, "If they won't treat you right, they won't teach you right." So their behavior actually served as a great lesson to me. It showed me what *not* to do in relationships where little eyes are looking up to me to guide them on their journey. I knew that I'd be prepared to do the right thing in future mentoring relationships in which I was the mentor. I needed to do the right thing, not just for them but for me as well.

Grandma used to quote a portion of a scripture from the Bible, "To whom much is given, much is expected." That is from the book of Luke, chapter 12, verse 48. It's a powerful passage that reminds me that I have a lot to offer the world, and even when I grow weary—and believe me, I do—I still have a responsibility to uphold my end of the bargain. Here's another treasure from the Bible that shows us how important it is to use what we've been given.

A master before traveling calls his servants and entrusts them with his assets. One he gives five coins, another he gives two and the last, one, each person according to that person's ability. The master leaves immediately.

After a long time, the master of those servants came back and asked for an accounting. The one who got five came forth and presented five other ones and said, "My lord, you gave me five coins, behold, I have earned five more on top of them." His master told him, "O, good and faithful servant, you were faithful with little, you shall be granted much. Enter your master's feast." The servant who'd been given two stepped forward. "My Lord, you gave me two coins, behold I too have multiplied them, here are the two you gave me, plus an additional two."

"Well done," the Lord said, "you have been given much, you will be blessed with much." Finally, the last servant appeared. He held out the one original coin. "Lord, I know that you are a hard-working master and that you value your assets. I didn't want to risk losing the one you gave me. I was afraid so I took it, dug a hole in the ground and hid it for you." The Lord replied, "Take the talent from this servant and give it to the one who has ten. For everyone who has, will be given more. He who does not multiply what he has will have it taken from him."

Matthew 25:14–29

What are you doing with your talents? Are you multiplying them or hiding them so they stay safe? Clearly, two of these servants understand wealth building. Which servant is most like you? The multiplier or the concealer?

Mom taught me a lesson that the wealthy have always known: Pay yourself first. Take care of home first and foremost. So that's what I did. As soon as I reached the point of earning income over and above what my family needed to live comfortably, I set out to make the world a better place. In my heart of hearts I knew I had to share the techniques and strategies for success that I'd learned from so many other mentors and experiences. NE^{2}W was about to help me make good on that promise.

I was still feeling the after-effects of UNEEC, but I knew it was time to put that behind me and move on with a clear vision of the future. More important, I had to heal the pain I felt when UNEEC crumbled. I was really hurt by that ordeal, mostly because I felt that it was never given the chance to blossom into a beautiful field of flowers. For a long time, I failed to see all of the blessings that came with the UNEEC experience. I was too busy focusing on the wreckage. But Mom kept telling me that all good businessmen have a few deals that go wrong. She said, "Be thankful that you were able to come out on the other side a better young man."

One of the many lessons I learned from my first entrepreneurial plunge was to solicit support from more people than you need. In other words, if I envisioned bringing twenty young entrepreneurs into NE^{2}W initially, I needed to interview at least a hundred. So that's what I did. I reached out to everyone, asking them all one question, "What is your passion? What do you want to do with your life?"

I looked for mentors and a board of advisors. I looked for partners and associates, anyone who could catch the vision of kids making a better life for themselves through entrepreneurship. I knocked on doors, made calls and mailed at least one thousand letters of request. I didn't need their money. I was looking for another Roi Tauer, someone who had a genuine interest in investing in

> *I think we should follow a simple rule: if we can take the worst, take the risk.*
>
> —Dr. Joyce Brothers

the souls of young America. Someone who was eager to provide advice, encouragement, hope and direction.

Sometimes adults would ask me, "What's NE^{2}W about?" I loved that question. NE^{2}W's message was crystal clear: we were a group of promising youth with dreams and a burning desire to become contributing members of our communities and society at large. The response was always the same, *"Well, well, well."*

But that response didn't translate into immediate support. Anybody can speak with passion. My potential partners wanted to see if I had any juice. Weeks passed with little response. No phone calls, no letters, nothing. Andrew Carnegie once said, "A wise man puts all of his eggs in one basket and watches the basket." I understood what Mr. Carnegie meant—you have to believe in your idea and put everything you have into it, but you also have to be vigilant and work hard to make sure your investments hatch. Yes, I know this takes time, but a return phone call would have been nice. Were there no stakeholders who were ready to invest in the leaders of tomorrow? Had I not written a powerful enough sales letter? Patience wasn't (still isn't) my greatest virtue, and the waiting was starting to get to me. I was fired up and ready to see NE^{2}W soar.

During downtime in my hotel room or on the plane I wrote out the NE^{2}W mission statement and developed presentations for potential investors. I even found an Einstein quote that I thought might get the attention of the people whose business cards were in my Rolodex. "Understanding a new idea is not like erecting a sky-scraper in the place of an old barn, but like climbing a mountain, gaining new and wider views, discovering unexpected connections and perspectives. We must go up into the high country of the mind and breathe the thinner air." I felt like I had taken a giant step in the direction of a new business. I had trekked into the Alps and was now breathing thinner air, but where was everyone else? Where were all of those men and women who'd said, "If you ever need any-thing, Farrah, don't hesitate to call me." Where were they now that I needed them?

I was starting to panic. I'd call my office to see if anyone had called, only to get a "not yet" from my assistant. I even made tons of calls from my hotel room, thinking that if I called at the right hour, I'd get through. Strangely enough, I could only get through to their secretaries and assistants. My contacts always seemed to be "out of the office" or "on another call." Finally, I decided to ask the gatekeeper if they remember seeing my letters. "No," most of them answered. What a wake-up call! Some assistants told me that it would be six to eight weeks before they could get to my letters. "What?" I said one day, not realizing that the words actually came out of my mouth. "Mr. So-and-So is a very busy man," they'd reply before taking my number . . . again.

I refused to be defeated. I wasn't as savvy with direct mail as I am today, so I didn't realize that people have to see your marketing materials four to five times before they truly notice it. I didn't have time to be sending five letters to the folks who'd told me to call them anytime, but the following month I sent letters to the original list again. I wrote a nice letter that had what I thought was a com-pelling quote on top of the letter-head: "Nothing is more important for the public wealth than to form and train youth in wisdom and virtue." That was Benjamin Franklin.

> *It is better to light a candle than to curse the darkness.*
>
> —Chinese proverb

I proudly dropped the letters into the mail bin, knowing that this batch of letters would render a huge return. I waited a few days, then a few weeks. Nothing. Not one phone call. Not one letter. Not one smoke signal.

I'd heard that the third time was a charm so I sent out another mailing to over nine hundred CEOs, senior executives and estab-lished entrepreneurs with the new NE^2W message: "Who will take responsibility for brightening the new economy with NE^2W busi-ness futures?" Apparently no one wanted to take responsibility because I got a grand total of zero responses. The postage and delivery bills were mounting, and so was my impatience.

It was time for me to have a family huddle with my people in Phoenix and Las Vegas and my extended family in New York City. They wanted to read and study the presentation just to see if I'd missed an important ingredient. The feedback was overwhelmingly positive. I'd written with sincerity and passion. The paper stock spelled quality, and I sounded like a serious young entrepreneur. My family urged me to get back on the phone. "It's a numbers game," Roi had said. "The more you call, the more likely you are to get a yes. Get back on the phone." So I did.

I telephoned hundreds of people, eventually getting about fifty of them on the phone. They all said the same thing. "Call us back when you have everything up and running." I was confused. Hadn't they told me to call them whenever I needed something? Well, I needed something, and that's why I was calling. Slowly but surely I was starting to understand the hidden code of business language. Those people didn't really want me to call them when I *needed* something; they wanted me to call them when I *had* something.

I had to grab myself by the collar and remember that I wasn't back calling the mom-and-pop shops in the 'hood. I was now tapping into a completely different group of businesspeople, folks who were overseeing multimillion- and billion-dollar corporations. Some of them found the kid in the business suit interesting or amusing. To them, I wasn't a major player in the game of business. I was just a kid who dressed to the nines and sat in first class on United Airlines.

Success is a numbers game. The more you call, the more likely you are to get a yes.
—Roi Tauer

I can still hear the questions. What in the world was NE^2W? And who was the man behind it? Sure, the company had a recognizable corporate business address but what did it do, and more important, what could it do for me? That's the question these busy executives' secretaries were really asking in a roundabout way. Because I couldn't get the decision makers on the phone, I didn't have a chance to infect them with my enthusiasm. If I could get just five minutes I'd share my story about a bunch of kids from single-parent homes who were about to turn the world on its ear. But as far as they were concerned, their corporation was already doing its part to help the kids. Wasn't that the reason they contributed generously to the Boys & Girls Clubs?

I had to think bigger. And I had to put my game face on. Getting support for NE²W was not going to be easy. That was fine for me. Nothing in life is a cakewalk (except an actual cakewalk at a carnival), and I didn't expect this to be any different.

First stop: Identify our mission and purpose. I spent days thinking about the uniqueness of NE²W. How we were going to set ourselves apart, and how we were going to be the model that future companies mimicked. I had it all mapped out. The next round of calls would be much better than the first. I was impressed with what happened when I buckled down and truly defined why NE²W needed to exist. Here's what I came up with.

NE²W acts as a catalyst to address issues important to early entrepreneurs, such as access to capital, strong role models, encouragement, recognition and credibility despite their youth or background, as well as to create networking opportunities to develop a wide range of business contacts early in their development. NE²W will use all resources available to create a complete network of early entrepreneurs, to provide the greatest moral support structure possible for bold and adventurous rookie entrepreneurs by providing core, age-appropriate knowhow and ethical practices for all ventures.

Second stop: Define the brand. NE²W's vision is to build and launch the next generation of America's market-based solutions. The ultimate goal is to positively contribute to the economic and social fabrics of our communities, cities and states, thus ultimately improving the economy and well-being of the entire nation.

Beginning the process at an early age is vital to the achievement of these goals as well as continual reinforcement of these basic foundations.

NE^2W = E5: Education—Economics—Entrepreneurship—Ethics—Empowerment; Home of the 21st-Century Business Futures. The purity of purpose and focus serves as a generator for added enthusiasm and as a moral compass for charting the next steps for Generation Next. It is the result of high intention, sincere effort, intelligent direction and skillful execution. NE^2W is quite simply the standard by which future companies will be measured.

Not bad, huh?

Third and final stop: Media attention. This next stage was going to take a little magic. I needed to pull a rabbit out of my hat because we'd need some high-profile attention. Now all I had to do was to find the right hat. My specialty was being in front of people, not publicity. I learned early on to know my limitations and always be willing to outsource in areas that aren't my strengths. I needed more than my face, name and bio to appear on the conference brochure. I needed some buzz, some serious juice and muscle behind NE^2W, so I hired a publicist.

With the public relations specialist on board to develop the Farrah Gray/NE^2W media campaign I was maximizing my time by recruiting and developing grassroots support. I still didn't have any large corporate supporters on board, but I've never been the type to give up.

I had enough business credibility to garner national media attention. I knew that my life would be different once my story hit the newswires. I'd have to put on a pair of giant boots to make strides on the big boy's landscape, or I wouldn't get any respect. I pasted Rudyard Kipling's poem "If" on my wall. It helped me focus on continuing to do the right things in the right way at the right time in the right spirit!

> *If you can keep your head when all about you*
> *Are losing theirs and blaming it on you;*
> *If you can trust yourself when all men doubt you,*
> *But make allowance for their doubting too;*
> *If you can wait and not be tired by waiting*
> *Or, being lied about, don't deal in lies,*
> *Or, being hated, don't give way to hating,*
> *And yet don't look too good, nor talk too wise;*
>
> *If you can dream—and not make dreams your master;*
> *If you can think—and not make thoughts your aim;*
> *If you can meet with triumph and disaster*
> *And treat those two imposters just the same;*
> *If you can bear to hear the truth you've spoken*
> *Twisted by knaves to make a trap for fools,*
> *Or watch the things you gave your life to broken,*
> *And stoop and build 'em up with worn-out tools;*
>
> *If you can make one heap of all your winnings*
> *And risk it on one turn of pitch-and-toss,*
> *And lose, and start again at your beginnings*
> *And never breathe a word about your loss;*
> *If you can force your heart and nerve and sinew*
> *To serve your turn long after they are gone,*
> *And so hold on when there is nothing in you*
> *Except the will which says to them: "hold on;"*

If you can talk with crowds and keep your virtue,
Or walk with kings—nor lose the common touch;
If neither foes nor loving friends can hurt you;
If all men count with you, but none too much;
If you can fill the unforgiving minute
With sixty seconds' worth of distance run—

Yours is the Earth and everything that's in it,
And—which is more—you'll be a man my son!

Now that you know what it takes to become a reallionaire, let's talk about how to get you into the mindset for creating your own empire. The first thing you have to do is, well, get real about where you are today. Yes, we touched on this at Step One, but now it's time to bring it all together, to mix all of the ingredients into one bowl and make one mean dish.

So I'll start by saying again that I know what I know, and I know what I don't know. I didn't know the formula for entrepreneurial success, but my journey honed my understanding of what it takes to be an achiever. I set my sights on something and then I go for it. Sounds simple and actually it is. Simple—but not easy. There's a difference.

I've spent years studying, mimicking and emulating people from all walks of life. I'm fascinated with how successful people think, act and react to challenges. My drive has allowed me to adapt and compensate for any unexpected setbacks or minor defeats I experienced along the way. Clearly, I've had my share of valleys, but I can honestly say that I've never doubted that success and wealth would one day be within my reach. I've wondered what was taking so long, but I never doubted that it would happen. Patience. I was going to have to learn to acquire a lot of *that* before it was over. Especially with Wall Street as my prize.

As I said in an earlier chapter, not everyone who knew me was a supporter. There were people in my camp who questioned why I wanted an office on Wall Street. "There are a million places to set up your office, why there?" My answer was clear. If you want to be a player in the financial world, where do you put your office? On Wall Street. End of paragraph, turn the page. Sure, there were other locations that probably would have welcomed NE^{2}W into their office buildings, but I wanted Wall Street. I'd seen IPO ceremonies on television. I'd read about the electricity you feel when you walk down the street. Plus, the mystique of Wall Street was almost as powerful as the Great Oz. The more I thought about it, the more I had to have it.

Of course, I could have followed the path of least resistance and thrown up my hands, saying, "If Wall Street doesn't want me, I don't want Wall Street." But that wasn't me. I might not win every battle, but I'll never raise the white flag without putting up a fight. And I was willing to fight to be on Wall Street.

The stress and expectations were starting to get to me. And the negative thoughts of "what if this" or "what if that" were starting to become more dominant than my usual mantra of *I can and I will.* I had to regroup and remember my mantra. *I can and I will.* I couldn't give up! NE^{2}W was counting on me to hang in there. Besides, I told myself, the worst that could happen was they'd deny me the space. I was big enough to handle the rejection. I didn't know if my family would be able to handle me after the rejection, but I was ready. I decided it was probably best to focus on the best thing that could happen. So that's what I did.

Within the next year, the move to Wall Street would either

happen or become a distant dream. I'm a firm believer that you have to claim what you want. So I started to share my vision of Wall Street in my speeches as I spread the good news about the features and benefits of NE^{2}W. When people asked me, "What are you doing now?" I pulled out my business card and my press kit, complete with press clippings and other media coverage.

I explained that Wall Street was the financial wheel that turns the world. I wanted to be right in the middle of the financial Mecca. When Wall Street coughed, Tokyo and London sneezed. I told them that I wanted to send a message to other aspiring youth that your background doesn't matter. Never be intimidated by anything. You don't have to be born in a palace to carry yourself like royalty.

Besides, Wall Street didn't intimidate me. It fascinated me. "Sooner than later my company will open its doors on Wall Street," I told one skeptic after a citywide small-business meeting in Vegas. His reply was, "Nothing wrong with dreaming." He found my goal rather amusing, which didn't bother me. But just as I was about to leave his presence I decided to leave him one small forget-me-not, "It ain't the size of the dog in the fight but the size of the fight in the dog." Then I barked and walked away.

To know the road ahead, ask those coming back.

—Chinese proverb

Time was of the essence. I was burning the midnight oil with the preplans for NE^{2}W, and at the same time I was running Farr-Out Foods (this was before I sold that business)! But there were only so many hours in a day, only so many speaking engagements I could squeeze into a thirty-day period. Something had to give, and it wasn't going to be the dream of going to Wall Street.

I reached out to Roi, who was always a sort of breakfast taco of a man—a lot of things rolled into one. He was an Einstein type: a scientist, engineer, inventor and astute businessman. He was what we call a Renaissance man. After carefully listening and assessing my current growth and patterns, he said I was right on the mark. "Just keep your eye on the prize," he said. "If you want Wall Street, then go get Wall Street." My conversations with Roi were often short but full of sage business advice and strategies I could take with me as I moved forward with NE^2W. It was time to score.

The public relations firm helped me prepare a simple, to-the-point, hard-hitting appeal letter to busy CEOs. They said the purpose of an appeal letter was to write the copy in such a way that those receiving it would "give a damn." They were right. The appeal letters worked.

I received more than twenty phone calls loaded with serious financial offers or referrals to potential backers. I learned there are varying degrees of everything. A little bit of money is a lot to people who don't have much. I was offered a "little money" once they received the executive summary. After six months, I had a commitment of up to three hundred thousand dollars. But remember, I had already had the experience of folks looking me straight in the eye only to ignore my calls later on down the line. I wasn't taking my chances, and I definitely wasn't quitting my day job and as a speaker CEO of Farr-Out Foods.

In April 1998, NE^2W was officially born. By August we had an Internet presence. The physical brick-and-mortar address was still unknown, but it was definitely in my sights. NE^2W was made up of me, Andre, a couple of students I'd met in one of my tutors' classes and a woman named Mildred Redding, who was a lifesaver, doing everything I needed in those early days. (Thank you, Mildred.) We kept working to get NE^2W up and running, and by September 9, 1998, my fourteenth birthday, financial gifts equaled my goal of securing six months of operating expenses on Wall Street. Again, I was flying high.

Although I'm sure a lot of people like to receive birthday, Valentine and Christmas gifts, receiving financial gifts is a little different. At least for me. I didn't want someone to "give" me money, because receiving it felt like they were saying "do what you will with this money. I don't expect you to do anything worthwhile with it. I'm willing to blow it." I didn't like that. So while I enjoyed getting those gifts, I accepted them with the mindset that the money I received was an investment, and each investor would receive their money back with interest. I wanted to show them they'd made a wise decision by investing in me and the young people of America.

I'll never forget how nervous I was the day I was scheduled to meet with building management at the office on Wall Street. I knew I would have three strikes against me from the jump: age, color . . . and age. Who does this kid think he is? Who does this black kid think he is? Who does this black businessboy think he is? I'm sure that's what they were thinking. I was trying to play it cool, but I was sweating bullets.

> *It ain't the size of the dog in the fight but the size of the fight in the dog.*
> —Old sports saying

Space was limited, and I knew the application process would be stringent. Only those who qualified (and had some solid referrals) would be considered. So I had my work cut out for me. Perhaps I shouldn't have felt this way, but I felt like the fate of many young men and women, especially minorities, rested on my shoulders. I had to make a good impression. I needed to make a lasting impression.

Andre and I flew to New York to scout out office space. We'd

heard there was availability at 67 Wall Street. Since I was all of fourteen years old at the time, I asked
Andre to become the company president and call the building management. They told him that a company
was subleasing built-out square footage
in their office. We made a few moves, and within a matter of
months the deal was done.

> *What do you want?*
> *And more importantly,*
> *what are you willing*
> *to do to have it?*

I wanted Wall Street. I got Wall Street. What do you want? And
more important, what are you willing to do to have it?

Open House

We opened our doors on November 30, 1998. There was no rib-
bon cutting or trumpets playing in the background—just the joy of
knowing that the lives of young entrepreneurs would be forever
changed. The news release read: "New Early Entrepreneur Wonders
(NE^2W) student venture capital fund opens doors for business." It
went on to say that we were operating from 67 Wall Street, just
doors from the New York Stock Exchange.

I wish I could tell you that the rest is history, but that sounds like
I'm dead, and thankfully, at the time of this writing anyway, I'm
not. As I look back on that fateful day in 1998, I know that NE^2W
was a miracle. Sometimes miracles come from seemingly nowhere,
but I believe you can sometimes make miracles happen. You can
facilitate miracles by staying true to your heart, being pure in your
intention, and treating those around you with kindness and respect.

It helps to know your purpose, and I was born for the NE^2W
mission. To achieve the objectives of NE^2W, I had to find and
recruit like-minded young entrepreneurs. Fortunately, I'd bumped

into thousands of them at my speaking engagements. We attracted dozens of junior-high and high-school students who I'd told to "stay in touch." They would have the responsibility of telling all of their friends to tell their friends about this new venture capital company that was for kids, by kids. An online chat room was set up for members to communicate at any time from anywhere.

My role was that of spokesperson. The PR firm was working overtime to get the word out on the new Wall Street tenants. And little by little, the inquiries started to pour in. It was happening. NE^2W was starting to garner "heat," a media term that meant people were talking about a particular person or news story. And since I was very comfortable in the kitchen, I could stand the heat.

NE^2W wasn't going to arrive at the party like a lamb, we were coming in like a lion! Our first big initiative was a national convention, a huge undertaking I admit, but I just felt in my gut this was the right move for us. The plan was to bring aspiring and existing young entrepreneurs together under one roof for the purpose of educating, socializing and networking. To raise capital to fund our ideas, we decided to form NE^2W as a limited liability partnership. The Idea and Investor Initiative Fund was established to identify individual angel investors.

But the money wasn't rolling in just yet. One of the most valuable lessons I learned from growing up poor was how to economize. I used to joke and say that Mom could stretch a dollar from the Atlantic Ocean clear across to the Pacific. She was that good. So instead of having an office for every single branch of my business, I decided to keep everything under one roof.

Each division would have its own space, but we'd all be in the same general office area. In other words, the Farrah Gray Foundation, Farr-Out Foods and NE^2W would be one big happy family so I could manage my operating expenses and overhead. Mildred, my assistant and chief bottle washer, was quite capable of handling calls for each business.

Grandma was (and still is) the bookkeeper who gets my financials ready for the certified public accountants so they can prepare annual reports and other documents for investors, stakeholders and partners. I knew my work would be under the microscope, especially since I had been so adamant about being on Wall Street. I didn't mind. What some people perceive as pressure, I see as opportunity. That's also the advantage of being a teenager.

> *Victory is a thing of the will.*
> —French Field Marshal Foch

Sometimes adults create so much drama and expectations they become paralyzed. When you're a kid you think everything is possible. You know no limits. I guess ignorance truly is bliss. And my bliss was just getting started.

The Apple or the Wind?

Sometimes I fly above the radar. I let my mind go as far as it wants, and then I reel it in if what I'm considering doesn't make good, sound business sense. Such was the case in 1999 as we began planning for the first NE^{2}W conference. As my team sat around the conference room table strategizing, I blurted out, "I think we should do the conference in New York." The room fell silent. Their facial expressions said it all: Are you crazy? What are you smoking? Is oxygen getting to your brain?

It was unthinkable to host the first NE^{2}W conference in New York for one simple reason—the Big Apple was too expensive. But I wanted to make a splash, so we couldn't have the event in an obscure location. Remember, we wanted to make a lion's entrance. This meant holding the event in a media Mecca, and there aren't many cities that fall into that category. The PR firm advised that I have some kind of connection to the city we chose. At the time, I didn't have an office in Los Angeles, so that left two logical choices—Chicago and Las Vegas. Instead of New York, we went with the Windy City. How perfect was that? The place where it all began. The spot where I'd sold cookies, lotions and lemonade before I could write my name.

At this time my brother Jonathan lived near Chicago. He was attending an information technology institute, which offered the perfect setting for the first annual conference. Once more, everything was falling into place. We settled on the location. Chicago was familiar turf. It was easier to travel in and out of by plane, bus, train or car. We developed a list of potential sponsors, and surely I'd be able to attract some media attention in my old 'hood. Plus, it was the perfect opportunity for a reunion with former UNEEC members. Unbeknownst to me, Jonathan had remained in touch with more than just a few of his friends from the 'hood. He'd kept in touch with 80 percent of the folks our family knew when we lived in Chicago. This was going to make things a lot easier for me once I started making calls.

When I arrived in Chicago, my first stop was the Chicagoland Chamber of Commerce to sign NE^2W up as a new member. I then contacted the former mentors and supporters of UNEEC to let them know their investment in my concept was going to pay off.

Many of them remembered me (never underestimate the power of your old contacts!) and were glad to hear that I had not fallen victim to the street game. More than five years had passed since they'd seen me, and many thought I'd either gone to prison or become a casualty of the 'hood. I still had fond memories of UNEEC, but I hadn't forgotten its unnecessary demise. Greedy parents had ruined a perfectly good opportunity for their kids. I couldn't blame my old friends; they simply did what their parents told them to do. That was the past. I was a little older and wiser this time around.

So I pulled out the trusty Yellow Pages and went to work. Among those on my list was a privately held supermarket chain in Chicago. The owner agreed to meet with me. And boy, did he greet me. When I arrived at his office there was a "Welcome" sign in the lobby. When he saw me his jaws dropped. I wasn't the squeaky-voiced kid he remembered. "You look well-heeled," he said. "Got rid of that bird body, I see." We laughed and shook hands. "Got quite a grip on ya too!"

In our meeting he said he didn't have the time to help me personally, but he offered to introduce me to a well-respected business notable he had known for a number of years, saying this gentleman was in a better position to make introductions and provide sound business advice. That introduction led to an introduction to Stedman Graham, a successful African American businessman and author. Mr. Graham met me in his office and autographed my copy of his latest book, *You Can Make It Happen: A Nine-Step Plan for Success*. He was generous enough to give me a few minutes of his time and pledge his support.

The meetings kept coming. I was introduced to a dignitary on the board of Sara Lee, who invited me to attend their annual shareholders meeting. I was feeling my Cheerios again and loving every minute of it. It seems that every week I was meeting three or four powerbrokers in finance, media, foods . . . you name it.

Although I was a veteran businessman by now, I was still very impressionable. As a kid, you think that "important" people are somehow exempt from petty or bad behavior. One executive—whose name I won't mention because the lessons are more important than his identity—was particularly bad about keeping his word. I admired, even idolized, this guy. Not only was that a mistake, it was also unfair. He was only human. I finally understood that, and it was that knowledge which helped me put the past behind me once and for all.

Not only is it a mistake to idolize "important" people, it is unfair. They are only human. You have to remain flexible and self-sufficient to succeed in the long-term.

By now I realized I needed to remain flexible, especially if I was going to be in business for a long time. Again, I tapped into the wisdom of the samurai, which said, "You've reached the wisdom of strategy when you cannot be deceived by men." While a part of me wanted to persecute those who had broken promises to me, I finally realized they had taught me a valuable lesson: your word is your bond. People will judge you based on your commitment to honoring your word. That's why I say what I mean and I mean what I say. It was now time for me to focus on the future and stop being bound by the flaws of a few people who probably didn't even remember the promises they'd broken.

A New Dawning

The inaugural Association of New Early Entrepreneur Wonders (ANE^{2}W) "Business Futures Exposed on Planet Wall Street" convention was scheduled for September 1999. It would require a mammoth effort to produce. I was about to lose more sleep than I realized. Our membership with the Chicagoland Chamber of

Commerce gave us access to the membership database to solicit sponsors and speakers. In just eight months, we raised one hundred thousand dollars.

Two months later the mayor of Chicago and governor of Illinois proclaimed September 24–26, 1999, the Association of New Early Entrepreneur Wonders (ANE^{2}W) Weekend. Our banner read *"ANE^{2}W—No Child's Play—The 1999 Business Futures Exposed Convention and Virtual Convention."* We were going to broadcast the event live over the Internet. By all accounts the event was going to be the largest gathering of its kind in North America, bringing together more than eight hundred high school and collegiate entrepreneurs from all over the United States.

For three days and three nights we took the city of Chicago by storm. We converged upon the Renaissance Hotel Chicago, and believe me, we were more than a handful. On Friday we kicked it off with the Chicagoland Chamber of Commerce mentor/young entrepreneur mixer. The Entrepreneurial Olympics Business Plan Competition followed. Teenagers submitted business plans that were judged for their originality and viability. Attendees spanned all races and ethnicities. There were students, teachers, parents, sponsors, stakeholders, mentors, benefactors, and business and community leaders. All of us gathering in the name of young entrepreneurship and empowerment. It was electric.

Saturday was a day for young business owners to show and sell their products in a real trade-show setting. The show started with business development sessions on topics such as opportunities, creative thinking, business planning, raising capital and launching a business. Student entrepreneurs, university business-major students, key business leaders and Chicago Economic Development officers headed these sessions.

One of the highlights of the weekend was the ANE^{2}W Gala Awards Banquet, with one thousand dollars cash to each of the ANE^{2}W award winners. WorldTel Interactive sponsored this award.

On Sunday, the last day of the event, we featured a power breakfast with a strong lineup of angel investors seeking bizkids with legitimate business ideas and enterprises. This panel gave way to the official launch of the Idea & Investor Initiative Student Venture Capital Fund, which raised more than one million dollars in committed funds. Because my story had been so well publicized, I was blessed to get tons of support from other entrepreneurs and especially other African Americans in the financial field who were generous enough to share sample documents and memorandums. Many of them either owned their own brokerage firms or were in key management positions at Morgan Stanley, Merrill Lynch, Citicorp or similar companies.

After the NE$^?$W conference I felt like I'd just run the New York Marathon. I also felt accomplished. Katherine Mansfield said that we can do whatever we wish, provided our wish is strong enough. The success of the conference gave me added leverage in the business world. I was more determined, more willful. My wish was *strong*. Folks who wouldn't take my calls before suddenly picked up the phone. The flip side was that I felt like Bruce Lee. I had folks coming at me from all angles, trying to break my stride and pull me down.

An athlete knows that he or she is only as good as the last competition, so it was back to the gym for me. I wanted to keep myself and the company in the media because I'd just seen how valuable a

little press could be. I'd learned a
lot cruising at thirty-three thousand feet as I traveled to and from
speaking engagements, and I had
an unquenchable thirst to know
what the business leaders were
discussing.

I don't believe leaders are born ... their life circumstances and how they respond to them carve out their leadership qualities.

I had to be like the glass door at the W hotel in New York—
always revolving. And always evolving. Leaders evolve. I don't
believe leaders are born; their personality traits and life circumstances carve out their leadership qualities. What newspapers and
magazines couldn't teach me I learned by asking questions of those
who had been there, done that. I was now the head of a financial
company. I had to be solid.

NE^2W, like every company, would be only as strong as its weak-
est link. Not only would I have to think outside the box; I'd also
have to construct new boxes for the twenty-first-century CEOs of
color to work out of.

REAL POINTS: Caring About the People Around You

There will come a point in your reallionaire journey when you can finally focus on those around you. This opportunity—not your Porsche—is the reward for your success.

1. **True giving is unconditional.** If you're giving and expecting something back, that's not giving at all. If you give something you don't need anyway, you're only halfway there. True giving is when you part with something truly important to you with no expectation of ever seeing it again.
2. **Everyone is a VIP.** You can make a difference in every life if you simply respect every life. Treat all whom you meet as if they matter—because they do. The person who buses the table at your favorite restaurant is just as important as the woman who owns it.
3. **Make a difference in the world.** Why else bother? Your personal legacy may begin with what you do to achieve greatness, but it will be defined by how you help others tap into *their* greatness.
4. **Inspire others.** I never wanted to be the only young businessman role model for poor African American kids. I wanted to create thousands of role models. Don't rest on your own success; inspire others to follow in your footsteps, and to even better your accomplishments.
5. **Don't be afraid to take, especially in the service of others.** This is the flip side of giving. Give with all your heart and without selfishness. The same is true of taking what others offer you. If their intentions are pure, there is no reason to turn them down.
6. **Don't hide your talents, but multiply them.** Resting on your laurels is not an option for reallionaires. Yes, you should take the time to enjoy life, but you must always strive to be better and to do more than you have already done.

7. **Don't settle for less than the best.** Many people will tell you to compromise, to be happy with halfway home. But if you really want something, there is no reason to settle for less. Set your sights on what you truly desire, then do everything in your power to make it happen.

8. **The four most important words you will ever utter are "thank you" and "I'm sorry."** You can never say these two phrases too much.

REALLIONAIRE AFFIRMATION

◆

Inside every seed is the potential for an incredible harvest.

Reallionaire Exercise:
Always Say "Thank You"

Expressing gratitude is an extraordinary opportunity that we sometimes let slip by. Not anymore. It's important to let people know they're appreciated, even people you don't know!

Take the next few minutes to make a list of at least ten people who have had a positive impact—small or large—on your life. These can be people who've been instrumental in any area of your life—spiritual, professional, personal, social—it could even be someone who offended you but whose behavior led to a greater lesson. Don't rush through this exercise; it is important to your journey as a reallionaire. And don't limit your gratitude!

Part two of the exercise involves dotting i's and crossing t's. Once you've made your list, you are going to do what some of you haven't done in a long, long time. Before the Internet invaded our lives, we used to write simple, heartfelt thank-you notes. Remember those days? Well, guess what, they're baaaaa-aaaaack!

Over the next thirty days, write a short, sincere thank-you note to everyone on your list. This exercise is as much for you as it is for the recipient. The act of saying "thank you" is one that feels good, but there's an extra boost you get when you commit those sentiments to paper, put a stamp on the envelope and send those good vibes into the universe.

It's a good idea to record any feelings you experience as you go through the entire exercise. I think you'll come away with some surprising insights. Have fun! And don't forget to dot your i's and cross your t's.

Me at age five with my first "briefcase"—my famous red lunchbox.

Me at age seven, just before starting my UNEEC business club. I'm wearing my one and only business outfit.

It's not all business all the time! Here's me at an amusement park, having fun.

A typical picture of my mom, on the phone and surrounded by paperwork.

My big brother Andre and I in 1995. My family had recently been through a stint on welfare and I'd seen the end of UNEEC, but my older brother always picked up my spirits.

Me and Andre with one of my idols and mentors, the boxing trainer Emmanuel Stewart, and his business entourage. Mr. Stewart is the one wearing matching jackets with me.

One of my first appearances as a cohost of *Backstage Live* in 1996. I'm eleven years old.

I admit it, I still get a kick out of meeting celebrities, especially when I love what they do and what they stand for. Here are two of my favorites, Queen Latifah and Eryka Badu.

Me (looking good) and Stephen Lachappelle, CEO of WorldTel. We successfully partnered to create Kidztel calling cards in 1997.

A meeting of the minds with Greg Calhoun, Leonard Harris, Mike Wright Jr. and Mike Wright Sr., food industry executives who helped me secure more than a million dollars in orders for my syrup products. This meeting took place at the Food Marketing Institute Convention in 1999. (photo credit Beverly Swanagan)

Me and some of the young entrepreneurs NE2W was designed to help. This meeting took place in our conference room on Wall Street.

A flyer for the product that made me a millionaire, Farr-Out Foods Strawberry Vanilla syrup. I sold Farr-Out Foods to a conglomerate that changed the name of the product.

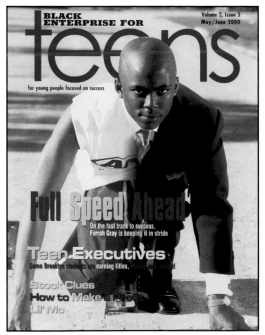

The cover of *Black Enterprise for Teens,* May 2000. I love the way they capture the two sides of my personality, the businessman and the fun-loving kid.

Michael Milken and me in 2000.

Speaking at the annual meeting of the NAACP.

Part of my happy family today: my brother and sister, my grandmother, and me.

One of the highlights of my career (so far) was meeting President Bill Clinton in the Oval Office of the White House in November 1999. (official White House photo)

Never Underestimate the Power of a Network

how I learned that what goes around comes around, that you should never neglect anyone you meet, and that you must always act as if someone is watching you— because someone always is

There's something special about athletes, especially elite athletes. They possess, or maybe acquire, something extra. Take, for instance, the case of the two Michaels. When Olympic gold medalist track star Michael Johnson ran he seemed to have a slice of heaven in his hand. He seemed to glide across the track, his feet barely touching the surface. His affable personality made him a crowd and media favorite, but I was struck by his humility during the 1996 Olympic Games. He shed tears as he crossed the line. His appreciation as he draped the American flag around his tired body for a gold-medal victory lap was inspirational. He was a true champion.

Then there's that other Michael. You know the one. The guy who's arguably the best basketball player to ever grace the game. The one who proved that character is what you do when no one is watching. He was physically talented, yes, but his mental toughness is legendary. Both of these champions left an indelible mark on their sports, but it's the following two quotes that are forever engraved in my mind.

> *"I have missed more than nine thousand shots in my career. I have lost almost three hundred games. On twenty-six occasions I have been entrusted to take the game-winning shots . . . and I missed. I have failed over and over and over again in my life. And that's precisely why . . . I succeed."*
>
> —Michael Jordan (five-time NBA league MVP)

> *"Life is often compared to a marathon, but I think it is more like being a sprinter; long stretches of hard work punctuated by brief moments in which we are given the opportunity to perform at our best."*
>
> —Michael Johnson
> (200 m and 400 m Olympic gold medal winner)

The two Michaels inspired me, so much so that by the time I started NE^{2}W, I was calling myself an athlete. A business athlete. I was working more than eighty hours a week. I was a dry sponge soaking up information and knowledge from everyone and every-thing around me. I was also earning more money because I was pulling double duty. Like every elite athlete, I was pushing my body beyond its limits. And like every elite athlete, I loved it!

I became so focused that I didn't notice how much I was chang-ing right in front of the people who loved and cared for me. I wasn't taking care of myself, they said. "Sound familiar?" Kiki asked one day. "You're working too hard, baby boy."

I knew what time it was. It was time to be grilled. Every single member of my West Coast blood family and New York adopted family pulled me aside. *You've gotta slow down. You need to slow down. You're too young to be going at this rate.* They were right, but by then I didn't know how to slow down. I had a fire in my belly and the eye of a ferocious tiger. I was not about to pull back. I was a strong, virile young man. Andre taught me how to keep my body strong, teaching me to do push-ups when I was eight years old, and I still keep that routine every day.

I was a youngblood, and you couldn't tell me very much. I listened respectfully to everything they had to say, but I was stubborn and I had my eye on the grand prize. My mother had given birth to me at age thirty-six, a great time in her life but also a challenging time. I saw her work like a dog to make sure we had clothes on our backs, food on the table and a roof over our heads. Do you think anybody could convince Mom that she wasn't acting in her or her family's best interest? No way! And I was the same way. We share an identical drive. In fact, everyone in my family is a type-A personality. We don't have an off switch. Of course, that means we must accept the consequences that accompany our frenetic pace. I'm not saying it's the right pace for everyone, but it works for me. Over time I've learned to take a nap—sometimes in the middle of the day—when I feel fatigued. But then I'm back up and at it until the wee hours of the morning. (It's three in the morning right now.)

I was shifting into a higher gear, and it was time for an upgrade in all areas of my life. For starters, I need a new look. I asked Andre, the international corporate clothes expert, to go shopping with me to pick out my new business wardrobe. Now, don't get it twisted, clothes don't make the man, but they do speak volumes on his behalf. Your attire is synonymous with your business brochure presentation. Clothes communicate your personal style. And as shallow as it sounds to most people, quality clothes can and often do open doors and minds to get your message across.

I understood that I would turn heads because I was still a "little man." I stood five feet, six inches tall so people did a double take when I walked past them. My fellow business travelers were curious

---

Clothes don't make the man, but they do speak volumes on his behalf.

about the "rookie CEO" in the suit with all the essentials: monogrammed shirt, cuff links and Allen-Edmonds shoes. Plus I had more accessories than a Donald Trump wannabe. I had the

Mont Blanc ink pen, leather briefcase and high-end luggage. I read the same books and newspapers businessmen and women read—the *Financial Times* or *The Art of War*. I could see people looking out of out the corner of their eyes. I could hear what they were thinking: *Is he for real?*

I was prepared for the millions of questions brave souls might ask en route from New York to Vegas. "So, what exactly do you do?" or "Is your father the president of your company?" or "You just sold your company to an international candy company?" I was game for whatever these inquiring minds wanted to discuss. I could cover the globe of conversations. You want to talk politics? Not a problem. Wanna talk about the stock market? Cool. Got thoughts about the state of minority entrepreneurship? Bring it on. In the span of one week, I'd dished about Warren Buffet, Sun Tzu, Michael Dell, Bill Gates, Deepak Chopra plus which artists had just gone platinum on the *Billboard* charts. I was, as Grandma would say, *qualified to be justified*. And that means that you always—I mean always—have to be informed about what's going on in your business and in the world around you.

Faith Moves Mountains . . . and a Few Valleys

I had reached a state of grace and peacefulness. I was being told that I made things look easy. But everyone who's had success knows that it only looks easy because a tremendous amount of time and effort has gone into making it look that way. Easy is simple and simple is easy when you find balance and harmony in your mind and heart. I don't want it to sound like my journey to this place was without challenges. That's not the case at all. Go back and read any of the previous steps if you think that. But I am in awe of how fluid my life became when I realized that I wasn't in control of anything outside of me. It's a beautiful place to inhabit.

All I could do was work on my thoughts, my belief system, and my perceptions and desires. I couldn't control whether people accepted me, wanted to do business with me or became my partners. At first I thought I could. I actually thought that if I delivered the perfect presentation or wore the right suit, everything would fall into place. Wrong! What I learned is that what's "supposed" to fall into place falls into place, period. And I was finally fine with that. I always knew that God would provide. So amid all of the rejection (and there was a lot of that!) I grew to have a quiet assurance that things would work out because I had accepted my mission on the planet.

Everyone who's had success knows that it only looks easy because a tremendous amount of time and effort has gone into making it look that way. Easy is simple and simple is easy when you find balance and harmony in your mind and heart.

Early in my career (when I was nine), I felt like a hamster running in place. I was going fast and it felt like I was covering ground, but I wasn't really going anywhere. Not where I wanted to go, anyway. But eventually, my name got around and people began to find me, rather than me having to find them. People like the president of the United States.

On November 1, 1999, I received an invitation from the White House addressed to Mr. Farrah Gray, chairman and chief executive officer, New Early Entrepreneur Wonders. It read:

> *The President and Mrs. Clinton request the pleasure of your company at a ceremony to be held at The White House on Tuesday, November 9, 1999, at two-thirty o'clock, on the occasion of the presentation of the Congressional Gold Medal to The Little Rock Nine. Please respond to The Social Secretary, The White House at your earliest convenience.*

On September 4, 1957, nine black children known as the Little Rock Nine voluntarily subjected themselves to the cruelty and bitterness of racial bigotry to become the first black students to set foot in the halls of Central High School in Little Rock, Arkansas. These students entered the school with President Eisenhower's support and the might of the 101st Airborne Division behind them, only to be shoved against lockers, tripped down stairways and excluded from activities. Their selfless acts seared the conscience of our nation and propelled the advancement of civil rights and equality. My great-grandmother had been born in Little Rock and attended segregated schools. The Supreme Court's decision had directly influenced my grandmother and mother.

It was a great honor to be invited to the White House, and of course I accepted, but I had no idea how my name came to the attention of the White House. Later, I was told that Minyon Moore, assistant to the president and director of political affairs (and a Chicago native) placed my name on the list of invitees. She had introduced me to many brothers with their own brokerage firms in Chicago and New York. We had not remained in contact, but she remembered me.

Let that be a lesson to you: Never underestimate the power or reach of your network. Never take any person you meet for granted. And also act as if someone is watching your every move, because guess what, someone is.

And networks, like a fruit flies, have a way of multiplying. Over the next ten months, I received three additional invitations and communications from the White House. These invitations ushered in a slew of other high-profile events. On November 11, 1999, I was invited to become part of the High Yield Capital Association conference with leaders from every segment of the investment community, including bankers, investors, accountants, lawyers and U.S. Department of Commerce officials. My special invitation came by way of Michael Milken, whom I'd met at the Las Vegas Chamber of Commerce meeting in October. I had been interviewed for a possible board of advisors seat after the local media picked up the news coverage of the ANE^{2}W conference in Chicago.

At the High Yield Capital conference I was seated at the table of Dr. Glen Yago, director of capital markets of the Milken Institute, an organization that seeks to create a more informed public, more thoughtful policymaking and improved economic conditions. The Institute's research areas include global capital markets, regional and demographic studies, human capital and job creation, access to capital, intellectual property studies,

You choose your profession, but you don't choose your mission. Your mission chooses you. Be open to it.

and enhanced understanding of economic issues. Institute scholars have held dozens of conferences and published hundreds of books, monographs and research reports.

Dr. Yago introduced me to the senior advisor to the director of the Minority Business Development Agency (MBDA) of the U.S. Department of Commerce, Kwame Brown. MBDA had plans on the table to establish two entrepreneurial institutes and incubators for the next generation of minority entrepreneurs. Eventually Courtland Cox, the director of MBDA, invited me to consult with and oversee the project. They made overnight hotel accommodations at the Marriot Hotel, and guess what, I slept in the hotel lobby because I was too young to check myself in. They just didn't get that someone so young could possibly head a youth summit and two national youth incubators.

On November 16, 1999, exactly a week after the White House visit, I found myself being invited to speak alongside Microsoft chairman, Bill Gates, Microsoft president, Steve Ballmer, and John Chambers, president and CEO of Cisco Systems, during COMDEX 1999, the world's largest computer technology show. All of my networking was paying big dividends. I was being invited to parties and meetings with heavy hitters. And just when I thought it might slow down something else happened.

In December, the president of the Las Vegas Chamber of Commerce invited me to become a member of the Las Vegas Chamber of Commerce board of advisors. I was fifteen at the time, and this honor gave me the distinction of being their youngest board member ever. I was ecstatic. The board consisted of powerful men and women, folks like the chairman of the board of Harrah's Las Vegas, Mirage Resorts and Casinos, Howard Hughes Corporation, and major bank executives. After the Las Vegas Chamber of Commerce invited me to sit on its board of advisors, similar offers started to come in. Chief among them was from the United Way of Southern Nevada, which offered me a three-year term on its board of directors, making me the youngest director making funding decisions in the United Way's then 113-year history.

By the end of 1999, I felt assured that I was finally making sense to people. They were starting to see what I brought to the table, and that felt good. I'd had a stellar year. I had taken the artist formerly known as Prince's advice: I'd partied like it was 1999. To cap things off, I received an invitation to the White House during the holiday season. I respectfully declined because I wanted to spend time with my family.

Make a Difference

On January 12, 2000, I received a phone call from the cohost of *Backstage Live.* She said that while attending a Vegas City Hall meeting she'd overheard a few people talking about a community-based program that would address Clark County's teen suicide death rate.

Ironically, around the same time I was asked by the executive director of the House of Blues Foundation to speak at the annual Dr. Martin Luther King Jr. "I Have a Dream" event at the Community College of Southern Nevada. A group of parents approached me and asked me if I'd consider funding and hosting a teen radio show. The effects of the Columbine High School massacre in April 1999 were still making parents, teachers and students nervous on high school campuses.

The Annie E. Casey Foundation sponsored a survey through the University of Nevada, Las Vegas called the *Nevada State Teen*

Suicide Death Rate Report. Those results were troubling. They revealed that the city of Las Vegas and Clark County reported the highest teen suicide death rate in the nation. I agreed to assist by establishing a radio program that youths could call their own. *The Teenscope 911 & 411* reality teen talk-radio program was a public service for teens, parents and stakeholders. Our motto: "Our Community's Best Resources Wear Sneakers."

I had never produced a show, but I did have cohosting experience from *Backstage Live.* Gary Campbell, my *Backstage Live* cohost, was also the general manager of the NBC radio affiliate in Las Vegas. He gave me guidance and support and opened up the door for me in the radio industry. The format was simple: a weekly thirty-minute call-in radio talk show airing live from the studios of KLAV 1230 AM and on the Internet at *www.youtham.com.*

Youths ages thirteen to eighteen tuned in to talk about topics that were especially relevant to young people and to get love, encouragement and respect from their fellow teens. The show, which aired weekly, was driven by questions and issues raised by teens. I liked that. I attempted to be in Vegas every Tuesday to host the show. I negotiated with a national radio syndicator and secured a distribution deal with Equity Radio Network to uplink to more than six hundred affiliates. Nevada Governor Kenny Guinn, the City of Las Vegas, Las Vegas Mayor Oscar B. Goodman and Lieutenant Governor Lorraine T. Hunt issued proclamations honoring the weekend of Teenscope's "Celebration of Youth."

Shortly thereafter I attended the Third Annual Wall Street Project, an event designed to promote minority participation in corporate America. The annual conference has featured Jesse Jackson ringing the opening bell on the New York Stock Exchange and playing host to the fundraising reception during Dr. King's birthday celebration. The event included a black-tie gala on the floor of the New York Stock Exchange.

At the Wall Street Project, President Bill Clinton and I struck up a conversation, which drew a lot of attention. When someone attempted to introduce me to him, President Clinton interrupted, "I know Farrah Gray, and we have already discussed his future. His motivation determines what he will do. His attitude determines how well he will succeed at making a difference!" Before the end of the event I was approached by a senior executive with *OneNetNow.com,* a culturally diverse online community seeking to increase the number of minorities using the Internet by providing relevant online content in a single Web site. Ronald W. Burkle, chairman of the Yucaipa Companies, LLC, provided funding.

OneNetNow.com's board boasted a prestigious lineup that included some of today's most influential business and community leaders, activists and celebrities: August A. Busch IV, Percy Sutton, Edward James Olmos, Andrew Shue, Reverend Jesse Jackson Sr., Kenneth "Babyface" Edmonds, Linda Johnson Rice, Monica Lozano and Sammy Sosa. In March 2000, I was invited to become the chair of the Young Adult Community of *OneNetNow.com.*

A Family Affair

My work schedule was now pushing the ninety-hour-a-week mark, leaving little time to visit my mother and grandmother in Phoenix. We talked two or three times a day; they were always on my mind, but we were ships passing in the night. In a few conversations I remember Mom dropping hints for me to back off on working so much. I didn't listen. I was too busy telling her about the latest deal or the most recent invitation I'd received from the White House.

And who was she to talk? I soon found out she was about to pack her bags and head to Los Angeles to join a technology start-up. She didn't bother to consult with her children. Before we knew it, she was gone. Her escapade lasted a total of two months because her health began to fail again. Grandma and Andre had to go and bring her back. She had been on heart medication for years but paid no attention to the swelling in her stomach area. That was her last full-time foray into the business world.

But Mom still had plans. She eased out of Phoenix and went to Los Angeles to assist a former business associate. She was scheduled to become the vice president of marketing and managing partner of The Virtual Network Company, a product developer with Hewlett Packard (HP), Canon and Extended Systems to deliver digital color documents. The founder and chairman of the company offered NE^{2}W a license for one-third the cost to become a distributor. We agreed to become a distributor because it was a win-win for both my mother and me, and because it was a natural fit for a mailing company I was considering buying for my grandmother. The owner had lost her husband and didn't want to struggle alone with her children to manage the three-thousand-square-foot mailbox rental and business service center with an approved U.S. Postal Service office station inside the store. I did my due diligence, and within a few months, the NE^{2}W Mail Post was born, with a distributor deal already in place.

Children are likely to live up to what you believe in them.
—Lady Bird Johnson

The media swarmed me with questions of how it felt to be able to buy businesses and provide financial support for my family members. My answer seemed to shock them. "This is what family's about," I said. "This feels good because my mom and grandma have always been there for me. At the end of the day, this gives me a great feeling because I don't care how much money you have in the bank or how much money your businesses are making. . . . You will always be with you, and there's no way you can get away from you, or run from you. In your quiet time, wherever you go, there you are."

More media inquiries flooded my office. *Las Vegas Image* magazine featured me in the March/April 2000 issue in a story titled, "Meet a Millennium Golden Child—Farrah Gray." I appeared as the cover story, "Full Speed Ahead—On the fast track to success, Farrah Gray is keeping it in stride," for the May/June 2000 issue of *Black Enterprise for Teens*. A staff writer with a magazine owned and published by Inner City Broadcasting Corporation called *INNERCITY* magazine wanted to cover a few speaking engagements around the country for a story in an upcoming issue. Two weeks after my sixteenth birthday, I delivered the keynote speech at the U.S. Department of Commerce. At that event I received several copies of the fall issue of *INNERCITY* featuring a story entitled "Farrah Gray: The Teenage Millionaire on Wall Street: Young, Rich and Handsome." Even the *National Enquirer* picked up the story.

Someone had been watching me. I could feel it. Not the voyeuristic watching that freaks you out. The kind of watching that lets you know a powerful wind is about to blow your way. At the Eighteenth Annual MEDWEEK Conference, I was seated at the head table with U.S. Department of Commerce Secretary Norman Y. Mineta, the undersecretary of commerce, the director of the Small Business Administration, the director of the MBDA, and other congressmen and senators. The closed-caption video presentation of the week's events and the comings and goings was

viewed by all, and there was only one keynote speaker spot-
lighted . . . me.

After the ceremony ended, folks swarmed me. I was happy to
shake everyone's hands, but what I wanted most was to get to the
nearest phone to call Mom and the rest of the family. As I broke
through the crowd, a stately graying gentleman stopped me. I
remembered him getting an award that night. That man was the
Honorable Percy Sutton.

I was sitting on the board with him of *OneNetNow.com* but had
not had the privilege of meeting him. I had seen him make the
opening remarks at the Wall Street Project. I was anxious to thank
him because his magazine, *INNERCITY*, had chosen to feature me
in its fall issue.

> *I can't say it enough:*
> *Never underestimate the*
> *power of your reputation,*
> *and never forget that* someone
> is watching you. *You better*
> *qualify to justify.*

"It was well-deserved," he said,
shaking my hand. "Young man,
you may not know this, but your
star is rising. You are destined for
greatness that you can't even
fathom." My knees went completely weak. This was the
Honorable Percy Sutton, lawyer,
civil rights activist, lecturer, government official, media founder
and the executive affectionately known as the "Godfather of Black
Business." This was the man who had been watching me.

I can't say it enough: Never underestimate the power of your
reputation, and never forget that *someone is watching you.* You better qualify to justify.

I took the entire month of December off to spend quality time
with my family in Phoenix and Las Vegas. This downtime allowed
me to visit my father for what turned out to be the last time. He

was a man of high intellect and oratory skills. Adopted at the tender age of two months old, he carried in his heart a deep sense of abandonment that prohibited close ties and attachments. But he proved to be a self-sacrificing servant with an abiding love for black people and the downtrodden. He sacrificed a life with his children in the name of his activism and service.

He knew the Bible and other Holy Books from cover to cover, and he had aspirations of becoming a Methodist minister. While studying other religions, he became a historian and was known for speaking the truth in fiery terms. I was told that people called him a black stallion that no one would ride.

I always lived apart from him but always felt a part of him. When I'd visit him I felt like I was seeking to understand who he was—or maybe I was trying to understand who I was. His unexpected death took something of mine to the grave with him. I will never have a chance to discover that part of me.

My father played an integral part in making my success possible. I wish I could have shown him how vital his existence was in my life, but he died a month after our last visit. In our last moments, he shared this story with me.

Life's Echo

A son and his father were walking in the mountains.

Suddenly, the son falls, hurts himself and screams: "AAAhhhhhhhhhhh!!!"

To his surprise, he hears the voice repeating, somewhere in the mountain: "AAAhhhhhhhhhhh!!!"

Curious, he yells: "Who are you?"

He receives the answer: "Who are you?"

Angered at the response, he screams: "Coward!"

He receives the answer: "Coward!"
He looks to his father and asks: "What's going on?"
The father smiles and says: "My son, pay attention."
And then he screams to the mountain: "I admire you!"
The voice answers: "I admire you!"
Again the man screams: "You are a champion!"
The voice answers: "You are a champion!"
The boy is surprised, but does not understand.

Then the father explains:
People call this Echo, but really this is Life. It gives you back every-thing you say or do. Our life is a reflection of our actions. If you want more love in the world, create more love in your heart. If you want more competence in your team, improve your competence. This applies to everything. Life will give you back everything you have given to it.

Thanks, Dad.

How Sweet It Is

As a director on the board of United Way of Southern Nevada, I received private party and networking invitations with the inner circle of movers, doers and decision makers in the city. Through these con-nections, I heard that a joint venture deal might be available with a Beverly Hills–based restaurateur who was looking for an investor to buy out his European partner. It seems that the guy had a dormant showroom available for a show production. I'd always wanted a show on the Strip, so I asked a few questions. Okay, I asked a lot of questions.

The circumstances seemed right. If I produced a family-oriented show my family could oversee it if I had to be away. The property was directly across from the Mirage and Treasure Island. Location,

location, location. The property had foot traffic of an average fifty-five thousand people per day traveling between the Venetian and Harrah Hotels and Casino. How could I go wrong?

I'd always been intrigued by hypnotists, so I put out the word that I was looking for performers. I hired an attorney to handle all the legal, construction and management issues. We invested four months getting the show up and running, completely redesigning the showroom. We tore down walls to expand the seating capacity. You name it, we did it. We were all pumped. The first few nights were awesome. We sold out the theater, and overnight were acclaimed a "Las Vegas must-see" and a "Las Vegas hot ticket" by *ShowBiz Weekly* and *What's On* magazines. Once again I was loving the magic and basking in the glow of this golden opportunity. I was only the second African American (after Redd Foxx) to own a show production on the Las Vegas Strip. I simply could not believe my fortune.

And then the wheels came off. For a few weeks, my mom had been complaining of pain in her lower abdomen. I'd encouraged her to go to the doctor to have it checked out, but she kept saying, "If it gets worse, I'll go. I promise. I promise."

It got worse. One week after the opening of my show, my mother began bleeding profusely. She'd been lying in her bed for most of the day, in what we later learned was excruciating pain. We'd grown up seeing my mom as this strong, vibrant woman who braved the most difficult storms, always making it to the other side. So when she said she was feeling fine, we believed her and didn't press the matter.

That night, though, she fell in her bedroom. Fortunately I heard the crash and rushed to her side. When I got there she was attempting to get up on her own. That's when I noticed she was bleeding. "Mom, are you okay?" I asked. "You're bleeding."

"I'm fine," she said. "I was just going to see what you were preparing for dinner and to get some V8 juice." I escorted her back to the bed and brought her a glass of vegetable juice, not totally convinced that she was okay but still not saying anything about it.

Mom lay back down and began to drink her juice. "Mom, you should rest. Don't try to get up. If you need anything, just yell, okay?" She nodded yes as she began to read the *Las Vegas Sun*. I went back to the kitchen to finish preparing dinner.

A few minutes later, while trying to get to the bathroom, she collapsed again, this time hitting her head on the wall. She was so weak that she didn't have enough strength to call out my name. Instead she crawled to the phone to call my sister, Kiki, who lived nearby. The next thing I knew, there was loud banging on the front door. Kiki had arrived at the house in a panic. I had not heard Mom fall, so when I answered the door I had no idea why Kiki looked so terrified. "Mom fell," she said as she brushed past me into the house and up to her room.

We hustled upstairs and found my mother nearly unconscious on the floor. We piled into the car and rushed her to the hospital, where we were immediately greeted with the busyness so common in emergency waiting rooms. Mom was losing more blood by the second. My two brothers Andre and Jonathan arrived at the hospital in a panic. They tried to keep Mom alert as I approached the receptionist's area for help.

"Excuse me," I said. "My mom is losing blood. She needs immediate attention." The overextended attendant sitting behind the desk handed me a clipboard without looking at me and said, "Fill this out and we'll be with you in a second."

I took the clipboard and turned to look at my mother, who by now seemed to be fading away. I turned back to the attendant.

"Look, we don't have time for this. Can't we fill this out while the doctors are taking a look at her?"

The attendant looked around the jam-packed waiting room full of crying babies, bleeding women and a host of other medical emergencies. Then she looked back at me rather unsympathetically. "The sooner you fill that out, the sooner we can take a look at your mother."

I was furious. It's not like we'd brought Mom in to have her tooth extracted. We didn't know what was wrong with her, but we knew that it couldn't wait. Shortly after we began completing the hospital paperwork, a young woman walked over to us. I'll never forget her kindness. Her name was Sabine Young and she was a registered nurse. "Let's get her hooked up to an IV," she said gently.

Instantly, I felt better. I knew Mom wasn't out of the woods, but Sabine's presence seemed to have a calming effect on all of us. After a few questions, Sabine noticed the gravity of Mom's situation. "We've got to get her in right away," she said as we watched her whisk our mother away, yelling as she entered the long hallway. "Code blue! Code blue!"

I couldn't stand the thought of losing my mother, so I went to the car, closed my eyes and tried to escape the thoughts of death that were still fresh on my mind from losing Dad that spring. I even found myself reflecting on one of the last conversations I had with my father when he'd said, "Son, take care of your mom."

I was flooded with a mixture of guilt and resentment. Guilt that I hadn't insisted that Mom go to the doctor sooner. Resentment that I might lose my mother and father within six months of each other. I cried out, "God, please don't cheat me out of my time with Mother." That had been my worst childhood fear.

Suddenly I heard knocking on the car window. It was Kiki

and Jonathan. "Mom's dying! Mom's dying!"

I jumped out of the car and headed into the hospital. "You can't come through here," the hospital administrator said rudely. "I'm sorry. You have to wait here." That's when Sabine walked out into the hallway. "Come this way," she said.

We walked into the room, and sure enough Mom was fighting for her life. The heart monitor was going crazy. Mom's eyes were rolling back in her head. Meanwhile, outside in the hallway, doctors were strolling by the room as if everything were normal. That's when Sabine literally began pulling doctors into the room to attend to Mom.

Hours later my mother would have two tumors the size of cantaloupes removed from her body. Two cantaloupes! Abdominal tumors so enormous they had shifted her other organs around. After her surgery the doctor told us that if Mom had lost one more ounce of blood, she would have died.

I have never been happier than I was the day I heard a soft-spoken "Happy birthday, sweetheart" flowing from my mother's lips as I entered her hospital room on September 9, my seventeenth birthday. My belated birthday gift came the next day when we were allowed to take Mom home.

We entered our home, so still after the hospital, preparing to start life with a renewed sense of optimism and appreciation. I helped Mom upstairs to her bed and propped her pillows for her, making sure she was totally comfortable. She had undergone at least eight blood transfusions and a major surgery. And even though her prognosis had improved, she was still very weak.

Ecstatic that my mom's health was improving and anxious to cook her an official homecoming meal, I went to the kitchen to prepare the gourmet dinner that had been interrupted the week before. After dinner my mom and I talked about the future. What we wanted to do more of, how we wanted to live our lives and how thankful we were that she was alive.

At six o'clock the next morning, my eyes opened with tears of joy rolling down my cheeks. My first thought was, *Today, my mother is alive. Hallelujah!*

I knocked gently on her door and entered with some fresh orange juice. "How about some CNN?" I asked as she sat up in her bed. "You didn't nickname me Chef Farrah for nothing. I'm gonna cook you breakfast. It won't be nearly as good as anything you got at the hospital though."

She laughed softly. "Thank you, Farrah. You don't know how good it feels to be home," she said.

"You don't know how good it feels to have you home," I said, kissing her on the cheek.

As I helped my mother settle into a comfortable position on her bed, I felt an amazing feeling of gratitude sweep over me. And I remember thinking how fleeting life is and how we never know how much time we have to fulfill our purpose on earth. In fact, since that day, I haven't been able to look at time in quite the same way. Maybe that's why I try to live each day to the fullest. People say that all the time, but no truer words have come from these lips. You don't come within inches of losing your anchor and not be changed forever.

After I got Mom in a comfortable position, I turned the television to CNN. On the screen was the footage of the horrific attacks on the World Trade Center. It was September 11, 2001.

As Mom and I watched the images with horror, I realized that I had been given another opportunity with my mother. She had been granted another chance at life, but so had I. We spoke no words but as our eyes met, we knew that our lives would be forever changed.

My life began to take a definite form after my mother's brush with death. I'd always been socially conscious; you can't grow up under poverty's cloak and not be aware of the world once you get out. Now I became acutely aware of how important it was to exhibit business values that were congruent with my personal belief system, which simply says that people matter in everything I do, no matter how small—and no matter whether anyone is watching or not. After all, if you're one person in public and a different person in private, then you're not an honest person.

As everyone knows, September 11 had many tragic and far-reaching implications. Tourism plummeted, and what I'd perceived as a sure bet in Las Vegas turned out to be a highly speculative investment risk. I lost every penny of my high-six-figure investment in showroom remodeling and show production. Even worse, the value of my investments in NE^{2}W took a nosedive, and new investors became hard to come by. Sadly, NE^{2}W closed operations near the end of 2001.

You must exhibit business values that are congruent with your personal belief system in everything you do, no matter how small—and no matter whether anyone is watching or not. After all, if you're one person in public and a different person in private, then you're not an honest person at all.

But the old saying goes, God doesn't close a door without opening a window. In my case, the window was the gift of time and perspective. Although my mother was allowed to come home after her surgical ordeal, she was extremely fragile and her health was still in danger. I began to nurse her back to health. Caring for Mom almost full-time for the next twelve months proved to be one of my greatest blessings, providing me with lessons I would have never learned had I been off doing my own thing in the business world. I couldn't necessarily save her life, but it felt good to be of service to the most important person in my life. No one does anything alone; don't believe the hype.

REAL POINTS: Real Perspective

Success isn't life. There will come a time when you have to decide what is most important to you, and if the answer is money and power and fame, then you have a long way to go before you are a reallionaire.

1. **Always watch your health.** Working yourself to death—or even just missing out on the pleasure of the moment because you're always looking to the future—robs you of the value of all that you possess.
2. **Hard work is important, but you can't control the world.** You have to know what is in your control and what is beyond your grasp. Then you have to let go of all that you can't control. The rest can sort itself out.
3. **Know your history.** You are here just for a moment. Value and study the great people who have come before you—from Martin Luther King Jr. to the Honorable Percy Sutton to the woman who started the local soup kitchen. Leave the world a better place for those who come after you.
4. **Give back to your family and friends.** I gave my grandma a business of her own, and I gave my mom a house. Your gift doesn't have to be that grand, but it needs to be from the heart. One of the greatest lessons I've ever learned is that the greatest gift you can give to those you love is your time. It's more precious than gold.
5. **Always act as if someone is watching you, because someone always is.** If you aren't honest when you think you're alone, then you're never truly honest. If you think of the consequences before doing something unethical, then you're not really ethical. The consequences don't matter; it's the act itself that counts. When you act ethically from the heart in all that you do, there will be consequences, and I guarantee you they will be positive.

6. A crisis can put everything in perspective, but why wait for a crisis? Think about what you would regret if someone important left your life suddenly. Now act so you will never have to experience that regret. There is no excuse for not living every day as if it were your last.

REALLIONAIRE AFFIRMATION

◆

Only what's real will last. I will last.

Reallionaire Exercise:
Developing Your Reallionaire Owner's Manual

I want to end the book with an exercise that will jumpstart your personal reallionaire journey. Now that you've ingested my nine principles, it's time to put them into action. It's time for you to become the da Vinci of your own reallionaire portrait.

The Reallionaire Owner's Manual is designed to share the steps, methods and eternal truths that empowered me to discover the values, goals, purpose and ability that enabled me to achieve results and experience profound fulfillment. There are seven steps to the exercise. Do them at your own pace. There is no time limit. They deserve your undivided attention.

Creating your Reallionaire Owner's Manual will help you understand how your life works and why parts of it may not be working. These seven operating steps will help you achieve dramatic new levels of success in all areas of your life and become rich from the inside out.

First, what does being rich from the inside out mean to you?

_____

_____

_____

_____

For me, being rich from the inside out means being aware of the great wealth and value that I posses naturally—with or without material gain. It means recognizing my talents and putting them to work to attain what my heart desires. This is my real meaning of success. That doesn't mean it has to be yours, but remember: we often mix up the dream with what it takes to achieve the dream, and that can sometimes throw off the definition of success. Let's talk about dreams.

My dream is to _____

_____

_____

If I could have any wish come true it would be _____

_____

_____

I wish I were _____

_____

_____

I wish I had _____

_____

_____

The thought of living a dream life seems like a fairy tale to many people, but the reality is that you can live the life you have always wanted just by knowing your real purpose. Once you change your mind about what's possible, you'll change your life.

Soul Searching

How well do you know yourself? Are you on the right path? What are your values? Your values are what you deem worthwhile or desirable. Begin your own exploration by filling in the following sentence.

I most value _____

_____

_____

What is important about . . . ?

1. The people in your life (family, friends, relationships)
2. Where you live
3. The things you do
4. The things you have
5. What you know

This is the key to your value system. These are the factors that will drive you to your purpose in life. Now let's talk about the less positive things. Let's ask: what do you want to change in your life and why?

I am unhappy with _____

_____

_____

I am distracted by _____

_____

_____

I desire fulfillment in _____

_____

_____

I desire greater meaning in _____

_____

_____

I desire independence in _____

_____

_____

I desire more options in _____

_____

_____

There's nothing wrong with wanting more. And there's nothing wrong with admitting that your life hasn't been a bed of roses. Everybody's got baggage! But how much are you still carrying with you? How big is your luggage? Can it be seen from a mile away? Is it a high-end matching set? A little bit of baggage is reasonable. By a little bit, I mean the size that can be stowed underneath the seat in front of you, not the size that takes over the whole overhead bin!

Whether you are aware of it or not, this baggage is like an emotional vampire, sucking you of energy and success. Until you empty your luggage, you will never find true prosperity and genuine happiness, and a lifetime of success will never be within your grasp.

Know Who You Are ... from the Inside

Your purpose is your passion. It is who you are. It is what you must and will do no matter what. It is what's going to allow you to commit to getting what your heart desires. Who are you? What scripts have society, family and friends written in your memory that you identify with or answer to? Is this who you are? For better or worse, the answer is yes. This is who you are. If you want to be something else, you have to change the script.

Circle all that apply to you—and don't be afraid to add others in the margin!

I AM . . .

Affectionate	Compelling	Free	Insightful	Practical	Sociable
Ambitious	Considerate	Friendly	Inspiring	Productive	Spirited
Amusing	Courageous	Fulfilled	Organized	Progressive	Strong
Analytical	Creative	Funny	Outgoing	Prosperous	Subtle
Artistic	Direct	Generous	Passionate	Purposeful	Successful
Balanced	Driven	Graceful	Patient	Realistic	Sympathetic
Blessed	Dynamic	Happy	Persistent	Resilient	Systematic
Caring	Empowering	Healthy	Playful	Responsible	Tenacious
Charismatic	Energetic	Honest	Positive	Rich	Wise
Compassionate	Fortunate	Humble	Powerful	Sensitive	Worthy

Often we define ourselves by what we do instead of who we are; yet who we are compels us to do what we do. Is a great lawyer great because he is compelling, or is he compelling because he is great?

When you define who you are, you will be able to align your vision with your true self, thus your true calling. You will be great because you will move in the direction that is native to your soul. So here are the important statements:

The three words I would honestly use to describe myself are

_____

_____

_____

The three words I'd like to define me are

_____

_____

_____

Okay, now that we got all of that out of the way, on to the seven steps.

STEP 1. DESIGN YOUR OWN DESTINY

Begin with the end in mind. The end is your vision; it will motivate you to achieve your purpose. Without motivation, inspiration and vision, nothing worthwhile will be achieved. Without personal organization, achievement will be like a winding road to nowhere. Your vision must resonate with your values if you are to enjoy the journey. If you are not excited about what you're doing with your life, you're probably not getting maximum results. This is a clear indication you are not living your life's purpose.

In life, we are either driven by promise or pain; the promise of an abundant future, or the immediate need to change a painful situation. Your immediate goals often relieve you of an undesirable situation; your long-term vision propels you toward great possibilities. State what you envision for yourself. No dates yet. We'll get to that in a second.

My immediate vision is _____

_____

_____

My short-term vision is _____

_____

_____

My midrange vision is _____

_____

_____

My long-term vision is _____

_____

_____

STEP 2. GET REAL!

You are blessed and highly favored; you have within you every-thing you need to achieve your goals. Learn how you work. How can you put your values, beliefs, assets, liabilities, strengths and weaknesses to work for you?

Your assets and liabilities are one and the same; it all depends on how you approach them. What can you do to maximize your strengths and minimize your liabilities?

Here are a couple of suggestions:
1. Identify personal characteristics, strengths and talents.
2. Name three opportunities for improving each strength and talent.
3. Establish an action plan to pursue these opportunities.
4. Focus your strengths on achieving your personal goals.

The next tool has been around for a while. That's because it's use-ful. Go through and assess where you are today using the SWOT method:

SWOT	Strength	Weakness	Opportunities	Talents
Mental				
Social				
Emotional				
Physical				

STEP 3. SET GOALS

A goal is a desire with a date on it. So get ready, set goals and run with expectation. Plan how you will use your SWOT inventory to acquire your vision. What additional knowledge do you have to master to get there?

Restate your VISION here.

_____

_____

Now make a commitment in the following format.

I undertake to:
Immediate vision _____
Completion date _____

I undertake to:
Short-term vision _____
Completion date _____

I undertake to:

Midrange vision _____

Completion date _____

I undertake to:

Long-term vision _____

Completion date _____

CONGRATULATIONS! Your commitment list is the first step toward fulfilling your dreams. You have made a commitment to yourself. You aren't going to let yourself down, right? Remember that a journey of a thousand miles begins with the first step.

Ask yourself the following:

- Does the goal completely describe what I want to accomplish?
- Is the goal measurable?
- Can the goal be clearly evaluated?
- Is the goal challenging?
- Does the goal require effort and discipline?
- Is the goal realistic?
- Can the goal be attained?
- How am I going to measure my progress?

STEP 4. FAITH IT TILL YOU MAKE IT!

Any person who says he or she's never been afraid of anything is straight-up lying! You're human. . . . Of course you experience fear and doubt and myriad other emotions. But fear doesn't have to immobilize you. It can actually propel you closer to your goals if you learn to manage it. I've found the best way to deal with fears is to acknowledge them. So let's get it all out in the open.

First, select a situation in which you experience fear. Now complete the following statements:

In this situation, I am afraid that _____

_____

_____

The worst thing that can happen is_____

_____

_____

The best thing that can happen is _____

_____

_____

Once you put them in perspective, it's sometimes funny how silly our fears can be. Repeat this exercise whenever you feel fear creeping up on you, and I guarantee you'll begin to replace that fear with peace.

STEP 5. PRAY FOR A GOOD HARVEST, BUT CONTINUE TO GARDEN

Don't worry about whether or not it's going to happen. It'll happen if you keep going. If you plant a tomato seed and you water it and make sure it gets sunlight and nourishment, guess what? Tomatoes will eventually grow. But you can't plant a tomato seed, hoping that petunias will grow. It's the same with your dreams. If you want success, you must plant for success instead of failure. You don't set out for Los Angeles from New York by walking east, do you? Of course not! You have to be walking in the right direction to get where you're going. Simple but true.

STEP 6. BE PATIENT

Set the vision. Do the work. Move in the right direction. Monitor your progress every week and every month. If it helps, make a chart. Don't change the goal, even if you fall behind. Change the course instead.

STEP 7. MAKE YOU COUNT

You are the only you that you've got, so don't take you for granted. Train, be disciplined, and honor your mind, body and spirit. Come to the table knowing that you bring value to everything you touch. And when you know this—not believe it, but *know* it—you will begin to see the fruits of your labor. You'll start to attract things and people who can help make your dreams a reality. Remember when I realized that "people were starting to listen to me"? They couldn't hear me until I heard myself. They couldn't see me until I saw me. They couldn't truly value me until I put a premium on myself. So put a premium on yourself.

BONUS PRINCIPLE:
Know Your Partner

I know, I know . . . I promised nine principles, but I've never been able to keep my mouth shut. That's especially true when I've got something important to say, and writing the end of this book has made me remember another element vital to reallionaire success: partners. Your mother, your family, friends, your God: They're always with you, and you better value them. You better not just value them, you better give to them: your time, your money, your heart.

Success isn't money, folks. Success is understanding and being happy with who you are, and it's taking the time to give back to those you care about most. If you enjoy yourself and enjoy those around you, you will enjoy life. That's the one thing I want you to remember after you read this book: only you can let yourself down, and the only way to do that is by not loving enough.

You don't think that's the real end to this story, do you? If all my businesses dried up at the age of seventeen, why am I writing a book about success? And why are you reading it? If you fell for that old gag, you haven't been watching enough movies.

Emotion can be the enemy; if you give into your emotion, you lose yourself. You must be at one with your emotion, because the body always follows the mind.

—Bruce Lee

Say what?

I'm a devout Bruce Lee fan, and I recommend Bruce Lee movies to all would-be entrepreneurs. Why? Because in every Bruce Lee movie he is outnumbered but exudes a cool, calm and collected defensive demeanor. He seems to instinctively know from which corner an attacker will come, and he'll summarily kick all twelve of their butts.

That's the movies, of course, but in real life Bruce Lee credited his success as a martial artist to same thing: he never let his emotions get the best of him. I'd like to add that he always remained calm under pressure and anticipated all the possible weaknesses (attack points) of his current position. And that is what you have to do as a successful businessperson.

Oh yes, and always, always, always pick the right partner. That's one of the great things about success: you get thousands of chances to invest your money, and there are a thousand different ways to turn that investment into more money. I'd been investing in all kinds of businesses along the way (too many to mention in one book, unfortunately), and many of them turned a nice profit. But it's not all about money, remember. It's also about helping people. And when you're in it to win it like I am, it's about helping the *right* people with the *right* ideas and the *right* character, and doing it the right way.

I can't tell you about all the people I've worked with, so I'll just mention one: Mary Spio. Mary was born in Syracuse, New York, to Ghanaian parents. When she was four, her parents moved back to Ghana, but they sent their daughter back to the United States to complete high school. Unfortunately, they sent her to South Carolina, where Mary was called "the African"—even by her teachers!—and teased because of her accent. Those teachers made her feel so bad about herself that after graduation she got a job at McDonald's because it was the only thing she felt confident she could do. But she knew in her heart she had more to give than a Happy Meal and a Coke. She joined the air force and eventually used the G.I. Bill to pay her way through Syracuse University, where she won the award for best project her senior year. This woman was a real survivor!

Of course, I didn't know all that when I met her in 2002. By that point, she had become one of the hottest young scientific minds in the country, having worked on heat-seeking probes for the NASA SETI (Search for Extraterrestrial Intelligence) program, designed orbits for rockets bearing communication satellites and sent a rocket into space with her signature on it. That's right, the Mary Spio I met had gone from "the African" everyone made fun of to rocket scientist.

Now she was looking for funding to pursue her dream of becoming an independent inventor. At COMDEX 2002 in Las Vegas, I became the exclusive holder of the licenses to her inventions, and Mary Spio got the capital to develop those inventions for practical use. Since then, we have worked together on new technology for Web sites, streaming video, television and other major media, and Mary's even had the chance to develop her dream project—a dating magazine and Web site for happening singles.

It's been a lucrative relationship for both of us, but even better, it's been the start of a true friendship. I didn't know I was helping such a worthy person when I invested in Mary Spio—I just saw a business opportunity and grabbed it—but this story is a wonderful example of my central philosophy: when you're living real, and you've got your heart in the right place, and you're investing in ideas and people, then you're going to be a success in life.

And that's advice you can take to the bank and cash.

Of course, it works the other way around too: when you live like a reallionaire, the right people are going to find you. And that's exactly what happened to me when, in late 2000, the opportunity—or should I say the partner—of a lifetime came knocking at my door.

"You got a call from the managing director of *INNERCITY* magazine," my assistant Gina Brooks told me that morning.

"Please call them back and thank them for the copies of the magazine. I got them."

"That's not what they want," she replied. "They want to know if you have any interest in acquiring the magazine."

"What?" I shook the water out of my ears.

"She said that if there was no such interest the magazine would probably cease printing indefinitely. Here's the number." Gina left the office almost as swiftly as she'd entered.

I stared at that slip of paper for a good ten minutes. Why would Inner City Broadcasting think I'd be interested in acquiring a magazine? I knew nothing about the magazine industry. Not to mention that my plate was so full it was spilling over. I didn't have an extra second to devote to another project.

I buzzed Gina. "Please call Inner City Broadcasting and tell them I'm going to have to regrettably decline."

"Will do," she said.

Fifteen minutes later Gina walked back into my office. "I told them you'd take the meeting."

"You did what?!"

"I think you should at least take the meeting," she said.

"Gina, are you crazy? You, of all people, know what my life is like. Why in the world would you tell her I'd take the meeting?"

"Call it instincts. Call it crazy," Gina replied, "but the meeting is next Wednesday."

We both stared at one another for a few seconds. Then all I could do was laugh. Gina had never gone directly against my wishes, but I knew there was wisdom in her judgment. You have to surround yourself with good people, and you have to trust their judgment, or you'll never go anywhere in life.

"I guess it's too much to think that you're joking, right?"

She wasn't. The following week I got the opportunity to visit at length with Mr. Pierre Sutton, the son of the Honorable Percy Sutton. That's right, the son and business heir to Mr. Percy Sutton, the legendary businessman who had had his eye on me for some time now. I had every intention of going to that meeting and graciously declining their generous offer, but when I got there, I knew I'd be coming home a different young man.

"We've been watching you for some time, Farrah," Mr. Sutton said. "You've been making moves since back in the day. Heard you made a mean pitcher of lemonade in your Chicago days."

I cracked up on that one. I'll never escape the UNEEC cookies-and-lemonade-stand days. At least I know I'll leave something for my kids and grandkids to tease me about.

"Mr. Sutton, I don't know anything about magazine publishing," I said humbly. "I know I've worn a lot of hats, but this is not a strength of mine."

"Yet," Pierre interjected.

"Yet?" I asked.

He nodded. "Yet."

"Oh," I said.

Over the next few weeks, I had numerous conversations with

Pierre Sutton. He asked me to critique the magazine. Tell him what I liked and disliked about it. What would I change? What would I do if I were to take it over?

"Just give us some feedback," Pierre Sutton said. "And then tell us what your price is." He was funny. "I know you, Farrah. I don't know you, but I know you. You're a businessman."

I was busted. I was already thinking about the changes I'd make when I took over the magazine. When I got on the elevator, I looked at myself in the door's reflection. *Are you crazy? You can't buy a magazine!*

But I did. The contract was executed on February 9, 2001. I received my copy on February 12, 2001, the same day I was informed of my father's brain aneurysm. During the contract nego-tiations I was informed that I had been the only candidate they were interested in meeting with. If I didn't want it, they were going to close it down. I couldn't believe it, but I'd done it. I was 80 per-cent owner of a magazine; Inner City Broadcasting retained 20 per-cent, but as the majority owner I'm responsible for its overall operations: editing, printing, advertising, sales and distribution. This was a very big deal—especially for a sixteen-year-old.

And the smartest thing I did in the whole venture—the key to making the venture work, really—was having the right partner. Inner City Broadcasting Corporation (ICBC) is the largest African American, privately held radio broadcasting corporation in the United States, with over $65 million in annual revenues. The orig-inator of "It's Showtime at the Apollo" and the urban contempo-rary radio format around 1970, Inner City Broadcasting owns and operates eighteen pure-play radio stations in seven U.S. markets with significant clusters in New York City; San Francisco; Jackson, Mississippi; and Columbia, South Carolina. It is a company that defines focus, integrity and entrepreneurial success—and especially black entrepreneurial success.

INNERCITY magazine was born in 1998 and was devoted to the urban music and entertainment scene in New York City. *INNERCITY* began small, but it always had huge dreams. Originally published quarterly, the plan was to become a national consumer magazine with a redefined demographic audience and slogan and an increased frequency and print run. ICBC came close to fulfilling its mission before the 2001 advertising recession dug in. The next step was a defining one. The magazine was put on hiatus to select the right partner to reinforce its commitment and presence in the publishing industry. According to the Suttons, I was that right partner. I still don't know why. And every time I read what Mr. Percy Sutton said about me in their press release, I bow in humility.

"We chose a young man who has tremendous drive and foresight. Gray's a young innovative leader and CEO who can push the magazine beyond what is comfortable to reposition and redefine the magazine's focus."

We've positioned *INNER CITY* as the ultimate urban entertainment magazine. It's the only national publication with a positive, upbeat dedication to all matters celebrity. We feature the chart-topping recording artists who electrify our radios, the box office record-breaking film stars, television actors who light up the screen, and the superstar athletes who dominate their sports and awaken our emotions and stimulate our fantasies. I think it is important to offer a behind-the-scenes, business approach (of course) so we profile songwriters, directors, producers, and other urban entertainment movers, shakers and dealmakers. The magazine's new direction is the perfect intersection of urban-oriented celebrity and entertainment-driven reporting. I like to say that *INNER CITY* is "where R&B and hip-hop collide!"

Since I took over the magazine, life has been more hectic than I ever imagined. I have much love and appreciation for people who run print publications. It's a circus! Even when you're closing one issue, you're already working on the next two or three. There's no such thing as downtime in this business. I thought my life was a roller coaster before, but now I realize it was a kiddie ride!

But I'm not complaining. I welcome the challenges, knowing that I'm growing as a businessman. Not only has my learning curve gone off the charts in publishing, but I've also learned a great deal about advertising, celebrity and entertainment reporting, target market penetration, and branding.

Now, let's be real for a second: taking over this magazine wasn't all fun and games. Not only did I take the magazine through a complete visual overhaul, I also had to make some much-needed but unfortunate layoffs. I had to learn a lot about the publishing world in a short period of time. As the managing editor I oversee all of the content down to the cover art. This is a business that never sleeps. That's probably why we're based in New York.

My challenge now is to continue finding ways to fund the publication in a shrinking advertising market. Not too many magazines are thriving in today's marketplace, but we're holding our own. To date we've snagged some of the top artists in the world for our cover, including platinum recording divas Ashanti and Janet Jackson. Not bad for a rookie, huh? We're not where I want us to be yet, but we're getting there, and each day I'm learning more about the business and becoming a better leader. Pick up a copy of *INNER CITY*. I'd love to know what you think.

And to think this all came about because one very important

man heard about me and continued to watch me. It just goes to show that you never know where opportunity will come from. When it knocks, be ready to move. That's my motto.

I have to say that I'm proud I was willing to tread new waters and take on new territory. I only wish I could share this with my father. He'd go bananas. It's funny, I've heard stories of men whose fathers passed away at crucial times during their lives, periods when they were undergoing a particular test of moral fiber. I've also heard stories of women who have lost their mothers during their pregnancies, only to give birth to a baby girl on their mother's birthday. Strange things have happened, if we want to call them strange.

I prefer to see them as being one with the universe and the divine order. Of being ready for all opportunities. Of having your heart in the right place. Of knowing yourself, where you want to go and how you want to get there. Of not fighting the flow, but instead swimming with the tide and letting the divine order guide you where you need to go.

And that's one more reason to make sure you pick the right partner.

As I write this, I have begun the next lap of my entrepreneurial race. I'm meeting with new investors for my magazine. I'm still scouting out new frontiers to do business, and I most definitely still have my eye on that talk show. Each day I'm learning more about the power of my choices. I continue to be amazed that faith and love can literally move mountains. My life is proof of that fact.

To achieve your dreams—to become a reallionaire—you must first have complete faith in yourself and in God, whatever God means to you. You must acknowledge that you can't control the world around you or the people in it; then you must work tirelessly to fulfill your purpose on Earth. If that's writing, then write. If it's cooking, then cook. If it's singing, sing. If it's healing, heal. Just do it. Don't do it for the money; the money will come if you do it for the right reasons. Do it with a quiet assurance that what you are creating will make the world a better place, and that it's already happening. That's knowing. Until next time, be you and be real.

About the Author

Farrah Gray's mission is to educate youth about career opportunities in business, while leading by example in the area of social responsibility. His inspirational spirit and grounded personality have made him a favorite youth motivator on the speaking circuit, where he speaks primarily to conferences, community organizations and churches. He contributes a portion of his income from speaking engagements to the Farrah Gray Foundation, a nonprofit organization that gives grants to after-school and summer programs for inner-city youths and underperforming students.

A self-made millionaire by the age of fourteen, Farrah Gray's business ventures have included Kidztel prepaid phone cards, Farr-Out Foods, the NE^{2}W Venture Capital Fund, the Teenscope interactive teen talk show, a comedy show on the Las Vegas Strip and *INNERCITY* magazine, a joint venture with Inner City Broadcasting Corporation. He has consulted with the United States

Department of Commerce Minority Development Department in the creation of a national youth entrepreneurship incubator.

Farrah Gray attributes his success to his unquenchable drive to accomplish his goals, a trait he learned growing up the youngest member of a poor but proud and hard-working single-parent household in inner-city Chicago. He currently divides his time between New York City and Las Vegas, Nevada.

To contact Farrah Gray, please write or e-mail him at this address:

67 Wall Street, Suite 2212
New York, NY 10005
(212) 859-5028
fg@farrahgrayfoundation.com